Poetry

Points of Departure

Henry Taylor

The American University

Winthrop Publishers, Inc.
Cambridge, Massachusetts

COVER BY SARAH EL BINDARI

Library of Congress Cataloging in Publication Data

Taylor, Henry   comp.
  Poetry: points of departure.

  1. American poetry (Collections)   2. English
poetry (Collections)   3. Poetry.   I. Title.
PS586.T3   821'.008   74-742
ISBN 0-87626-678-2

PS
586
T3

Copyright © 1974 by Winthrop Publishers, Inc.
  17 Dunster Street, Cambridge, Massachusetts 02138

Contents

3. **Shadow in the Deepening Shade:** Personal Interpretations of Tradition 125

4. A Bliss in Proof: Love and Sex 157

5. The Book of Lies: Language Barriers and Credibility Gaps 184

8. **With Multitudinous Will:** War 241

9. **Seeking What Is Yet Unfound:** Frontiers and Illusions of Progress 259

10. One Name Is Pain: Sports 275

An Epilogue 335

Index of Titles and Authors 337

Index of Terms 345

Preface

This book is intended primarily for use in classrooms, as an introduction to the pleasures to be gained from studying poetry. Two basic assumptions underlie its organization. First, contemporary poems are often more accessible to beginning readers than are older poems, especially if the contemporary poems are presented along with older representatives of the Anglo-American poetic tradition. Second, an anthology arranged according to the poems' nominal subjects, rather than their themes or historical periods, can reveal some important aspects of poetic thought.

The first of these assumptions is open to debate, but it is clear that contemporary poets are largely responsible for poetry's increasing popularity. However, no poet can work successfully without taking some stance toward the poetry that has preceded his own; our understanding of today's poetry is enriched when we see how it stands in comparison to Shakespeare's or Keats's. Furthermore, an examination of poetic techniques in works whose language is clearly our own can facilitate examination of similar techniques in older poems.

For these reasons, about half of the 265 poems in this book are by poets who have established their reputations since World War II. The remaining poems are divided between poets of the earlier part of this century and poets from the fourteenth century to the nineteenth century. I have chosen the poems on the basis of my own teaching experience: most of the poems are here because of their excellence, some are here because of their interesting or amusing badness, and all are here because examination of them yields more than the silence of bafflement or admiration. Finally, in choosing the older poems, I have considered the degree to which each one represents the tradition out of which it was written.

The arrangement of the anthology also needs some further explanation. There are many thematic anthologies of poetry; most of them suggest, doubtless unintentionally, that a poet habitually sets out to write about such great themes as mutability, love, death, or the problem of evil. This is sometimes the case, as when Milton set out to justify the ways of God to man; but more often a poet begins with uncertainty about his theme and finds it during the course of composition. So I have arranged the poems according to their nominal subjects, to demonstrate that one poem about movies, for example, will have nostalgia as its theme, while another may be concerned with the nature of heroism. However, some great themes have been attractive to poets as points of departure; to illustrate this, four sections of the anthology are devoted to nominal subjects which traditionally have the status of great themes: love, nature, war, and art.

For purposes of thematic discussion, the twelve sections of the anthology are arranged in three groups of four. The first four sections contain poems arising from that which endures, or that which is inescapable. The next four sections contain various forms of protest or reaction against the inescapable. The last four sections are concerned with kinds of escape or transcendence.

Most of the subject headings are self-explanatory, but I should point out that there are hundreds of other possibilities and that some of the subjects greatly limit the range of selection. Obviously the section on movies can contain no poems written before movies were invented; I have included the section because a number of fine movie-poems have been written and because the way movie-mythology operates in them can remind us of the relevance and immediacy that more traditional myths have had to earlier poems. Thus the movie-poems can shed light on many of the poems in Section 3, "Personal Interpretations of Tradition," which contains poems arising from the struggle to blend personal beliefs and inherited beliefs—as in Milton's mixture of classical and Christian ideas in "Lycidas."

The arrangement of poems within sections is not chronological; it is intended instead to promote discussion by juxtaposing poems which it is interesting to compare.

The six introductory chapters deal with the basic elements of poetry; they may be read as a self-contained unit. My own attitude is that this material should be mastered as soon as possible, to leave time for the informed discussion of poems. However, the questions which refer to poems in the anthology will facilitate a more leisurely approach which combines one chapter with many poems in the anthology. The order of the chapters confronts elementary stumbling blocks early and refinements later. Chapters 1 and 2 are concerned with kinds of resistance to poetry and with the popular misconception that poetry is always the poet's expression of his inner self; Chapters 3 and 4 deal with images, figures of speech, and diction; Chapters 5 and 6 treat the more difficult matters of form, structure, and technique. Chapter 6, "The Process of Revision," contains all the drafts of one of my own poems, with comments following each draft. I use my own work here because I can comment on it with more authority than I could bring to the drafts of some better poem by another poet. Furthermore, the drafts of, say, "Ode on a Grecian Urn" or "Sailing to Byzantium" contain almost supernatural leaps of improvement, and so baffle discussion at certain points; "The Hughesville Scythe," on the other hand, should not prove discouraging to people who have hopes of writing their own poems.

In addition to the introductory chapters, there are notes on allusions in certain poems, and on words that seem modern but are not, and on words not readily found in standard college dictionaries. An index of the terms that are in boldface type in the introductory chapters serves as a glossary.

I became indebted to other people soon after starting work on this book. Here I would like to mention Edward Lueders, Diana Major, and Philip Sullivan, all of the University of Utah English Department; they suggested some of the subject headings for the anthology. Michael Rudick, of the same department, H. Ramsey Fowler, of Memphis State University, and George R. Thompson, of Kansas State Teachers College, read drafts of the manuscript and made many valuable suggestions, as did several other people whose anonymity, I am sorry to say, is preserved according to a tradition among publishers. Finally, my wife, Frannie, has been incalculably helpful with all stages of preparing the manuscript; there is no end to her claims on coauthorship of this book, and so there can be no end to my gratitude to her.

Acknowledgments

John Alexander Allen. "A Word to a Father, Dead" from THE LEAN DIVIDER by John Alexander Allen. Copyright © 1970. Reprinted by permission of Golden Quill Press.

W. H. Auden. "That night when joy began" copyright © 1937 and renewed 1965 by W. H. Auden. "Musée des Beaux Arts" and "The Unknown Citizen" copyright © 1940 and renewed 1968 by W. H. Auden. Reprinted from COLLECTED SHORTER POEMS 1927–1957 by W. H. Auden by permission of Random House, Inc.

Ben Belitt. "The Spool" copyright © 1964 by Ben Belitt. Reprinted from THE ENEMY JOY (University of Chicago Press) by permission of Ben Belitt. "Moon Walk" copyright © 1970 by Ben Belitt. Reprinted from NOWHERE BUT LIGHT (University of Chicago Press) by permission of Ben Belitt.

John Berryman. "Dream Song #14," "Dream Song #29," and "Dream Song #105" are reprinted with the permission of Farrar, Straus & Giroux, Inc., from THE DREAM SONGS by John Berryman. Copyright © 1959, 1962, 1963, 1964, 1965, 1966, 1967, 1968, 1969 by John Berryman.

John Betjeman. "A Subaltern's Love Song" from COLLECTED POEMS by John Betjeman is reprinted by permission of John Murray (Publishers) Ltd. and Houghton Mifflin Company.

John Peale Bishop. "A Recollection" is reprinted by permission of Charles Scribner's Sons from THE COLLECTED POEMS OF JOHN PEALE BISHOP, edited by Allen Tate. Copyright © 1948 by Charles Scribner's Sons.

Robert Bly. "Counting Small-Boned Bodies" copyright © 1967 by Robert Bly; "Those Being Eaten by America" copyright © 1966 by Robert Bly. Reprinted from THE LIGHT AROUND THE BODY by permission of Harper & Row, Publishers, Inc.

Fred Bornhauser. "The Wishbone" copyright © 1960 by Fred Bornhauser; first appeared in FIVE POETS, published by the Cornell University Contemporary Arts Festival. Reprinted by permission of Fred Bornhauser.

John Malcolm Brinnin. "Nuns at Eve" copyright © 1951, from THE SORROWS OF COLD STONE, is reprinted by permission of the author.

Gwendolyn Brooks. "We Real Cool" from WORLD OF GWENDOLYN BROOKS copyright © 1959 by Gwendolyn Brooks. Reprinted by permission of Harper & Row, Publishers, Inc.

Fred Chappell. "Skin Flick" and "Spitballer" copyright © 1971 by Fred Chappell, from THE WORLD BETWEEN THE EYES, by Fred Chappell. Reprinted by permission of Louisiana State University Press.

Kelly Cherry. "A Song for Sigmund Freud" copyright © 1970 by Kelly Cherry; first published in THE MILL MOUNTAIN REVIEW. Reprinted by permission of the author.

G. K. Chesterton. "The Rolling English Road" reprinted by permission of Dodd, Mead & Company, Inc., from THE COLLECTED POEMS OF G. K. CHESTERTON. Copyright © 1911, 1932 by Dodd, Mead & Company, Inc. Copyright renewed.

Tom Clark. "Sonnet" ("The orgasm completely") from STONES by Tom Clark. Copyright © 1968 by Tom Clark. Reprinted by permission of Harper & Row, Publishers, Inc.

Austin Dobson. "A Kiss" reprinted by permission of Oxford University Press and A. T. A. Dobson as Executor for the estate of Austin Dobson.

Alan Dugan. "On Hurricane Jackson" copyright © 1961 by Alan Dugan. From POEMS, 1961, Yale University Press. Reprinted by permission of Alan Dugan.

Richard Eberhart. "The Fury of Aerial Bombardment" from COLLECTED POEMS 1930–1960 by Richard Eberhart. Copyright © 1960 by Richard Eberhart. Reprinted by permission of Oxford University Press, Inc.

T. S. Eliot. "Preludes" is from COLLECTED POEMS 1909–1962 by T. S. Eliot copyright © 1936 by Harcourt Brace Jovanovich, Inc.; copyright © 1963, 1964 by T. S. Eliot. Reprinted by permission of the publisher.

Robert Francis. "The Base Stealer" and "Hallelujah: A Sestina" copyright © 1948, 1960 by Robert Francis. Reprinted from THE ORB WEAVER by Robert Francis by permission of Wesleyan University Press.

Robert Frost. "Desert Places," "Mending Wall," "Range-Finding," "The Silken Tent," and "Stopping by Woods on a Snowy Evening" are from THE POETRY OF ROBERT FROST edited by Edward Connery Lathem. Copyright 1916, 1923, 1930, 1939, © 1969 by Holt, Rinehart and Winston, Inc. Copyright 1936, 1942, 1944, 1951, © 1958 by Robert Frost. Copyright © 1964, 1967, 1970 by Lesley Frost Ballantine. Reprinted by permission of Holt, Rinehart and Winston, Inc.

George Garrett. "Salome" from FOR A BITTER SEASON by George Garrett copyright © 1967 by George Garrett. Published by University of Missouri Press. "Goodbye, Old Paint, I'm Leaving Cheyenne" from ABRAHAM'S KNIFE by George Garrett copyright © 1961 by George Garrett. Reprinted by permission of the University of North Carolina Press.

Brewster Ghiselin. "Vantage" and "Marlin" from COUNTRY OF THE MINOTAUR copyright © 1968, 1969, 1970 by Brewster Ghiselin. Reprinted by permission of the publisher, the University of Utah Press.

Gary Gildner. "First Practice" is reprinted from FIRST PRACTICE by Gary Gildner copyright © 1969 by permission of the University of Pittsburgh Press.

Allen Ginsberg. "A Supermarket in California" copyright © 1956, 1959 by Allen Ginsberg. Reprinted by permission of City Lights Books.

Edwin Godsey. "Hoppy" from CABIN FEVER copyright © 1967 by Edwin Godsey. Reprinted by permission of Mrs. Edwin Godsey and the University of North Carolina Press.

Steven Graves. "The Rendezvous" copyright © 1974 by Winthrop Publishers, Inc. Included by permission of the author.

John Haines. "Denali Road" copyright © 1965 by John Haines. Reprinted from WINTER NEWS by John Haines. "The Legend of Paper Plates" copyright © 1969 by John Haines. Reprinted from THE STONE HARP by John Haines. Both are reprinted by permission of Wesleyan University Press.

Bruce Haley. "The Rime of the Ancient Mariner" copyright © 1969 by Bruce Haley. First appeared in WASATCH FRONT. Reprinted by permission of Bruce Haley.

Jerry Hammond. "Feature Time" copyright © 1974 by Winthrop Publishers, Inc. Included by permission of the author.

Thomas Hardy. "Channel Firing," "In Time of 'The Breaking of Nations,'" and "The Ruined Maid" are reprinted with permission of The Macmillan Company from COLLECTED POEMS by Thomas Hardy. Copyright © 1925 by The Macmillan Company.

Samuel Hazo. "The Day They Ate the Baritone" is reprinted from BLOOD RIGHTS by Samuel Hazo copyright © 1968 by permission of the University of Pittsburgh Press.

Anthony Hecht. "Lizards and Snakes" from THE HARD HOURS by Anthony Hecht. Copyright © 1959, 1967 by Anthony E. Hecht. Reprinted by permission of Atheneum Publishers. "Epitaph" first appeared in COUNTER/MEASURES. Copyright © 1971 by Anthony Hecht. Reprinted by permission of the author.

Conrad Hilberry. "Poet" from ENCOUNTER ON BURROWS HILL copyright © 1968 by Conrad Hilberry. Reprinted with permission of Ohio University Press. "Sleeping Out in Vermont" copyright © 1974. Included by permission of Conrad Hilberry.

Ralph Hodgson. "The Bells of Heaven" is reprinted with permission of The Macmillan Company from POEMS by Ralph Hodgson. Copyright © 1917 by The Macmillan Company, renewed 1945 by Ralph Hodgson.

John Hollander. "Movie-Going" from MOVIE-GOING AND OTHER POEMS by John Hollander. Copyright © 1962 by John Hollander. Reprinted by permission of Atheneum Publishers.

R. Ernest Holmes. "Black Lady in an Afro Hairdo Cheers for Cassius" copyright © 1971 by R. Ernest Holmes. Reprinted by permission of R. Ernest Holmes.

Ray Holt. "My Morose Master-Sergeants" copyright © 1974 by Winthrop Publishers, Inc. Reprinted by permission of Bernice Holt.

A. D. Hope. "Conquistador" from COLLECTED POEMS 1930–1965 by A. D. Hope. Copyright © 1963, 1966 in all countries of the International Copyright Union. All rights reserved. Reprinted by permission of The Viking Press, Inc.

A. E. Housman. "I Did Not Lose My Heart" from THE COLLECTED POEMS OF A. E. HOUSMAN. Copyright 1936 by Barclays Bank Ltd. Copyright © 1964 by Robert E. Symons. Reprinted by permission of Holt, Rinehart and Winston, Inc. "To an Athlete Dying Young" and "Loveliest of Trees" from "A Shropshire Lad," Authorized Edition, from THE COLLECTED POEMS OF A. E. HOUSMAN. Copyright 1939, 1940, © 1965 by Holt, Rinehart and Winston, Inc. Copyright © 1967, 1968 by Robert E. Symons. Reprinted by permission of Holt, Rinehart and Winston, Inc.

Barbara Howes. "City Afternoon" copyright © 1959 by Barbara Howes. Reprinted from LIGHT AND DARK by Barbara Howes by permission of Wesleyan University Press. "Out Fishing" copyright © 1966 by Barbara Howes. Reprinted from LOOKING UP AT LEAVES by Barbara Howes by permission of the author.

T. E. Hulme. "The Embankment" from SPECULATIONS by T. E. Hulme. Reprinted by permission of Harcourt Brace Jovanovich, Inc.

David Ignatow. "The Bagel" copyright © 1966 by David Ignatow. Reprinted from POEMS 1934–1969 by David Ignatow by permission of Wesleyan University Press.

Randall Jarrell. "Next Day" copyright © 1963, 1965 by Randall Jarrell and "Well Water" copyright © 1965 by Randall Jarrell are reprinted with permission of The Macmillan Company from THE LOST WORLD by Randall Jarrell.

Robinson Jeffers. "Shine, Perishing Republic" copyright © 1925 and renewed 1953 by Robinson Jeffers. Reprinted from SELECTED POETRY OF ROBINSON JEFFERS by permission of Random House, Inc.

Dan Johnson. "Stray Things" copyright © 1974 by Winthrop Publishers, Inc. Included by permission of the author.

Erica Jong. "Here Comes" from FRUITS & VEGETABLES by Erica Jong. Copyright © 1971 by Erica Mann Jong. Reprinted by permission of Holt, Rinehart and Winston, Inc.

Donald Justice. "The Grandfathers" copyright © 1961 by Donald Justice. Reprinted from NIGHT LIGHT by Donald Justice by permission of Wesleyan University Press. This poem was first published in POETRY.

X. J. Kennedy. "Nude Descending a Staircase" copyright © 1960 by X. J. Kennedy from the book NUDE DESCENDING A STAIRCASE. Reprinted by permission of Doubleday & Company, Inc.

Edward Kessler. "The Dodo" copyright © 1974 by Winthrop Publishers, Inc. Included by permission of Edward Kessler.

Paul Lawson. "The Ambassadors" copyright © 1969 by Paul Lawson. Originally published in THE NEW MEXICO QUARTERLY. Reprinted by permission of Paul Lawson.

Philip Legler. "Love and an Old Western at the Starlite Drive-In Theater" from A CHANGE OF VIEW copyright © 1964 by Philip Legler. Reprinted by permission of Philip Legler.

Denise Levertov. "What Were They Like?" from THE SORROW DANCE. Copyright © 1966 by Denise Levertov Goodman. Reprinted by permission of New Directions Publishing Corporation.

Robert Lowell. "In the Cage" and "The Quaker Graveyard in Nantucket" from LORD WEARY'S CASTLE copyright © 1946 by Robert Lowell. Reprinted by permission of Harcourt Brace Jovanovich, Inc.

William Matthews. "Oscar Robertson: Peripheral Vision" copyright © 1974 by Winthrop Publishers, Inc. Included by permission of William Matthews. An earlier version was published in PEBBLE in 1967.

William Meredith. "Two Figures from the Movies" copyright © 1948 by Princeton University Press. Reprinted by permission of William Meredith. "Earth Walk" copyright © 1969 by William Meredith and "An Old Field Mowed for Appearances' Sake" copyright © 1961 by William Meredith are reprinted from EARTH WALK: NEW AND SELECTED POEMS by William Meredith by permission of Alfred A. Knopf, Inc.

James Merrill. "Laboratory Poem" from THE COUNTRY OF A THOUSAND YEARS OF PEACE by James Merrill. Copyright © 1958 by James Merrill. Appeared originally in POETRY. Reprinted by permission of Atheneum Publishers.

W. S. Merwin. "When the War is Over" and "Caesar" from THE LICE by W. S. Merwin. Copyright © 1967, 1964 by W. S. Merwin. Reprinted by permission of Atheneum Publishers. "Caesar" appeared originally in THE ATLANTIC MONTHLY.

Josephine Miles. "Reason" is reprinted from PREFABRICATIONS by Josephine Miles by permission of Indiana University Press.

May Miller. "Bell at Midnight" copyright © 1962 by May Miller Sullivan; reprinted from INTO THE CLEARING by May Miller Sullivan by permission of the author. "The Direction" copyright © 1974 by Winthrop Publishers, Inc.; included by permission of May Miller Sullivan.

Howard Moss. "Going to Sleep in the Country" from SELECTED POEMS by Howard Moss. Copyright © 1965, 1971 by Howard Moss. Reprinted by permission of Atheneum Publishers.

Valery Nash. "Working for Dr. No" copyright © 1972 by Valery Nash. First published in THE FILM JOURNAL. Reprinted by permission of Valery Nash.

Howard Nemerov. "To the Governor & Legislature of Massachusetts" from THE BLUE SWALLOWS. Copyright © 1967 by Howard Nemerov. "September, the First Day of School" from GNOMES AND OCCASIONS by Howard Nemerov. Copyright © 1973 The University of Chicago. Reprinted by permission.

Bink Noll. "Landscape with Pervert" by Bink Noll. Copyright © 1967 by Bink Noll. Reprinted from his volume THE FEAST by permission of Harcourt Brace Jovanovich, Inc.

Wilfred Owen. "Anthem for Doomed Youth" from COLLECTED POEMS by Wilfred Owen. Copyright Chatto & Windus, Ltd., 1946, © 1963. Reprinted by permission of New Directions Publishing Corporation.

William Packard. "The Teacher of Poetry" copyright © 1971 by William Packard.

First published in COUNTER/MEASURES. Reprinted by permission of William Packard.

Kenneth Patchen. "In Order to" from COLLECTED POEMS by Kenneth Patchen. Copyright © 1954 by New Directions Publishing Corporation. Reprinted by permission of New Directions Publishing Corporation.

Sylvia Plath. "Face Lift" from CROSSING THE WATER by Sylvia Plath. Copyright © 1962 by Ted Hughes. Reprinted by permission of Harper & Row, Publishers, Inc.

Ezra Pound. "In a Station of the Metro" from PERSONAE by Ezra Pound. Copyright © 1926 by Ezra Pound. Reprinted by permission of New Directions Publishing Corporation.

Paul Ramsey. "Marilyn Monroe," "The Physical Imperfections of Old Films," and "Willie Mays" copyright © 1972 by Paul Ramsey. Reprinted by permission of the author. "The Physical Imperfections of Old Films" first appeared in SOUTHERN POETRY REVIEW.

Julia Randall. "The Writer Indulges a Hobby" copyright © 1968 by Julia Randall Sawyer. Reprinted from ADAM'S DREAM by Julia Randall by permission of Alfred A. Knopf, Inc.

John Crowe Ransom. "Bells for John Whiteside's Daughter" copyright 1924 by Alfred A. Knopf, Inc. and renewed 1952 by John Crowe Ransom. Reprinted from SELECTED POEMS, 3rd Edition, Revised and Enlarged, by John Crowe Ransom, by permission of Alfred A. Knopf, Inc.

Henry Reed. "Naming of Parts" copyright © 1947 by Henry Reed. Reprinted from A MAP OF VERONA by Henry Reed by permission of Jonathan Cape Limited.

Thomas Reiter. "Dinoland" copyright © 1974 by Winthrop Publishers, Inc. Included by permission of the author.

Edwin Arlington Robinson. "Mr. Flood's Party" is reprinted with permission of The Macmillan Company from COLLECTED POEMS by Edwin Arlington Robinson. Copyright © 1921 by Edwin Arlington Robinson, renewed 1949 by Ruth Nivison. "How Annandale Went Out" is reprinted from THE TOWN DOWN THE RIVER by Edwin Arlington Robinson with permission of Charles Scribner's Sons. Copyright © 1907 by Charles Scribner's Sons; renewal copyright 1935 by Ruth Nivison.

Theodore Roethke. "Dolor" copyright 1943 by Modern Poetry Association, Inc.; "In a Dark Time" copyright © 1960 by Beatrice Roethke as Administratrix of the Estate of Theodore Roethke. Reprinted from THE COLLECTED POEMS OF THEODORE ROETHKE by permission of Doubleday & Company, Inc.

Norman Rosten. "Nobody Dies Like Humphrey Bogart" copyright © 1965 by Norman Rosten. Reprinted by permission of Trident Press/Division of Simon & Schuster, Inc.

Saint Geraud. "Hair Poem" from THE NAOMI POEMS, BOOK ONE: CORPSE AND BEANS by Saint Geraud. Copyright © 1968 by William Knott. Used by permission of Follett Publishing Company, division of Follett Corporation.

Carl Sandburg. "Useless Words" from GOOD MORNING, AMERICA copyright © 1928, 1956 by Carl Sandburg. Reprinted by permission of Harcourt Brace Jovanovich, Inc.

May Sarton. "Baroque Image" reprinted from A PRIVATE MYTHOLOGY, NEW POEMS by May Sarton. By permission of W. W. Norton Company, Inc. Copyright © 1966 by May Sarton.

James Seay. "No Man's Good Bull" copyright © 1968 by James Seay. Reprinted from LET NOT YOUR HART by James Seay by permission of Wesleyan University Press.

Clarice Short. "Imperfect Sympathies" and "Taking Leave of the Old" from THE OLD ONE AND THE WIND. Reprinted by permission of Clarice Short and the University of Utah Press. Copyright © 1972 by Clarice Short.

Jon Silkin. "Death of a Son" copyright © 1954 by Jon Silkin. Reprinted from POEMS NEW AND SELECTED by Jon Silkin by permission of Wesleyan University Press.

Louis Simpson. "On the Lawn at the Villa" copyright © 1963 by Louis Simpson. Reprinted from AT THE END OF THE OPEN ROAD by Louis Simpson by permission of Wesleyan University Press.

David Slavitt. "Ride the High Country" from THE CARNIVORE copyright © 1965 by David Slavitt. Reprinted by permission of the University of North Carolina Press.

M. J. Smith. "Cataract" copyright © 1965 by The New Yorker Magazine, Inc. Reprinted by permission of Margoret J. Smith and The New Yorker Magazine, Inc.

William Jay Smith. "The Closing of the Rodeo" copyright © 1947 by William Jay Smith, originally published in POEMS; "Morels" copyright © 1964 by William Jay Smith, originally published in THE NEW YORKER; and "What Train Will Come?" copyright © 1970 by William Jay Smith, originally published in THE NEW REPUBLIC. All from NEW AND SELECTED POEMS by William Jay Smith. A Seymour Lawrence Book/Delacorte Press. Reprinted by permission of the publisher.

W. D. Snodgrass. "After Experience Taught Me . . ." from AFTER EXPERIENCE by W. D. Snodgrass. Copyright © 1964 by W. D. Snodgrass. Reprinted by permission of Harper & Row, Publishers, Inc.

Gary Snyder. "To Hell with Your Fertility Cult" from THE BACK COUNTRY. Copyright © 1959, 1964, 1968 by Gary Snyder. Reprinted by permission of New Directions Publishing Corporation. "Riprap" from RIPRAP AND COLD MOUNTAIN POEMS copyright © 1958, 1969 by Gary Snyder. Reprinted by permission of the author.

Stephen Spender. "An Elementary School Classroom in a Slum" copyright © 1942 and renewed 1970 by Stephen Spender. Reprinted from SELECTED POEMS by Stephen Spender by permission of Random House, Inc.

William Stafford. "Prairie Town" and "Thinking for Berky" copyright © 1962 by William Stafford, from TRAVELING THROUGH THE DARK by William Stafford. Reprinted by permission of Harper & Row, Publishers, Inc.

Ann Stanford. "Edward Hicks: 'The Peaceable Kingdom'" copyright © 1970 by Ann Stanford; "The Late Visitor" copyright © 1966 by Ann Stanford; both from THE DESCENT: POEMS by Ann Stanford. Reprinted by permission of The Viking Press, Inc.

Wallace Stevens. "Disillusionment of Ten O'Clock" and "Sunday Morning" copyright © 1923 and renewed 1951 by Wallace Stevens. "The Idea of Order at Key West" copyright © 1936 and renewed 1964 by Holly Stevens. Reprinted from THE COLLECTED POEMS OF WALLACE STEVENS by permission of Alfred A. Knopf, Inc.

James Tate. "The Book of Lies" and "Coming Down Cleveland Avenue" are reprinted by permission of Yale University Press from THE LOST PILOT by James Tate. Copyright © 1967 by Yale University.

Henry Taylor. "The Hughesville Scythe" copyright © 1970 by Henry Taylor; reprinted from THE SOUTHERN REVIEW.

Dylan Thomas. "Do Not Go Gentle into That Good Night" and "Fern Hill" from THE POEMS OF DYLAN THOMAS. Copyright 1946 by New Directions Publishing Corporation. Copyright 1952 by Dylan Thomas. Reprinted by permission of New Directions Publishing Corporation.

1
Approaching
Poems

To begin with, what is poetry? No study of the subject can ignore the question, even though it cannot be answered very satisfactorily. Attempts to define poetry have failed in the same ways that attempts to define life or love have failed: they make sense only to people who already have their own ideas about the concept. Here, for example, are three well-known definitions of poetry:

William Wordsworth [1770–1850]

I have said that poetry is the spontaneous overflow of powerful feelings: it takes its origin from emotion recollected in tranquillity.

Samuel Taylor Coleridge [1772–1834]

I wish our clever young poets would remember my homely definitions of prose and poetry; that is, *prose*: words in their best order; *poetry*: the best words in the best order.

Emily Dickinson [1830–1886]

If I read a book and it makes my whole body so cold no fire can ever warm me, I know that is poetry. If I feel physically as if the top of my head were taken off, I know that is poetry.

These statements are somewhat **subjective**: intentionally or not, their emphasis is on the personality making the definition, not on the object being defined, and so they communicate very little to the reader who knows nothing about poetry. Furthermore, the reader who does have some notions about poetry will find in these statements more about Wordsworth, Coleridge, and Dickinson than he will find about poetry itself.

But definitions of poetry that seek to be **objective**, or impersonal, abstract, and accurate, are even more troublesome; they ask to be hammered at until they reveal their subjective loopholes. For example, J. V. Cunningham (b. 1911) has written that "Poetry is the definitive statement, in meter, of something worth saying." A moment's examination reveals that this statement, though objective in tone, is as subjective as the three above. Many readers will find that the way something is said will have a great deal to do with whether it seems to have been worth saying.

Fortunately, we do not have to say with finality what poetry is before we can begin to read it with enjoyment. Most of us can look at words on a page and decide whether we are looking at poetry, though there are times when we will disagree. This book is not intended to resolve those disagreements, many of which are indispensable to the creative life; but some of the material here can provide the reader with ways of stating and defending his own point of view.

A more pressing question may be, why should anyone read or study poetry? People who make a habit of reading poems seem to do so for all kinds of personal reasons, many of which are difficult to explain. At the deepest level, the encounter between poem and reader is nonrational and private and cannot be fully shared. (This is known even on Madison Avenue; a recent television commercial, whose aim is to suggest that using a certain cologne makes women more mysterious, implies that the kind of woman who wears it takes long, silent walks in the rain and enjoys unrhymed poetry.) The study of poetry, however, can be shared, because it is largely a rational enterprise. Whether studied systematically in the classroom, or informally wherever interested people gather, the best poems reward examination with more lasting reverberations at the nonrational level.

Most good poems contain some difficulties for the untrained reader. Even the simplest of short poems, if they arrest our attention on a first reading, will yield additional pleasure on further examination. More difficult poems, those that refer to people, places, or events with which we are unfamiliar or that use language in ways that are at first hard to follow, can come to give the kind of pleasure more quickly gained from simpler poems. There is even some pleasure in unraveling the difficulties; what W. B. Yeats (1865–1939) called "the fascination of what's difficult" applies to reading poems as well as to writing them, as it applies to learning an athletic skill or a complicated dance step.

But the rational "reading equipment" acquired in classrooms or from books like this one is only a starting point. Reading and enjoying a difficult poem involves more than mere translation or puzzle-solving. Unfortunately, many readers seem not to realize this; some feel that analysis "ruins" a poem, robbing it of its spontaneous glory, while others examine a poem only for its "deep hidden meaning," which they manage to state as flatly as possible, confident that the poem has given them all it has to give.

The reader who thinks of analysis as a form of cruelty fails to notice the poem's own durability. A good poem can withstand the most brutally minute examination. We must remember that learning what can be said about a poem can give us a fuller appreciation of what cannot be said about it, such as why parts of it come to mind at unexpected moments, surprising us with their appropriateness to our situation or our feelings.

Robert Frost [1874–1963]

STOPPING BY WOODS ON A SNOWY EVENING

Whose woods these are I think I know.
His house is in the village, though;
He will not see me stopping here
To watch his woods fill up with snow.

My little horse must think it queer   5
To stop without a farmhouse near
Between the woods and frozen lake
The darkest evening of the year.

He gives his harness bells a shake
To ask if there is some mistake.   10
The only other sound's the sweep
Of easy wind and downy flake.

The woods are lovely, dark, and deep,
But I have promises to keep,
And miles to go before I sleep,   15
And miles to go before I sleep.

Few people can get through high school without encountering this poem, and for that reason it presents a special kind of problem in analysis. A poem that has been in the back of the mind for years takes on values and meanings that do not arise from the poem itself. This poem will remind one reader of the scenery outside a schoolroom window on a day in the distant past, and another of a teacher's false teeth, which clicked over a particular line. Such immediate associations lead to a whole assortment of vaguer impressions that can profoundly influence the reader's attitude toward the poem.

These impressions must be examined and separated from the poem itself; the poem must be seen as if for the first time. Try reading it aloud, listening for intonations which irrelevant attitudes may have produced. An extreme approach, which works for a few poems, is to sing the words to some incongruous popular tune—in this case, say, "Hernando's Hideaway"—and then to notice that the words have withstood even so heartless an attack as that upon their integrity.

Another difficulty in analyzing poetry is that caused by suspect interpretations which have been forced on you by someone who applies one particular approach to all literature. Though intelligent psychoanalytical criticism is quite useful, there are people who can find psychological symbolism in anything; such a person may have told you that the speaker of "Stopping by Woods on a Snowy Evening" is revealing his initial feelings of attraction to the dark wood (sexual involvement) and then his decision to avoid such entanglements. Some readers may reject analysis completely if that is what comes of it; a better reaction might be to exorcise the suspect interpretation by concocting another, albeit equally suspect. For example, "Stopping By Woods" might be about Santa Claus, pausing at a weary moment in his annual journey. Since Santa's sleigh is pulled by reindeer, the "little horse" is a minor obstacle to such an interpretation; but this type of realization may make you better able to look for flaws in the interpretation you are trying to discredit. Such a train of thought must finally lead to intuitive judgments: "It's just *not* about Santa Claus; any fool can see that." Such judgments are hard to defend, except in the light of wider reading in poetry.

But what is going on here? The answer to that question must be arrived at through a clear understanding of the poem's literal meaning: On a winter evening, someone in a horse-drawn vehicle stops to enjoy the beauty of a wood in snow. He is tempted to stay there, perhaps to go into the wood, but he must go on. Before searching too deeply for "hidden meanings," it is well to remember that the literal meaning, artfully stated, seems to some readers "something worth saying."

It is the last four lines which lead us to think that the woods may represent something more than just a bunch of trees. The identical last two lines strongly suggest that there is more than one way to interpret the conclusion of the poem. Life is often characterized as a journey which concludes with the sleep of death; it seems easy to say, then, that the woods, "lovely, dark, and deep," represent death and its attractiveness, while the "promises to keep" represent life's responsibilities. Such an interpretation seems convincing, but it should not be regarded as final or complete. As we shall see, a poem's total effect depends on more than its "message."

Some poems produce irrelevant responses on a first reading; the careful reader will recognize when this is happening and concentrate his attention on the words before him.

Saint Geraud (Bill Knott) [b. 1940]

HAIR POEM

Hair is heaven's water flowing eerily over us
Often a woman drifts off down her long hair and is lost

This is a mysterious little poem. But there is an approach to it which will deepen its effect on us; this approach is useful in dealing with most poems. First of all, read the poem aloud, emphasizing its "prose sense," its literal meaning. Read the poem this way two or three times before checking a dictionary for any unfamiliar words.

Once the prose sense of the poem is as clear as you can make it, start letting your oral performance of the poem be influenced by line-endings and, in this case, the lack of punctuation. Each line of "Hair Poem" can be read as a sentence; but the absence of terminal punctuation suggests that your voice should not be dropped quite as much as you would drop it at a period. When you drift away from the prose reading, your voice takes on a certain incantatory quality, which is reinforced by the series of short o sounds in the second line.

Gradually the poem's internal logic becomes clear. It is hard to **paraphrase**, or restate in your own words. the idea that "Hair is heaven's water flowing eerily over us"; but if we accept the image of hair flowing over us like liquid, then the second line seems a natural outgrowth of the first. The image is **surrealistic**: its components are drawn from the actual world, but they are combined in ways that go beyond the actual into realms of the incongruous or fantastic.

"Hair Poem" stubbornly resists the kind of criticism whose goal is a flat statement of what the poem means. An appropriate response to poetry is partly intellectual, but it is also partly emotional. Understanding our emotional responses helps us to understand a poem whose meaning may remain difficult to state except by repeating the poem itself.

This is not to say that the study of poetry ultimately becomes a vague discussion of emotion. Instead, we try to examine our emotional responses in a rational way, asking questions that seem likely to have reasonable answers. By this method we arrive at a firmer notion of the poem's effect. For example, discuss these questions about "Hair Poem":

Does the idea of hair as water flowing over us seem frightening or otherwise disturbing?

Does the statement that it is "heaven's water" make the idea more acceptable?

Does the picture evoked in the first line become clearer when we are presented with the long-haired woman in the second line?

Is the woman's drifting off to be lost something to be pitied? Envied?

Does the poem suggest that women with long hair have a quality of "lostness" which other people do not have?

Discussion of such questions helps us to see not only the poem's effect but also what it is that makes it a memorable statement of a surprising idea which may at the same time be oddly familiar.

William Shakespeare [1564–1616]

SONNET 73

That time of year thou mayst in me behold
When yellow leaves, or none, or few, do hang
Upon those boughs which shake against the cold,
Bare ruin'd choirs, where late the sweet birds sang.
In me thou see'st the twilight of such day   *5*
As after sunset fadeth in the west;
Which by and by black night doth take away,
Death's second self, that seals up all in rest.
In me thou see'st the glowing of such fire,
That on the ashes of his youth doth lie,   *10*
As the death-bed whereon it must expire,
Consum'd with that which it was nourish'd by.
  This thou perceiv'st, which makes thy love more strong,
  To love that well which thou must leave ere long.

A paraphrase of this sonnet's first four lines might sound like this: "You see in me that time of year when only a few yellow leaves, or none at all, hang on the branches shaking in the cold; those branches, where only recently birds were singing, are like bare, ruined choir-lofts in abandoned churches." This paraphrase is intended to clarify small difficulties caused by unfamiliar uses of language, rather than to give a capsule version of the statement contained in the poem. A more general paraphrase of the whole poem might be, "I'm getting older, as you may have noticed. That should make you love me more strongly, since you know that we must soon be parted by death." This kind of restatement is difficult to devise unless the more detailed kind has been worked out first.

Both the detailed and the general paraphrase leave out much that is contained in the poem itself. Restating a poem can clarify difficulties and bring up useful questions for discussion, but it cannot replace the poem. For example, the detailed paraphrase above clarifies the sense of the phrase "bare, ruin'd choirs," but it does not fully explain the phrase's effectiveness in the poem.

M. J. Smith [b. 1902]

CATARACT

I

The lashes of my eye are clipped away,
the eyelids pinned back with
diamond hatpins.
Tomcats pad in; their tiger tails
don't show under those starched smocks.   5
Grinning like balloons, they rise
and nudge the ceiling. They have been trained
to pick cobwebs from human eyes.

I lie under the beam of God's kilowatts,
a cloud of opium raining down like soot.   10
A well, murky with hoarded reflections,
is uncovered. Will they find me there—
with the drowned woodchuck, the white-eyed snake?

I've watched a glacier grinding
through the tumid ranges of the brain,   15
dropping silt
over my inner eye. Words flick
out of the haze like angry birds,
or crawl, wings torn off,
peeping feebly. . . .   20
But I cannot remember what saints and martyrs
have said under far worse circumstances.

II

When I was nine, strapped down
by nightmares, I screamed for
my sleeping father. Big as the hunter's moon,   25
he loomed in his nightshirt.
"Father, please chase those cats out of
the poppy trees, kick them into the dark
where I can't hear them hissing
'She . . . She . . .'   30
Don't let their prickers slip, Daddy!
Light a cigar."

I see the shadow of ivy on a plaster wall,
yellow roses climbing, my son's chestnut thatch
polished by a barn lantern—   35
don't let the blackbirds in the window!
A hand is turning the white doorknob.

God, dear, I am not ready. I am ashamed
to entertain you here at the beginning,
at the bottom of the well.   40
All I have for tea are these mud pies,
rich with stone raisins, pressed into rusted
cake tins. I set them out to dry, a row a day,
when the sun was hot on my gingham back,
and I pulsed like a tree toad in June,   45
mixing sweets, baking cakes,
enough, more than enough, for everyone.

This poem makes obvious the rewards of rereading. The first time
through, it may be confusing, though the richness of the details
gives it a certain energy or intensity. Some of the problems in it can
be approached by noticing the poem's overall organization.

The poem is in two parts, of three verse paragraphs each. The first
paragraph, together with the title, leads us to expect a description of
eye surgery to remove cataracts. That the doctors are seen as tomcats
seems odd, but the first verse paragraph of Part II gives us the reason:
the speaker, under stressful circumstances, has had frightening
dreams about cats.

The second paragraph of Part I continues the description of sur-
gery, with its "cloud of opium," the anesthetic, obscuring the
speaker's consciousness. And in this paragraph, the speaker's
blindness is first likened to being at the bottom of a well. Why is
God introduced here?

The third paragraph of Part I introduces the notion that the eye
operation is not to be taken entirely on the literal level. The phrases
"inner eye" and "saints and martyrs" make us wonder if the eye
operation is fictitious, and meant to stand for the restoration of some
other kind of vision, or actual, but still suggestive of the removal of
spiritual blindness.

The first paragraph of Part II, as suggested above, helps us under-
stand the vision of doctors as cats; the recollection of youth leads us
to the second paragraph, in which a series of images appears, either
in the speaker's memory or in the speaker's eyes as vision is restored.
We then return, in the final paragraph, to the image of the well, and
to God. It appears that the speaker has been occupied with matters

("mud pies") which seem insignificant when compared to the things restored sight has suddenly made visible.

The foregoing suggestions should provide the basis for discussion. How are we to take the eye operation? In other words, is this a poem about an eye operation which led to a deep, spiritual appreciation for sight, or is it about a religious experience which the poet makes real by describing it as an eye operation?

In poems like this, such questions are not always resolvable; but finding reasons to decide which way the poem's emphasis lies is one way of coming to know the poem better.

2

Speakers
and
Masks

Early in the study of an unfamiliar poem, it is necessary to determine who is to be imagined as the speaker. This may seem elementary, but very intelligent people sometimes fail to see that the speaker of a poem may be someone other than the poet. The late John F. Kennedy is reported to have said, during a speech commemorating a boundary treaty between the United States and Canada, "As Robert Frost has put it, 'Good fences make good neighbors.'" There is no doubt that that line appears in a poem by Robert Frost; but it may possibly be inaccurate, even so, to attribute the line to Frost himself.

Robert Frost [1874–1963]

MENDING WALL

Something there is that doesn't love a wall,
That sends the frozen-ground-swell under it
And spills the upper boulders in the sun,
And makes gaps even two can pass abreast.
The work of hunters is another thing: 5
I have come after them and made repair
When they have left not one stone on a stone,
But they would have the rabbit out of hiding,
To please the yelping dogs. The gaps I mean,
No one has seen them made or heard them made,   10
But at spring mending-time we find them there
I let my neighbor know beyond the hill;
And on a day we meet to walk the line
And set the wall between us once again.
We keep the wall between us as we go.   15
To each the boulders that have fallen to each.
And some are loaves and some so nearly balls
We have to use a spell to make them balance:
"Stay where you are until our backs are turned!"

We wear our fingers rough with handling them.   20
Oh, just another kind of outdoor game,
One on a side. It comes to little more:
There where it is we do not need the wall:
He is all pine and I am apple orchard.
My apple trees will never get across   25
And eat the cones under his pines, I tell him.
He only says, "Good fences make good neighbors."
Spring is the mischief in me, and I wonder
If I could put a notion in his head:
"Why do they make good neighbors? Isn't it   30
Where there are cows? But here there are no cows.
Before I built a wall I'd ask to know
What I was walling in or walling out,
And to whom I was like to give offense.
Something there is that doesn't love a wall,   35
That wants it down." I could say "Elves" to him,
But it's not elves exactly, and I'd rather
He said it for himself. I see him there,
Bringing a stone grasped firmly by the top
In each hand, like an old-stone savage armed.   40
He moves in darkness as it seems to me,
Not of woods only and the shade of trees.
He will not go behind his father's saying,
And he likes having thought of it so well
He says again, "Good fences made good neighbors."   45

The person in this poem who calls himself "I" may be Frost, or
someone not unlike him, but we cannot be certain. The safest course
is to refer to this person as the speaker of the poem. The speaker
seems to disagree with his taciturn neighbor; he sees in the latter's
stubborn reiteration of "his father's saying" a kind of ignorance
verging on savagery.

But what was Frost's own point of view, if we cannot with cer-
tainty ascribe the speaker's position to the poet? Frost himself was
not much help with this question; here are some remarks he made
about the poem during a reading at the Library of Congress in Octo-
ber, 1962:

The first time I got back to America — in 1915 — I met an old college
president; Rollins College, I guess. He was a grand old fellow. I'd known
him a little before. But he came up and took both my hands for my
pacifist triumph, see. And I looked a-sly at him, and he said, "Oh, I
see you said both sides of the fence, but I can tell which side you were
on," and so I left it that way.

And then, in England, two or three years ago, Graham Greene said to me, "The most difficult thing I find in recent literature is your saying that good fences make good neighbors."

And I said, "I wish you knew more about it, without my helping you."

We laughed, and I left it that way.

These remarks demonstrate that the poet himself is not necessarily a trustworthy interpreter of his poem. In this case, Frost seems actually unwilling to commit himself; he would rather tease his audience into going back to the poem than give them a flat statement which might make them stop being interested in it. A famous example of this attitude was expressed by Robert Browning when he was asked the meaning of one of his more difficult poems: "When I wrote that poem, only God and Robert Browning knew what it meant; now, only God knows."

So we must return to the poem itself, not asking what Frost wanted to say, but what the poem actually manages to say. It is tempting to conclude that the poem sides with the main speaker, since it is he who speaks in the first person. It is he who derides the wall-mending as a game, who repeats the line "Something there is that doesn't love a wall." He sees his neighbor as a savage, as we have noticed. On the other hand, it is also he who arranges the meeting between the two men: "I let my neighbor know beyond the hill." Perhaps when Frost told Graham Greene that he wished Greene knew more about it, he meant that one needs to know more about the different ways in which "Good fences make good neighbors" may be taken.

For our purposes, the problem of the speaker and the poet is best contended with by remembering these elementary guidelines:

1. Unless, by wide reading in a single poet's work, you have learned to decide when the poet is speaking for himself, it is best to attribute what is said in a poem to its speaker.
2. There is, however, no reason to avoid discussing certain technical matters in terms of the poet's apparent intentions. Obviously, "The poet chose this word" usually makes more sense than "The speaker chose this word."

In matters of content, then, the speaker does the saying; in matters of technique, the poet does the doing. This distinction is quite clear in poems which obviously do not side with their speakers; such a poem is "My Last Duchess" (p. 179). The situation in this poem is that of the typical **dramatic monologue**: the speaker is someone other than the poet, and he addresses a silent listener who is clearly within earshot. In this case, the speaker is the duke of Ferrara, and he is addressing the emissary of his next father-in-law.

Browning exploits **irony** in this poem, in that we discover from the duke's statements certain aspects of his personality that he has not intended to reveal. For example, in ranking the duke's "gift of a nine-hundred-years-old name/ With anybody's gift," the young duchess revealed more generosity than the duke did in bestowing the "gift" in the first place.

"My Last Duchess" provides a convenient approach to the speaker/ poet problem, for the speaker has a name. It makes sense to say, "Ferrara, in what he seems to think is a friendly show of hospitality, unwittingly reveals his pride ('I choose/ Never to stoop'), his petti-ness ('who passed without/ Much the same smile?'), and his greed ('no just pretense/ Of mine for dowry will be disallowed')." But it also makes sense to say, "Though Browning wrote this poem in iambic pentameter couplets [see pages 44, 45, and 49], he makes the language sound conversational. He does this partly by letting the sense of a sentence or phrase run over from the end of one line to the beginning of the next, so that the rhyme is not noticeable enough to interrupt the flow of the speech." By maintaining the speaker-poet distinction, we heighten the ironic discrepancy between what the speaker knows and what Browning, God, and the reader know.

Even in a poem not spoken by someone who calls himself "I," the personality and attitude of the speaker are important parts of the poem's meaning. It is necessary to determine whether the speaker is addressing a specific listener, the anonymous reader, or himself, and what his attitudes are. Some poems are more complicated in this respect than the foregoing examples.

John Vernon [b. 1943]

WHAT IS SALT?

Thank you for asking this question.
Salt is what makes potatoes taste
bad when you haven't put any on them.
This is true as well as funny. Our
taste buds seem to crave salt. The   5
reason for this, if you look at the
picture, is said by the little salt
shaker man. We must take in salt
to replenish supplies which are soon
used up in our chemical workings.   10

Mary Ann Steinchrohn of Colton, Ohio
wins a prize for asking this question.
In the blood, in cells, we need salt.
It is well that we do. As I write this,
my body is squeezing out salt. This   *15*
is called sweating. The day is hot.
The light droops over the branches of
trees, a curious fact. What is salt?
Thank you for asking. Salt comes in
thousands of tiny cubes, if you look   *20*
at the picture. A woman once changed
to a pillar of salt for disobeying
the words of our Lord. This is true
as well as funny. Pillars are not
always made out of salt. A pillar   *25*
is used to hold up a building, a
curious fact. What is salt? It is

soon used up in our chemical workings.
The reason for this, if you look
at the picture. What is salt?   *30*
Salt pours out of the holes of the
ocean. What is salt? What is salt?

This poem is clearly based on one of those newspaper columns for young people in which answers are given to questions about the nature of things. Parts of the poem appear to be quoted directly from such a source; this is a convention of "found poetry," writing not originally intended as poetry, which becomes interestingly transformed when offered as poetry by the finder. However, this is not strictly a "found poem," because there is material in it that appears not to have been in the original source.

If some of the material has been found, and some has been added, who is the speaker? It might be useful to think of him as the personality that becomes more strongly apparent in the second verse paragraph. This person may be thought of as presenting the original to us in the first verse paragraph, and then enlarging on it and satirizing it by shifting the context of some of its phrases.

The impact of the poem lies in the effect the original material is having on the speaker. He begins by quoting, then soon starts to satirize; but he ends by revealing that his way of seeing has been somehow altered. His repetition of the question in the last line suggests that there are, as far as he is concerned, important aspects of the question that cannot be answered satisfactorily. This is true, and less funny than some earlier passages in the poem.

Much of this interpretation is derived from the poem's **tone**, the attitude it takes toward its subject and toward the reader. The shift in tone at the end, for example, is a major clue to the poem's meaning. But there are limits beyond which we cannot allow our interpretation of tone to take us.

Jon Silkin [b. 1930]

DEATH OF A SON

[*who died in a mental hospital aged one*]

Something has ceased to come along with me.
Something like a person: something very like one.
    And there was no nobility in it
        Or anything like that.

Something was there like a one year   5
Old house, dumb as stone. While the near buildings
    Sang like birds and laughed
        Understanding the pact

They were to have with silence. But he
Neither sang nor laughed. He did not bless silence   10
    Like bread, with words.
        He did not forsake silence.

But rather, like a house in mourning
Kept the eye turned in to watch the silence while
    The other houses like birds   15
        Sang around him.

And the breathing silence neither
Moved nor was still.

I have seen stones: I have seen brick
But this house was made up of neither bricks nor stone   20
    But a house of flesh and blood
        With flesh of stone

And bricks for blood. A house
Of stones and blood in breathing silence with the other
    Birds singing crazy on its chimneys.   25
        But this was silence,

This was something else, this was
Hearing and speaking as though he was a house drawn
   Into silence, this was
      Something religious in his silence,   *30*

Something shining in his quiet,
This was different this was altogether something else:
   Though he never spoke, this
      Was something to do with death.

And then slowly the eye stopped looking   *35*
Inward. The silence rose and became still.
The look turned to the outer place and stopped,
   With the birds still shrilling around him.
      And as if he could speak

He turned over on his side with his one year   *40*
Red as a wound
He turned over as if he could be sorry for this
And out of his eyes two great tears rolled, like stones, and he died.

    The tone of this poem is **confessional**, in that the speaker is concerned with his deep personal reactions to a painful experience. Such poets as Robert Lowell, Anne Sexton, and Sylvia Plath have recently come to be called confessional poets, because many of their poems *appear* to be based on direct experience of suffering, evil, and so on. In cases in which the language and technique of the poems are as important as the experiences they relate, they have been powerfully successful; but when they rely too heavily on the intrinsic horror of their subject matter, they read, as Anne Sexton has put it, "like a fever chart for a bad case of melancholy."

    Our reaction to the confessional tone may lead us, erroneously, to pity the poet, because we assume that the experience related actually happened to him. The question is irrelevant; whether the poet suffered the experience or not, the poem cannot succeed unless the experience is fully imagined in the poem. For example, we cannot be absolutely certain, from a reading of "Death of a Son," whether Jon Silkin actually had a son who died in a mental hospital at the age of one. But we do not need to be certain: whether the experience is "real" or "imaginary," it has been *imagined* again. We can partake of it without feeling a need to know more about Silkin's personal life.

    Because the "I" of a poem may or may not be the poet, or may be only a representative from a certain province of the poet's personality, it is risky to base general statements about the poet's beliefs on the reading of one poem. For example, compare Frost's "Stopping by Woods" with his "Desert Places" (p. 270). How can you reconcile the moods which snow arouses in the speakers of the two poems? Actually, there is little need for such a reconciliation. Each poem speaks for itself and succeeds on its own terms. Only by long and detailed study of a poet's complete works can one arrive at reliable general statements of his beliefs; such statements would have to account for apparent contradictions between individual poems.

---

1. The obvious discrepancy between speaker and poet creates irony. The effect of this irony may be satirical, but it may also serve other purposes of characterization. Both "We Real Cool" (p. 220) and "Counting Small-Boned Bodies" (p. 252) are spoken in the first person plural. In each poem, furthermore, it is possible to guess intelligently at the author's attitude toward his speakers. How are the two poems different? Is one more satirical than the other? Are there significant similarities between the two poems?

2. Read the following poem. Sylvia Plath is often called a confessional poet, but the speaker of this poem may be a character created by Plath. Plath died at the age of thirty-one; cosmetic face-lifting is usually performed on somewhat older people. However, the tone of the poem is confessional. Compare this use of the confessional tone with that in "Salome" (p. 180), in which it is obvious that the poet and the speaker must be different people.

Sylvia Plath [1932–1963]

FACE LIFT

You bring me good news from the clinic,
Whipping off your silk scarf, exhibiting the tight white
Mummy-cloths, smiling: I'm all right.
When I was nine, a lime-green anesthetist
Fed me banana-gas through a frog-mask. The nauseous vault   *5*
Boomed with bad dreams and the jovian voices of surgeons.
Then mother swam up, holding a tin basin.
O I was sick.

They've changed all that. Traveling
Nude as Cleopatra in my well-boiled hospital shift,   *10*
Fizzy with sedatives and unusually humorous,
I roll to an anteroom where a kind man
Fists my fingers for me. He makes me feel something precious
Is leaking from the finger-vents. At the count of two

Darkness wipes me out like chalk on a blackboard . . .   ¹⁵
I don't know a thing.

For five days I lie in secret,
Tapped like a cask, the years draining into my pillow.
Even my best friend thinks I'm in the country.
Skin doesn't have roots, it peels away easy as paper.   ²⁰
When I grin, the stitches tauten. I grow backward. I'm twenty,
Broody and in long skirts on my first husband's sofa, my fingers
Buried in the lambswool of the dead poodle;   .
I hadn't a cat yet.

Now she's done for, the dewlapped lady   ²⁵
I watched settle, line by line, in my mirror—
Old sock-face, sagged on a darning egg.
They've trapped her in some laboratory jar.
Let her die there, or wither incessantly for the next fifty years,
Nodding and rocking and fingering her thin hair.   ³⁰
Mother to myself, I wake swaddled in gauze,
Pink and smooth as a baby.

---

3. Read "Ozymandias" (p. 195). The first word in the poem is "I," but this speaker very quickly presents the words of another person, a "traveller from an antique land," who speaks the rest of the poem. What is the effect of this device? What would be lost if the poem were spoken entirely by the second speaker?

4. With the above question in mind, read "'next to of course god america i" (p. 190). The first thirteen lines of the poem are spoken by a political orator; the last line is spoken by someone who appears to have been observing the orator's performance. How does the observer's sudden appearance affect your response to the poem? Does it help in any way to explain the orator's incoherence?

5. Read "The Unknown Citizen" (p. 193) and "Shame" (p. 200). It is fairly easy to see that the main object of the satire in each poem is a collective state of mind; Auden's poem satirizes the age of depersonalization, and Wilbur's satirizes a kind of dishonest humility. However, a secondary target of the satire in each poem is the abuse of language. What kind of writing seems to have influenced each poem?

6. Read "Fashionable Poet Reading" (p. 331). What would happen if the poem were rewritten in the first person, with the poet himself as speaker? Would it be possible to believe in him? Would the sharp satirical tone be significantly altered?

3
Imagery
and
Figures

Once we have established the prose sense of a poem, and determined who is speaking it, we can isolate certain elements for detailed examination. It is often useful to begin by examining the poem's imagery, for it may provide important indications of the poem's meaning. **Imagery** is nearly as hard to define as poetry. On the most basic level, it may be thought of as a collective term for images, the verbal records of sensory impressions. On a more complex level, though, imagery engages the intellect as well as the senses. Figurative language, discussed later in this chapter, is often regarded as a kind of imagery. The function of imagery, however, is fairly constant in all poetry. It helps to make vividly concrete what might otherwise be vaguely abstract, so that when we read a poem, we comprehend its concrete aspects fairly readily, coming more gradually to a recognition of its abstract implications.

It is important to note that this movement from the concrete to the abstract is made often by the reader but not necessarily by the poet. True, some poets begin with images and arrive at an abstract theme during the process of composition; but some poets go the other way, searching for images which will make clear an abstract idea with which they have begun. If the poem is successful, it is neither possible nor desirable for the reader to decide whether the poet began with an idea or with images.

Matthew Arnold [1822–1888]

DOVER BEACH

The sea is calm tonight.
The tide is full, the moon lies fair
Upon the straits;—on the French coast the light
Gleams and is gone; the cliffs of England stand,
Glimmering and vast, out in the tranquil bay.   5

Come to the window, sweet is the night-air!
Only, from the long line of spray
Where the sea meets the moon-blanched land,
Listen! you hear the grating roar
Of pebbles which the waves draw back, and fling,   10
At their return, up the high strand,
Begin, and cease, and then again begin,
With tremulous cadence slow, and bring
The eternal note of sadness in.

Sophocles long ago   15
Heard it on the Aegean, and it brought
Into his mind the turbid ebb and flow
Of human misery; we
Find also in the sound a thought,
Hearing it by this distant northern sea.   20

The Sea of Faith
Was once, too, at the full, and round earth's shore
Lay like the folds of a bright girdle furled.
But now I only hear
Its melancholy, long, withdrawing roar,   25
Retreating, to the breath
Of the night-wind, down the vast edges drear
And naked shingles of the world.

Ah, love, let us be true
To one another! for the world, which seems   30
To lie before us like a land of dreams,
So various, so beautiful, so new,
Hath really neither joy, nor love, nor light,
Nor certitude, nor peace, nor help for pain;
And we are here as on a darkling plain   35
Swept with confused alarms of struggle and flight,
Where ignorant armies clash by night.

28, *shingles:* coarse stones thrown up at the sea's edge; by extension, the shores
themselves.

Although it is not difficult to see that the speaker of this poem is
with the woman he loves, overlooking the English Channel, and that
his primary concern is that they maintain their love in the face of

the world's dispassionate brutality, there are some difficulties in the references to Sophocles and the Sea of Faith. Sophocles (496–406 B.C.), Greek dramatist, makes comparisons in *Antigone* and *Oedipus at Colonus* between the sea's motion and the tragic, cyclical nature of human life. (In this passage, it might be noted, the speaker is experiencing the kind of sudden literary association discussed in Chapter 1, p. 3.) The "Sea of Faith" passage reminds us of the Middle Ages, when Christian faith was a powerful force.

These references help make the poem's theme clear, but the force with which the theme strikes us is achieved largely by means of the carefully controlled imagery. The first verse paragraph opens with an appeal to our sense of sight; the impression of beauty and tranquillity is reinforced, in the sixth line, by an appeal to our senses of touch and smell ("sweet is the night-air!"). With the word "Listen!" sound images are introduced and "bring / The eternal note of sadness in."

The second verse paragraph cites Sophocles's tragic interpretation of the sea's sound; then, almost entirely in terms of sound, the third paragraph depicts the retreat of the Sea of Faith. The suggestion here is that there was security in the medieval world of devout Christian belief, but that the coming of the modern age has brought a decrease in faith.

The fourth paragraph, beginning with the speaker's expressed hope that love may prevail, sets forth a visual image of the world's apparent beauty, then an abstract statement of its emptiness. It concludes with another sound image: the armies clash by night, unable to see each other; the primary impression is of "confused alarms of struggle and flight."

The effect of the poem, then, depends partly on a cyclical movement from visual to auditory imagery. What the speaker sees turns out to be what *seems* to be; his ideas of what is real are introduced and amplified in passages which rely heavily on auditory imagery. There may be a thematic statement implied by this organization; what is available to our sense of sight may be an illusion, to be corrected by what our other senses can grasp. Such an interpretation parallels the more obviously stated theme of the poem, and it is clear that the contrast between visual imagery and auditory imagery creates a tension in the poem which makes the primary theme come through forcefully and with immediacy.

At times, the imagery of a poem may seem to be the whole poem; whatever abstract implications the poem has, if any, must be arrived at by a less direct interpretation than the one above.

Wallace Stevens [1879–1955]

DISILLUSIONMENT OF TEN O'CLOCK

The houses are haunted
By white night-gowns.
None are green,
Or purple with green rings,
Or green with yellow rings,   5
Or yellow with blue rings.
None of them are strange,
With socks of lace
And beaded ceintures.
People are not going   10
To dream of baboons and periwinkles.
Only, here and there, an old sailor,
Drunk and asleep in his boots,
Catches tigers
In red weather.   15

The reader's first task may be to determine that ceintures are waistbands. Once that task is done, he can begin to consider the imagery of the poem. For example, he might readily see that the poem takes an attitude toward imagery itself. The title, first of all, suggests that the speaker is disillusioned with the inhabitants of the houses because they lead lives devoid of color and strangeness. And there may be an ambiguity in the title, if we can take "disillusionment" to mean not only a disappointing realization of the way things are, but also a removal of the people's illusions. The people in the houses have been divested of their dreams, their illusions. Only the sailor, the one person in the poem who is given any identity, has any interesting dreams.

The imagery of the poem conveys meaning in another noteworthy way: the first part of the poem might be called a verbal optical illusion, for what we are made to imagine is not so much a village full of white night gowns as a village full of strange, brightly colored nightgowns; we imagine what we are told is not there. The speaker's dissatisfaction with the people is conveyed by dwelling on what they are not. This demonstration of the power of images strengthens the speaker's plea for a world made lively by imagination.

Though imagery has always been a major source of power in poetry, the poem which relies almost entirely on imagery is a relatively recent development. Early in this century, several British and American poets banded together and called themselves imagists; their aim was to produce poetry which was free of the sonorous vagueness they found in English poetry of the late nineteenth and early twentieth centuries. T. E. Hulme's "The Embankment" (p. 28) and Ezra Pound's "In a Station of the Metro" (p. 232) are both products of the imagist movement. More recently, certain poets have explored the uses of what they call the "subjective image," which is less tied to the literal world than is most descriptive imagery. Bill Knott's "Hair Poem" (p. 5) is an example of the subjectivist approach; surrealistic imagery is often used in these poems, on the assumption that certain kinds of images, no matter how odd or fanciful, will arouse predictable responses in most readers.

The assumption made by the subjectivists is not new. Certain images are all but guaranteed to arouse rather specific associations: a white-bearded man in a red suit trimmed with fur; a six-pointed star formed of two interlocking triangles; a black fist raised above the head. Such images are **symbols,** in that they stand for things with which a great many people are familiar. But notice the difficulty of saying in a few words what is meant by Santa Claus, the Star of David, or the Black Power salute. The meaning of a symbol is richer and harder to define than the meaning of a mere sign, like 2, which stands for one plus one. Furthermore, though a symbol will have largely the same associations for most of the people acquainted with it, an individual's response to the symbol will not be predictable. To some, the Black Power salute symbolizes unity and pride; to others, it means violence and outrage.

But the literary symbol is not always as **conventional**, or generally accepted, as those discussed above; more often, an image will become a symbol in the context of the work in which it appears. Before Sir Arthur Conan Doyle created Sherlock Holmes, the deerstalker cap and the calabash pipe were not immediately associated with the art of criminal detection; even now, they do not mean much to readers unfamiliar with Holmes. Many symbols, then, have predictable associations or meanings, but the opportunity to create new symbols remains available. Consider the poems about movies in Section 11 of the Anthology: for some poets, film is a symbol of dream, illusion, nostalgia; for others, it is a symbol of advances in our artistic consciousness. But beware of trying to come too quickly to conclusions about whether an image is a symbol; over-enthusiastic symbol-hunting can lead rapidly to excessive concentration on a poem's "deep hidden meaning," which may not, after all, be there.

Like symbolism, **figurative language** is a kind of image-making which is of primary importance to poetry. Figurative language is language containing any of the following **figures of speech**, in which the denotative, or literal, meanings of words are de-emphasized in favor of other meanings.

The most frequently used figures are **simile** and **metaphor**, in which, for the purposes of fresh perception, one thing is compared to another. In a simile, the comparison is stated: "Joan is as sharp as a tack." Here, two meanings of *sharp* must be borne in mind, or the statement makes no sense. Not all statements in this form are similes, since in some comparisons the shared quality does not shift meanings: "John is as tall as Fred." But to say, "That story is as tall as the Empire State Building" calls on our knowledge of the phrase *tall story*, shifting the meaning of *tall* between the two terms of the comparison. In **metaphor**, the comparison is made without any such connection as *like* or *as*: "Wilfred is a jackass."

This distinction between simile and metaphor is the traditional one, but it does not always seem satisfactory. To say that someone is "like a snake in the corncrib" carries metaphorical force, even though the standard definition of simile is satisfied by the presence of the word *like*. Another way of distinguishing between them is to say that in simile, the comparison is restricted to one or two features shared by the two terms, while metaphor draws several parallels between them. To say that someone is as "devious as a snake" is to refer mainly to the snake's way of traveling; to call someone a snake is to refer to many qualities: lowliness, sliminess (unfair to snakes, by the way), treacherousness, venomousness, and so on.

John Donne [1572–1631]

A VALEDICTION: FORBIDDING MOURNING

As virtuous men pass mildly away,
  And whisper to their souls, to go,
Whilst some of their sad friends do say
  The breath goes now, and some say, no:

So let us melt, and make no noise,   5
  No tear-floods, nor sigh-tempests move,
'Twere profanation of our joys
  To tell the laity our love.

Moving of th' earth brings harms and fears,
  Men reckon what it did and meant,   10
But trepidation of the spheres,
  Though greater far, is innocent.

Dull sublunary lovers' love
  (Whose soul is sense) cannot admit

Absence, because it doth remove   15
  Those things which elemented it.

But we by a love, so much refined
  That our selves know not what it is,
Inter-assured of the mind,
  Care less, eyes, lips, and hands to miss.   20

Our two souls therefore, which are one,
  Though I must go, endure not yet
A breach, but an expansion,
  Like gold to airy thinness beat.

If they be two, they are two so   25
  As stiff twin compasses are two,
Thy soul the fixed foot, makes no show
  To move, but doth, if th' other do.

And though it in the center sit,
  Yet when the other far doth roam,   30
It leans, and hearkens after it,
  And grows erect, as it comes home.

Such wilt thou be to me, who must
  Like th' other foot, obliquely run;
Thy firmness makes my circle just,   35
  And makes me end, where I begun.

8, *laity*: in the church, laymen are those not ordained; the speaker suggests that he
and his beloved have been ordained into the mysteries of a higher form of love than
that shared by most people. 13, *sublunary*: beneath the moon; i.e., earthly.

This poem makes extensive use of simile and metaphor. The first
stanza introduces a comparison between the parting of the lovers
and the parting of a good man and his soul; the implication is that
neither parting will have dreadful consequences. The third stanza
develops this argument. "Moving of th' earth" is an earthquake,
which causes alarm and speculation about its meaning. "Trepida-
tion of the spheres" is the movement of the concentric spheres that,
according to ancient astronomers, surrounded the earth; such move-
ment, though harmless, would be a far vaster phenomenon than an
earthquake. The implication here is that earthly love is subject to all
sorts of physical inconveniences, but love of a higher order is free
from parting's sorrows. After all, as the sixth stanza argues, the lovers

in this poem are not parting forever; when the speaker must leave on some errand, the bond between the two lovers does not break, but expands, like a piece of gold beaten out to thin foil.

The last three stanzas of the poem make up a **metaphysical conceit.** It is an extended simile, because of the explicit *as* in the second line of the passage; but because the comparison shows similarities of several kinds, it may be said to be metaphorical in effect. Such extended similes and metaphors were attacked in the eighteenth century by Samuel Johnson, who felt that they were strained and overwrought; when he applied the term metaphysical conceit to the devices of certain seventeenth-century poets, including Donne, he intended to deride their excessive playing with philosophy and the overingenuity of their figurative analogies. But modern readers have found much to admire in the poetry of Donne and his colleagues; the term *metaphysical* is still applied to them, but it has lost its derogatory connotations.

Other figures of speech important to poetry include **understatement** and **overstatement,** or **hyperbole,** which enable poets to achieve different tones by expressing the same basic idea in slightly varied ways. When E. A. Robinson's speaker describes a dying man in "How Annandale Went Out" (p. 273), he understates when he says "the sight was not so fair / As one or two that I have seen elsewhere." The effect is similar to Swift's famous understatement in *A Tale of a Tub:* "Last week I saw a woman flayed, and you will hardly believe how much it altered her person for the worse."

Hyperbole, on the other hand, exaggerates in order to heighten a serious effect or produce a comic effect. Christopher Marlowe employs this figure of speech seriously in "The Passionate Shepherd to His Love" (p. 157), when his speaker makes promises like this:

And I will make thee beds of roses
And a thousand fragrant posies.

Gregory Corso has used hyperbole to heighten the hysterical tone of "Marriage" (p. 167), as in the passage describing the newlyweds' arrival at Niagara Falls (lines 34–49).

Personification and **apostrophe** are often confused, because there are passages in which they both appear. Personification is the representation of an animal, an inanimate object, or an abstract concept as having human qualities, as in this stanza from Thomas Gray's "Elegy Written in a Country Churchyard" (the whole poem may be found on pp. 83–87):

Let not Ambition mock their useful toil,
   Their homely joys, and destiny obscure;
Nor Grandeur hear with a disdainful smile
   The short and simple annals of the poor.

Apostrophe, on the other hand, consists of a direct address, either to a person or to something else, as when Shelley opens his "Ode to the West Wind": "O wild west wind, thou breath of Autumn's being." When a person is apostrophized, it is assumed that he is not within earshot of the poem's speaker. When Ferrara addresses the count's emissary in "My Last Duchess," he does not employ apostrophe, for the emissary is able to reply if he likes; but when Wordsworth begins a sonnet by saying, "Milton! thou shouldst be living at this hour," it is clear that Milton will not respond. Thus apostrophe can sometimes emphasize, rather than diminish, the silence or distance of the thing or person being addressed.

Two more figures of speech which are often confused are **metonymy** and **synecdoche**. The distinction is subtle: synecdoche may be regarded as a subclass of metonymy. Metonymy substitutes for the thing in question another closely associated with it; examples are the substitution of a writer's name for the body of his work— "Have you read Hemingway?"—and the substitution of *light* for *vision* in the first line of Milton's sonnet on his blindness (p. 140). Synecdoche is a more specific kind of substitution, in which the whole signifies the part—"Here comes the law!"—or vice versa— "The hired hands are hungry."

The **pun**, often derided as "the lowest form of wit," can be a useful figure in poetry, for to take advantage of the similarity in sound between two words with different meanings often enriches the effect of a poem. Most of us are acquainted with bad puns intended to be humorous: "Waiter, this coffee tastes like mud!" "That's because it was ground this morning." But in Dylan Thomas's "Do not go gentle into that good night" (p. 55), we find the phrase "Grave men, near death, who see with blinding sight. . . ." Here, *grave* is used to mean *serious*; but because the men are near death, another meaning of *grave* comes easily to mind.

"Blinding sight" is an oxymoron, a kind of paradox. **Paradox** is the general term referring to a contradiction beneath which some larger truth may lie; **oxymoron** refers only to those paradoxes constructed by joining two contradictory words. "Blinding sight" suggests that men near death may be blinded to their accustomed earthly visions by some sudden vision of things beyond this world. Paradox is also the controlling figure in these concluding lines from Donne's "Holy Sonnet XIV" (p. 139):

Take me to You, imprison me, for I,
Except you enthrall me, never shall be free,
Nor ever chaste, except you ravish me.

The analysis of figures of speech, and of varieties of imagery, consists of more than mere identification. It is true that a reader must know what the figures are before he can go through a poem and point them out; but to do no more than that would be to imply that these devices are merely ornaments hung on an abstract frame. In fact, most uses of these figures make possible the apprehension of things not stated with great explicitness in the poem. For example, pun and paradox contribute significantly to a poem's tone, the attitude its speaker takes toward its subject. Although the paradoxes in Donne's sonnet are rationally constructed, their very profusion helps to convey the emotional intensity of the speaker's desire that God re-enter his soul.

Various figures of speech contribute to a poet's distinctive style. When we read a number of poems by Robert Frost, we discover that understatement gives force to much of his work. The low-key description in "Mending Wall" makes the speaker's comparison of his neighbor to a savage particularly striking; to make such a statement in a matter-of-fact tone renders it more believable than if Frost had let his speaker develop the comparison in an obtrusive attempt to frighten us. Most of these figures of speech can also sharpen a poem's effect by compressing it, making possible in a few lines the inference of many different meanings.

---

1. The following two poems depend heavily on imagery. How do the images convey whatever abstract implications the poems may have? Is anything gained by thinking of the third line of "The Embankment" as containing a pun on "eye"? Is the plum-pit at the end of Hilberry's poem used in a metaphorical sense? If so, how?

T. E. Hulme [1883–1917]

THE EMBANKMENT

[*The fantasia of a fallen gentleman on a cold, bitter night*]

Once, in finesse of fiddles found I ecstasy,
In a flash of gold heels on the hard pavement.
Now see I
That warmth's the very stuff of poesy.
Oh, God, make small   5

The old star-eaten blanket of the sky,
That I may fold it round me and in comfort lie.

Conrad Hilberry [b. 1928]

SLEEPING OUT IN VERMONT

A river rattles its money
In the dark. A crow coughs.
Lightning talks low over the Adirondacks.
Pines let their needles fall,
The first drops of rain.   5

You sleep in flat country.
I miss your gullies, the cricket
Music of your legs.

This is the last of the plums
You sent with me. I hold   10
The pit in my hand,
Seed out of its flesh.

---

2. Examples of the figures of speech discussed in this chapter appear
in the passages below, each of which is taken from a poem in the
Anthology. Locate each example in its context, and discuss its effect.
(For the sake of convenience, each page number refers to the page on
which the example actually appears, not necessarily to the page on
which the poem begins.)

SIMILE:
Day after day, day after day,
We stuck, nor breath nor motion;
As idle as a painted ship
Upon a painted ocean.

> Coleridge, "The Rime of the Ancient Mariner" (p. 108)

METAPHOR:
What is our life? A play of passion . . .

> Ralegh, "What Is Our Life?" (p. 75)

UNDERSTATEMENT:
The grave's a fine and private place,
But none, I think, do there embrace.

> Marvell, "To His Coy Mistress" (p. 165)

HYPERBOLE:
Here once the embattled farmers stood
  And fired the shot heard round the world.

Emerson, "Concord Hymn" (p. 247)

PERSONIFICATION:
The land was taken for taxes,
the young people cut down
and sold to the mills.

Haines, "The Legend of Paper Plates" (p. 123)

APOSTROPHE:
Western wind, when will thou blow . . .

Anonymous, "Western Wind" (p. 157)

METONYMY:
The English archery
  Stuck the French horses.

Drayton, "The Ballad of Agincourt" (p. 246)

SYNECDOCHE:
Blind mouths! That scarce themselves know how to hold
A sheep hook, or have learned aught else the least . . .

Milton, "Lycidas" (p. 146)

PUN:
Therefore I lie with her, and she with me,
And in our faults by lies we flatter'd be.

Shakespeare, Sonnet 138 (p. 190)

OXYMORON:
The nightmare Life-in-Death was she . . .

Coleridge, "The Rime of the Ancient Mariner" (p. 110)

PARADOX:
Thus, though we cannot make our sun
Stand still, yet we will make him run.

Marvell, "To His Coy Mistress" (p. 165)

3. What figures of speech predominate in the following poems? How do they function?

Chidiock Tichborne [1558?–1586]

ELEGY

Written with his Own Hand in
the Tower Before his Execution

My prime of youth is but a frost of cares,
   My feast of joy is but a dish of pain,
My crop of corn is but a field of tares,
   And all my good is but vain hope of gain:
The day is past, and yet I saw no sun,   *5*
And now I live, and now my life is done.

My tale was heard, and yet it was not told,
   My fruit is fall'n, and yet my leaves are green, ✎
My youth is spent, and yet I am not old,
   I saw the world, and yet I was not seen: *10*
My thread is cut, and yet it is not spun,
And now I live, and now my life is done.

I sought my death, and found it in my womb,
   I looked for life, and saw it was a shade,
I trod the earth, and knew it was my tomb,   *15*
   And now I die, and now I was but made:
My glass is full, and now my glass is run,
And now I live, and now my life is done.

3, *corn, tares:* In British usage, even today, *corn* is a small grain such as wheat or barley. *Tares* is a name given to a kind of weed which too often grows in corn fields.

J. V. Cunningham [b. 1911]

THE AGED LOVER DISCOURSES IN THE FLAT STYLE

There are, perhaps, whom passion gives a grace,
Who fuse and part as dancers on a stage,
But that is not for me, not at my age,
Not with my bony shoulders and fat face.
Yet in my clumsiness I found a place   *5*
And use for passion: with it I ignore
My gaucheries and yours, and feel no more
The awkwardness of the absurd embrace.

It is a pact men make, and seal in flesh,
To be so busy with their own desires 10
Their loves may be as busy with their own,
And not in union. Though the two enmesh
Like gears in motion, each with each conspires
To be at once together and alone.

4
Word Choice
and
Word Order

We use the term **diction** to refer to a poet's selection of words, or to the words in a particular poem.

Since poems are made of words, it might seem that diction would cover nearly all aspects of poetry. In fact, however, when we consider a poem's diction, we are concerned with questions that might help us to see what the words have in common: is there some underlying principle, or group of principles, according to which they have been selected? And so we examine the words to see whether they are predominantly formal or colloquial, archaic or modern, in common use or restricted to some specialized body of knowledge, monosyllabic or polysyllabic, and so on. Whatever the results of these examinations, the words in a good poem will be notable for their precision. It will also become clear that each poem creates its own set of criteria for a word's appropriateness.

Because it is largely the business of poetry to render images, sounds, and ideas in a way that will be memorable and fresh, a poet expends a great deal of time and effort looking for the right word for a particular passage, or waiting for the poetic context which will suit a word that has caught his interest.

William Jay Smith has given an amusing account of a poet's desire to claim for his own a word that has struck his fancy. He was being visited by Richard Wilbur, who noticed a little book about mushrooms and mushroom-gathering on Smith's coffee table. As Wilbur picked it up and began leafing through it, Smith said, "Oh, now, there's nothing very interesting in that. I'll put it out of the way."

"Wait a minute," Wilbur said. "Here's an interesting word; it's been underlined."

"Yes, I know. *Duff*. I found it, and it's mine."

"What do you mean, it's yours? It's in this book, isn't it?"

"You know perfectly well what I mean," Smith said. "It's my word. You can't use it. I'm going to use it."

As it happened, Wilbur used the word first, in a poem entitled "To

Ishtar."[1] A few years later, Smith found a place for his use of it, in "Morels" (p. 97). It is worth noting that in neither poem does the word call particular attention to itself; it is no more or less startling than the words around it. In "Morels," for example, it appears effortlessly, as the only word that precisely refers to what the speaker is talking about: "the partly decayed organic matter on the forest floor," to quote a dictionary definition.

Why, then, did Smith and Wilbur seize on the word with feelings of territorial aggression? Evidently many poets are alert to the possibilities inherent in words: their **denotations**, or exact literal meanings, and their **connotations**, or the suggestions they often carry beyond their denotations. Propagandists, too, are sensitive to denotation and connotation; when it is reported that "the Southeast Asian conflict has been escalated," we hear a tone of objectivity, almost as if no people were involved; consider the effect on public opinion if such reports said instead, "In Southeast Asia, more and more people are killing each other."

William Shakespeare [1564–1616]

SONNET 87

Farewell! thou art too dear for my possessing,
And like enough thou know'st thy estimate;
The charter of thy worth gives thee releasing;
My bonds in thee are all determinate.
For how do I hold thee but by thy granting?   *5*
And for that riches where is my deserving?
The cause of this fair gift in me is wanting,
And so my patent back again is swerving.
Thyself thou gav'st, thy own worth then not knowing,
Or me, to whom thou gav'st it, else mistaking;   *10*
So thy great gift, upon misprision growing,
Comes home again, on better judgment making.
    Thus have I had thee, as a dream doth flatter,
    In sleep a king, but, waking, no such matter.

Several of the words in this poem are drawn from legal terminology: *estimate*, value; *charter*, special privilege or exemption; *bonds*, claims; *determinate*, expired; *patent*, document granting a privilege;

---

[1]In Richard Wilbur's *Advice to a Prophet and Other Poems.* New York: Harcourt, Brace & World, 1961. Pp. 48–49.

misprision, mistake or misconduct. The presence of so many legal words draws attention to the legal and financial connotations of other words; *dear,* for example, seems at first to mean *beloved,* but in the context of the poem it takes on its other meaning, *costly.* This use of legal and financial diction gives the poem a somewhat cynical tone. Though the speaker seems to feel sorrow and disillusionment at the end of the relationship, his choice of words implies that the relationship was based on too worldly a foundation.

Since the poet makes demands on the words he uses, the words in turn often make demands on the reader. The precision with which a poet uses words will be lost on the reader who has little knowledge of a poem's diction. The examination of diction requires caution: because language is always changing, we must be particularly careful when we interpret words in poems written before the twentieth century. For example, here is the second stanza from Part V of "The Rime of the Ancient Mariner" (p. 105), published in 1798:

The silly buckets on the deck,
That had so long remained,
I dreamt that they were filled with dew;
And when I awoke, it rained.

How can a bucket be silly, in the usual sense of giddy or foolish? *Webster's Third New International Dictionary* indicates that *silly* derives from a Middle English word meaning happy or blessed and that another archaic meaning of the word is rustic, simple, plain; the example quoted in the dictionary entry is Coleridge's line. Given the context of the passage, though, either *rustic* or *blessed* might work. This is a simple example of **ambiguity**, or simultaneous occurrence of more than one meaning.

In expository prose, which must be clear, ambiguity is not usually an admirable quality. But in poetry, the simultaneous operation of more than one meaning in a word or phrase can add to the richness of the poem's content—as long as all the plausible meanings make sense, or function rewardingly, in the poem.

A complex and fruitful ambiguity occurs in Henry Reed's "Naming of Parts" (p. 241). As in "Mending Wall," there are two speakers in the poem, though there are no quotation marks to differentiate them. The first is a drill sergeant, who is explaining the parts of a rifle to a group of recruits. His speech is rough, sometimes ungrammatical, and obsessively to the point. The second speaker is one of the recruits; he does not speak aloud, but the last sentence of each of the first four stanzas, and all of the fifth stanza, reveal what is happening in his mind: he is distorting the drill sergeant's words, letting them be twisted by the images that occupy his daydreaming. The contrast between the two speakers suggests that the recruit's sensitivity to beauty will not permit the drill sergeant's brutal single-mindedness to take over his consciousness. All this is clear enough from the denotative meanings of the words in the poem.

The contrast between the two speakers is effectively heightened, however, when we detect the connotations of certain words and phrases. To begin with the point that is most obvious, the end of the fourth stanza carries sexual connotations (italics added):

. . . And *rapidly backwards and forwards*
The early *bees* are *assaulting* and *fumbling* the *flowers:*
    They call it easing the Spring.

The recruit, in mentally repeating snatches of the drill sergeant's monologue, is giving them a sexual meaning which could not be farther from the drill sergeant's mind. But once it is clear that this is happening, many of the words and phrases in the gunnery lecture appear to have been chosen for their openness to sexual interpretation, so that the gulf between the two speakers can be further emphasized. That the recruit can read sexual innuendo into the drill sergeant's speech suggests that the recruit can conquer this death-dealing monologue with a restless urge toward creation. In this poem, then, the denotation killeth, but the connotation giveth life.

Certain words and phrases take on special connotative force by recalling some event, person, or literary context which existed prior to the poem in which they appear. Such references are called **allusions**. Like figurative language and ambiguity, allusion can compress the poet's thought into a few words, by taking advantage of the reader's previous knowledge.

Some critics prefer to think of allusion as a figure of speech rather than as a device of diction. But allusion is discussed in this chapter because the kind of attention the beginning reader must devote to it is similar to the attention he must give to other matters of word choice. For example, look at these two lines from Part II of Pope's "Essay on Criticism" (p. 320):

When Ajax strives some rock's vast weight to throw,
The line too labours, and the words move slow.

The point of the couplet—to arrange words in such a way that they are difficult to speak smoothly and quickly—would not be greatly altered by substituting "someone" for "Ajax." But the reference to Ajax, one of the bravest of the Greek warriors portrayed in Homer's *Iliad*, conjures up a far more vivid and concrete image.

Obviously, allusion gives most pleasure when it causes the least inconvenience at the moment we encounter it. If, as most poets apparently intend, we already know the reference, we can take pleasure in the device and in a recognition of shared knowledge. But what if we do not immediately understand the allusion? Some time and energy must be devoted to looking it up in a dictionary, encyclopedia, or some more specialized reference tool such as a synopsis of mythology; or we can ask for help from someone who is likely to know the reference. In any case, this seems at first like more work than a poem ought to require of us. But as allusions become clearer and knowledge is increased, and the poem's impact can be more strongly felt, the labor seems worth it. True, some poems outlive the impact of their allusions; Shelley's "England in 1819" (p. 205) requires more knowledge of English history than many contemporary readers possess. But even though we cannot become passionate at the injustice of the Test Act, we can think of contemporary analogies to that particular restriction of human freedom.

Denotation, connotation, sound, ambiguity, allusion. If we must consider all these aspects of language when we look at a poem, may we conclude that there is a special class of words in every language that is reserved in a **poetic diction**? Many poets have thought so. In eighteenth-century England especially, poets went to unusual lengths to exclude from their serious work those words which carried suggestions of commonness, of the everyday. Alexander Pope, in a broadly ironic treatise called "The Art of Sinking in Poetry" (1728), ridiculed poets who used common words, as in these lines:

And his scorched ribs the hot Contagion *fried.*

Should the whole frame of nature round him break,
He unconcerned would hear the mighty *Crack.*

A few pages further on, however, Pope makes fun of poets who use exalted, consciously poetic language to convey "vulgar and low actions of life" by circumlocution or allusion or both. Here are two of his examples, headed with his own paraphrases:

SHUT THE DOOR.
The wooden guardian of our privacy
Quick on its axle turn. . . .

LIGHT THE FIRE.
Bring forth some remnant of *Promethean* theft,
Quick to expand th' inclement air congealed
By *Boreas'* rude breath. . . .

Pope's position is not quite paradoxical, for both kinds of unintentional humor **(bathos)** where high seriousness is sought are caused by diction inappropriate to the context. Today it is generally felt that an appropriate poetic context may be found for any word; there is no reason, for example, to object to the word *moll* in Norman Rosten's "Nobody Dies Like Humphrey Bogart" (p. 295); on the other hand, *lady*, a perfectly serviceable word in some writing, would seem odd in the same context.

Word order is not, strictly speaking, an aspect of diction, but rather of style. Because English does not operate on a system of inflected endings like Latin, we depend on word order for sense. "This water is cold" may not mean the same thing as "Cold is this water"—especially if, in the second sentence, the speaker is using cold water to show the meaning of *cold* to someone who does not know the language very well. However, it is possible to shift words from one position to another in a sentence in order to achieve a desired emphasis. "Ask not . . ." begins President Kennedy's famous inaugural exhortation; this sounds better than "Don't ask . . . ." Keats's "On First Looking into Chapman's Homer" (p. 329) contains several such **inversions** of syntax; for example, the first line, "Much have I traveled in the realms of gold," places the emphasis on the amount of travel, rather than on the speaker of the poem; it is therefore more to the point than "I have traveled much in the realms of gold."

Partly because this technique was often used to excess in English and American poetry before 1910, and partly because English word order has become more rigid with the passage of time, inversions are rare in recent poetry. However, just as any word may find its place in the right poem, so unusual word order may be used to good effect in contemporary poetry.

The following nineteenth-century poem contains many examples of inverted word order. In a broad sense, the examples are typical of the inversions which were generally used in poems from the same period.

"A. Sailor" (Robert Peter) [fl. 1875]

O! WHEREFORE

O! wherefore pensive heaves that sigh?
  Why is thy face o'ercast with sorrow?
Thy throbbing bosom heaving high;
And wherefore should thy grief-dimmed eye
  That tint of melancholy borrow?   5

....

'Tis thus with me; I cherish dear
  Each fond memorial of affection;
My heart the impress still shall wear—
Though fate doth now asunder tear
  Those ties, the cause of my dejection.   *10*

For soon the dark, deep, rolling waves
  Of wild Atlantic shall us sever;
And while around me ocean raves,
Still warm remembrance friendship craves;
  Thee, M. M. Woods, forget I'll never!   *15*

Even if we make allowances for the fact that inversions of this sort
were common in nineteenth-century poetry, there are certain lines
here which suffer because they are inverted: many of them have been
wrenched out of normal order merely in order to force a rhyming
word into position at the end of a line.

   The poem below, on the other hand, uses inversions for other pur-
poses, even though some of the lines rhyme. It is a contemporary
poem, part of a book-length sequence entitled *The Dream Songs.*[1]
The central character of the sequence is a man named Henry; he is
also the speaker of most of the poems. Sometimes, as here, he speaks
of himself in the third person.

John Berryman [1914–1972]

DREAM SONG # 29

There sat down, once, a thing on Henry's heart
só heavy, if he had a hundred years
& more, & weeping, sleepless, in all them time
Henry could not make good.
Starts again always in Henry's ears   *5*
the little cough somewhere, an odour, a chime.

And there is another thing he has in mind
like a grave Sienese face a thousand years
would fail to blur the still profiled reproach of. Ghastly,
with open eyes, he attends, blind.   *10*
All the bells say: too late. This is not for tears;
thinking.

---

[1] John Berryman's *Dream Songs.* New York: Farrar, Straus & Giroux, 1969.

But never did Henry, as he thought he did,
end anyone and hacks her body up
and hide the pieces, where they may be found.
He knows: he went over everyone, & nobody's missing.
Often he reckons, in the dawn, them up.
Nobody is ever missing.

15

Here, the tortured syntax clearly arises from the speaker's tortured state of mind. Trying desperately to identify the guilt that nags him, Henry speaks sometimes in phrases that recall black slang and sometimes in learned, allusive phrases like "grave Sienese face"—a reference to the conservative art of medieval Siena, in Italy. Both erudition and slang can lead to shifts in word order which help to convey Henry's hysteria.

These examples suggest that there is nothing intrinsically successful or unsuccessful about inverted word order in poetry. What makes inversion succeed or fail is its effect, from which we can deduce its apparent purpose. In "O! Wherefore" the inversions appear to have been mere conveniences for the versifier, because there is nothing else in the poem's diction which gives a convincing expression of the grief which the speaker says he feels. Most of the words having to do with the speaker's feelings are no more than abstract names for emotions: *sorrow, grief, melancholy, affection, dejection, remembrance, friendship.*

Berryman's Henry, on the other hand, never uses an abstract word; he speaks of his feelings in terms of what they do to his mind and body. We can sense the guilt without needing to see the word *guilt.* The inversions, because they appear to have arisen from Henry's emotional state, seem like necessities rather than conveniences.

---

1. Read "The Fury of Aerial Bombardment" (p. 253). How would you characterize the diction of the first three stanzas? The last stanza? What is the effect of this shift?
2. In the following poem, what is the effect of the shift in diction between the first part of the poem and the last two sentences?

Robert Lowell [b. 1917]

IN THE CAGE

The lifers file into the hall,
According to their houses—twos
Of laundered denim. On the wall

[40]*Poetry: Points of Departure*

A colored fairy tinkles blues
And titters by the balustrade;   5
Canaries beat their bars and scream.
We come from tunnels where the spade
Pick-axe and hod for plaster steam
In mud and insulation. Here
The Bible-twisting Israelite   10
Fasts for his Harlem. It is night,
And it is vanity, and age
Blackens the heart of Adam. Fear,
The yellow chirper, beaks its cage.

---

3. Discuss the diction of the following poem. Pay particular attention to those words which are directly concerned with the speaker's feelings.

John Crowe Ransom [b. 1888]

BELLS FOR JOHN WHITESIDE'S DAUGHTER

There was such speed in her little body,
And such lightness in her footfall,
It is no wonder her brown study
Astonishes us all.

Her wars were bruited in our high window.   5
We looked among orchard trees and beyond,
Where she took arms against her shadow,
Or harried unto the pond

The lazy geese, like a snow cloud
Dripping their snow on the green grass,   10
Tricking and stopping, sleepy and proud,
Who cried in goose, Alas,

For the tireless heart within the little
Lady with rod that made them rise
From their noon apple-dreams and scuttle   15
Goose-fashion under the skies!

But now go the bells, and we are ready,
In one house we are sternly stopped
To say we are vexed at her brown study,
Lying so primly propped.   20

5
Form
Sound
and
Structure

Though we have established the difficulty of defining poetry, most of it is easily distinguishable from other kinds of writing. In prose, the length of the line is immaterial, and may be changed without altering the meaning of the passage. Most poetry, however, is written in **verse,** a kind of writing in which some principle other than the width of the page determines the length of each line.

In **formal verse** in English, the length of each line is determined by counting stressed syllables, or all the syllables, or units composed of stressed and unstressed syllables. In **free verse,** the length of each line is determined intuitively, as the poet senses the poem's rhythmical requirements. However, once a free-verse poem is finished, changing the length of any line will alter the effect of the poem.

Stress is the emphasis or increased pitch which falls on certain syllables in a word, phrase, or sentence. If the poet decides at the outset that each line of his poem will contain four stresses, he might come up with something like this (stress marks added):

An áxe ángles
               from my néighbor's áshcan;
It is héll's hándiwork,
             the wóod not híckory,
The flów of the gráin
             not fáithfully fóllowed.

These three lines begin Richard Wilbur's "Junk" (p. 230), a contemporary imitation of Anglo-Saxon verse. Its **meter** (from the Greek *metron,* measure) is the oldest in English verse: Anglo-Saxon poems were written in four-stress lines, with a heavy pause, or **caesura,** between the second and third stresses. The number of syllables in each line was not formally predetermined; likewise in Wilbur's poem the lines vary from eight to twelve syllables.

In **syllabic verse,** the situation is just the opposite: each line contains a predetermined number of syllables, but the number of stresses per line may vary (stress marks in first stanza added):

Ray Holt [1941–1970]

MY MOROSE MASTER-SERGEANTS

Nów, súddenly, they shów úp
In dréams of a dístant pást.
Will they bárk óld órders ónce
Agáin? Swímming the céiling,
They dróp forgótten námes, óld   5
Cómrades and nightmare evénts.

But when I sit up to speak,
I cannot hear their voices,
And distance lies between us
Like the Pacific. Over   10
There, terrible fire still falls
As silently as fireworks

Looked at through a telescope;
It lights my room whenever
My morose master-sergeants   15
Float into my darkened room
To make their disinterested,
Silent sales-pitch for the dead.

Each line of this poem contains seven syllables, though the number of stresses varies from two to four. The next-to-last line is an example of the occasional necessity of determining a line's meter by looking at the rest of the poem. By itself, the line could be said to contain either seven or eight syllables, depending on whether one says *dis-in-ter-es-ted* or *dis-in-t'res-ted.* The point is that meter, even syllable-counting, is not totally mathematical; one must sometimes make judgments based on the context of the line.

"Fern Hill" (p. 134) is a more complex example of syllabic verse, in that the predetermining principle is based on a whole **stanza** — a group of two or more consistently organized sets of lines, bound together by some formal element, usually rhyme. With a few exceptions, the lines in the same position in each stanza contain the same number of syllables; even the exceptions are placed with a certain symmetry.

By far the most usual unit of meter in verse written in English is the **foot,** a combination of stressed and unstressed syllables. There are four basic feet:

1. the **iamb:** one unstressed syllable and one stressed syllable, in that order, as in prŏfóund, dĭstínct, ălóne. The adjectival form of iamb is **iambic.**
2. the **trochee:** one stressed syllable and one unstressed syllable, in that order, as in úndĕr, míttĕn, éssĕnce. Adjectival form: **trochaic.**
3. the **anapest:** two unstressed syllables and one stressed syllable, in that order, as in ĭntĕrfere, ĭntĕrtwine, dĭsáppear. Adjectival form: **anapestic.**
4. the **dactyl:** one stressed syllable and two unstressed syllables, in that order, as in hórrĭblĕ, Cárnăbў, fínĕrў. Adjectival form: **dactylic.**

In addition to these basic feet, there are a number of others that have been identified and named by students of **prosody,** the theory and principles of versification. These are used as substitutes for one of the basic feet in a line; few poems have employed them throughout. The most usual are:

1. the **spondee:** two stressed syllables, as in bóokcáse, wínegláss, or in pairs of monosyllabic words like stríke twó. Adjectival form: **spondaic.**
2. the **pyrrhus:** two unstressed syllables together. Some prosodists are reluctant to classify this as a foot, since it contains no stress; but it needs to be kept in mind, since it turns up as a substitute for an iamb, as in the third foot of this line: Dównward/ to dárk/ ness, on/ extén/ ded wíngs. Adjectival form: **pyrrhic.**

These prosodic designations derive from Greek and Roman metrical systems, in which it was not stress but duration that characterized the primary syllable of a prosodic unit. In those languages, certain syllables were long, not in the phonetic sense, but in actual time elapsed in pronunciation. Because these classical prosodic systems have been adapted to a stressed language, they admit a certain number of artificialities. The most obvious of these is the tacit assumption that there are only two degrees of stress in the language. Since there are actually many gradations of stress, it is nearly impossible to find a line of five iambs in which each of the five stresses receives equal emphasis. As a way of slightly alleviating this difficulty, we admit into our system of scansion the **half-stress** (˘), used when we wish to call attention to a syllable which falls in a stress-receiving position but which normally would not be heavily stressed — as in this line of five iambs: Frŏm Kénnĕbúnkpŏrt to Schĕnéctădў.

In naming a line of verse composed of the feet listed above, we use a two-word term made up of (1) the adjectival form of the name of the foot used in the line, and (2) a noun which indicates the number of feet in the line. These nouns are:

monometer: one foot
dimeter: two feet
trimeter: three feet
tetrameter: four feet
pentameter: five feet
hexameter: six feet
heptameter: seven feet
octameter: eight feet

Here, then, are some such terms, together with examples of the line each describes.

Anapestic tetrameter:
Thĕ Aŝsýriăn came dówn lĭke thĕ wólf oṅ thĕ fóld,
Aṅd hĭs cóhŏrts wĕre gléamĭng iṅ púrpĺe aṅd góld.

Dactylic trimeter:
Júmp frŏm thĕ édge ŏf ă précĭpice,
Nérvŏuslў múttĕriṅg dóggĕrĕl.

Iambic tetrameter:
a. Whŏse wóods thĕse áre Ĭ thĭnk Ĭ knów.
b. He'd reáched thĕ pínnăclĕ ŏf fáme
   Whĕn tò thĕ précĭpice hĕ cáme.

Iambic pentameter:
a. Shăll Í cŏmpáre thĕe tò ă súmmĕr's dáy?
   Thóu àrt mŏre lóvelў, aṅd mŏre témpĕràte.
b. Thĕ lóng rèd úndĕrwèar ŏf Rándŏlph Scótt,
   Thĕ góld-rìmmed spéctăclès ŏf Jóel McCréa,
   Úndĕrscòre áge, aṅd thrŏugh thĕ réverĕnd plót
   Thĕ óld gúnfìghtĕrs ríde fŏr óne móre dáy.

Trochaic tetrameter:
Táke thў hát, mў líttlĕ Láură,
Fíx ĭt bу̀ thĕ lóop ĕlástĭc.

Armed with these terms and a knowledge of how to place the little scansion marks, you look at a poem and wonder what to do. Prosodic analysis, in the strictest sense, is merely breaking down the prosodic elements in the poem; but it is of little critical value unless it leads to critical conclusions. Many students seem to feel an obligation to devote some portion of each paper they write about poetry to pointing to prosodic phenomena, in paragraphs that sound like mere lists: "This poem is written in fifteen lines of iambic pentameter, with trochaic substitutions in lines 4, 7, and 9, and with a spondee in the fifteenth line." Unless we can say something about the way those substitutions operate, there is not much point in drawing attention to them. In the following piece of doggerel nonsense, there are a few blatant metrical variations which bear some relation to the "content" of the passage in which they appear.

A little story I will tell
Of one man's rise, and how he fell.
He worked his fingers to the bone
Striving to make his name well known.
He wrote the most fantastic letters   5
To curry favor with his betters;
When one of these he chanced to meet,
He groveled at the great man's feet.
At last his fame was recognized,
Though no one yet quite realized   10
Just what the nature of his gift
Might be; no one had heard him lift
His voice in song, or seen him paint;
He'd reached the pinnacle of fame
When to the precipice he came: 15
The substance of the general public complaint
Against him was that he just wasn't worth much of anything after
   all, and so he settled into a quiet, embarrassed obscurity.

A cursory syllable- and stress-count reveals that the majority of these lines are iambic tetrameter. The variations of interest are these:

1.   Ŏf óne màn's ríse, aňd hów hĕ féll.

The second foot here is nearly spondaic, and this strengthens the pause at the comma, thereby emphasizing the comparative briskness of the following four syllables; the line tumbles toward the announcement of the protagonist's fall.

2.   Stríviňg tŏ máke hĭs náme wèll knówn.

The first foot is trochaic, so *striving* against the prevailing meter;

the final near-spondee emphasizes the magnitude of the protago-
nist's goal.

3. Hĕ wróte thĕ móst făntástĭc léttĕrs
    Tó cúrrў fávŏr wìth hĭs béttĕrs.

The extra unstressed syllable at the end of each line is not a func-
tional variation. It is a convention of metrical writing called the **femi-
nine ending**, formally defined as an unstressed syllable occurring
after the final stress in a line of anapestic or iambic verse.

4. Thŏugh nó oñe thén quìte rĕălízed
    Jùst whát thĕ ñatuře òf hĭs gíft
    Mĭght bé; nò óne hăd heárd hím líft
    Hĭs vóice ĭn sóng, ŏr séen hĭm páint.

The lines preceding this passage are all end-stopped, either by
punctuation or prose sense. Reading these lines as end-stopped,
however, would distort the sense; these lines are enjambed, or run
on. The effects of **enjambment** are to vary the overall rhythm of the
poem, keeping it from falling into quite predictable units of eight
syllables each, and to make the rhymes somewhat less obtrusive.

5. Hĕ'd réached thĕ pínnăclè ŏf fáme
    Whèn tŏ thĕ précĭpĭce hĕ cáme.

The example on page 45 illustrating dactylic trimeter contains the
word *precipice*, and yet the word also appears here in what is sup-
posed to be iambic tetrameter. How can this be? The iambic con-
text here, well established by the time these lines appear, puts the
half-stress on the third syllables of *pinnacle* and *precipice*, but these
half-stresses are quite audible, so that there is an emphasis on fame
in the first of the lines, and a rush toward catastrophe in the second,
before the poem, like the man's career, trails off ignominiously into
prose.

These brief analyses demonstrate two cardinal rules of prosodic
analysis. First, never point out a prosodic feature unless you are pre-
pared to find out something more about it than the fact of its exist-
ence. Second, remember that abstract metrical patterns rarely convey
any meaning. For meter to add to meaning, as in the "rush toward
catastrophe" above, the meaning must be contained in the words
themselves.

Rhyme, like meter, is a basic organizing element in formal verse. Whereas meter alone can make possible a line-by-line formal progression in a poem, rhyme at the ends of lines makes possible a progression in larger units called **stanzas.**

For example, Godsey's "Hoppy" (p. 298) is written in unrhymed iambic pentameter **(blank verse)**. In terms of form, then, it develops a line at a time, though in broader structural terms it falls into seven **verse paragraphs**, which are distinguished from stanzas in that they are not similarly rhymed or of identical length.

"Baroque Image" (p. 196), on the other hand, proceeds formally in four-line stanzas which are all similar in some respects. Here is the first stanza:

He angled the bright shield
To catch the setting sun,
And dazzled the whole field,
Enemy, friend, as one.

The **rhyme scheme** of this stanza, represented by assigning a letter of the alphabet to each occurrence of a rhyme-sound, would be *a b a b*. The metrical scheme of the stanza remains constant throughout the poem: each line is iambic trimeter (note that there are feminine endings in the second stanza, which is why some of the iambic trimeter lines contain seven syllables). This stanza is an example of a **quatrain**, a stanza which in its numerous forms has become more popular than any other stanza in English and American verse. A quatrain is defined as a stanza of four lines; three common types of the quatrain are:

1. **ballad stanza** (stress marks added):

O móther, móther, máke my béd!   a   x
O máke it sóft and nárrow!   b   a
Since mỳ love díed for mé todáy,   c OR x
I'll díe for hím tomórrow.   b   a[1]

2. **elegiac stanza** (stress marks added):

The cúrfew tólls the knéll of párting dáy,   a
The lówing hérd winds slówly ó'er the léa,   b
The plówman hómeward plóds his wéary wáy,   a
And léaves the wórld to dárkness ànd to mé.   b

---

[1]The *xaxa* rhyme scheme is used only when a poem has a large number of unrhymed lines appearing at regular intervals. In such cases it is sometimes useful to mark each unrhymed line with an x, and then mark the rhymed lines. This readily reveals the pattern according to which the unrhymed lines are placed.

3. **envelope quatrain** (variously metered):

Though beauty be the mark of praise,	a
And yours of whom I sing be such	b
As not the world can praise too much,	b
Yet is't your virtue now I raise.	a

The **tercet** is a three-line stanza, variously rhymed and metered. When each line ends with the same rhyme-sound, it is sometimes called a **triplet. Terza rima,** the rhyme scheme of Dante's *Divine Comedy,* links rhymes from one tercet to the next: *aba bcb cdc,* etc.

The **couplet,** two rhymed lines, seems different from other rhyme units in the way it affects the formal progression of a poem: couplet-by-couplet progression is an extension of line-by-line progression, since it merely doubles the length of each unit. But the couplet, tercet, and quatrain combine to make many of the other stanzas in English and American verse; here, for example, is the first stanza from "The Eve of St. Agnes," by John Keats (1795–1821); it is an example of the **Spenserian stanza,** named for Edmund Spenser (ca. 1552–1599), who first used it in *The Faerie Queene.*

St. Agnes' Eve—Ah, bitter chill it was!
The owl, for all his feathers, was a-cold;
The hare limped trembling through the frozen grass,
And silent was the flock in wooly fold:
Numb were the Beadsman's fingers, while he told   5
His rosary, and while his frosted breath,
Like pious incense from a censer old,
Seemed taking flight for heaven, without a death,
Past the sweet Virgin's picture, while his prayer he saith.

Notice the stanza's "rules": it consists of nine lines, the first eight being iambic pentameter, the last being iambic hexameter. Its rhyme scheme links the two quatrains, and the last line rhymes with the eighth: $a\ b\ a\ b\ b\ c\ b\ c\ c.$

We can see these organizing principles as a progression. First, the abstract metrical scheme provides a base against which the poet counterpoints the actual meter of his line. In other words, since very few lines of poetry are *precise* examples of a regular metrical pattern, a pleasing tension arises between the regular beat of the abstract pattern and the slight irregularities of the line itself. Second, the line-by-line accumulation of the abstract metrical scheme provides a base against which the poet can counterpoint varying sentence structures, shifts in diction, and so on. Third, rhyme provides an abstract pattern against which the poet counterpoints by means of structural and metrical variations. The slight discrepancies between abstract patterns and actual patterns produce part of the energy which gives a poem liveliness.

In a successful poem, these formal elements operate at a level of the mind different from that at which the poem's surface content is operating. They create almost unconscious rhythmical responses, patterns of anticipation and fulfillment, while the conscious mind is absorbed with what is being said. This is not to suggest, however, that "form" and "content" can be separated, except for the convenience of discussion; our unconscious responses to formal elements have some bearing on the effect of the content. This is why, as we noted in Chapter 1, a paraphrase cannot be viewed as a substitute for the poem.

If rhyme and meter were the only sound devices that could affect our sensibilities in these ways, free verse would be an impossibility, since it would not differ from arbitrarily chopped prose. However, a number of other uses of sound add variety to the poet's resources.

Alliteration is the repetition of initial consonant sounds: "Howard hums horribly." The Anglo-Saxon four-stress line uses alliteration to emphasize some of the stressed syllables, as in Wilbur's "Junk" (p. 230). **Hidden alliteration** is the repetition of consonant sounds within words: "I told him to follow the hallway." **Assonance** is the strict term for the repetition of vowel sounds, though when they occur initially in three or more words, they may be called alliteration. Assonance and alliteration can draw our attention to the relations between words, or to a whole line; as Spiro Agnew has demonstrated, they can make a phrase more memorable: "Nattering nabobs of negativism."

Consonance is the repetition, at the ends of lines, of consonant sounds. It differs from rhyme because the vowels preceding the consonants need not sound alike. For example, *heat* and *beat* rhyme, but *heat* and *hat*, or *heat* and *let*, are examples of consonance. Consonance is one kind of inexact or **slant rhyme**; the other kind employs line-end assonance, in pairs like *scream* and *Queen*. The following poem contains interesting patterns of both kinds of slant rhyme:

W. H. Auden [1907–1973]

That night when joy began
Our narrowest veins to flush,
We waited for the flash
Of morning's levelled gun.

But morning let us pass, 5
And day by day relief
Outgrows his nervous laugh,
Grows credulous of peace,

As mile by mile is seen
No trespasser's reproach, 10
And love's best glasses reach
No fields but are his own.

The slant rhyming here is complex; none of the end words rhyme exactly, but in each stanza they share similar sounds. The first and fourth lines are related by final consonance, as are the second and third. Based on consonance, then, the rhyme scheme is *abba*. But there is assonance at work too, relating first and third lines and second and fourth lines, so that a rhyme scheme based on assonance would be *abab*. The poem even contains **internal** slant **rhymes**, such as *trespasser's* and *best glasses*. Such a dense texture of sound helps this poem to stay in the mind even before its meaning becomes clear. It can reverberate in the mind without causing too much discomfort at incomplete understanding, gradually becoming clearer as we carry it about in our heads.

Onomatopoeia is a term for words whose sounds echo what they mean: *bang*, *whizz*. It is a tricky term, however; it must be distinguished from **euphony** and **cacophony**, which characterize the general effect of a series of sounds. Euphony is smooth and flowing, and cacophony is rough and jarring. All these kinds of sound are at work in the following poem:

e. e. cummings [1894–1962]

Buffalo Bill's
defunct
        who used to
        ride a watersmooth-silver
                        stallion 5
and break onetwothreefourfive pigeonsjustlikethat
                                Jesus
he was a handsome man
                        and what I want to know is
how do you like your blueeyed boy 10
Mister Death

The third, fourth, and fifth lines of this poem are euphonious, in that the long vowel sounds in *used, to, ride,* and *watersmooth* combine with the *l*'s of *silver* and *stallion* to reinforce an effect of smoothness and speed. The next line, with its two sets of words run together, is cacophonous, but not unpleasant, for we can see the function of the cacophony in the sense of speed and violence it helps to convey. The line may also be said to employ onomatopoeia, since the staccato movement of the syllables echoes the rapid-fire precision with which the great marksman shattered clay pigeons.

At this point it must be noted that these sounds alone do not *create* these effects, they merely emphasize them; for without meaning, sound alone does not convey smoothness or rapid-fire precision or anything else.

Though this poem is in free verse, its effects are as carefully controlled as those in a good formal poem. One illustration will make this point clear. Move the word *Jesus* to the left-hand margin, for example:

and break onetwothreefourfive pigeonsjustlikethat
Jesus
he was a handsome man

This change, simple as it may seem, breaks down important connections between the first and third of the quoted lines. In our placement, *Jesus* precedes the third line; in Cummings's placement, it follows the first. Cummings's placement makes *Jesus* an exclamation of admiration for the sharpshooting first, and a lead-in to the next line second, so that *handsome* may be seen as a description of performance as well as appearance.

So far, we have maintained a distinction between **form** and **structure**, declaring form to consist of repetitive patterns that may exist prior to the poem in which they appear, and structure to consist of the individual, overall pattern which evolves as the poem proceeds. Some ways of structuring a poem, however, have become **conventions**—generally accepted elements of poetic composition. Some of these we now regard as **fixed forms.**

The **limerick** is the most obvious example of a fixed form in English:

Bruce Haley [b. 1933]

THE RIME OF THE ANCIENT MARINER

If I only had something to drink
I'd be fairly happy, I think;

Still, I'm sometimes made gloomy
By this bird that's tied to me:
It's heavy, and starting to stink.   5

The metrical pattern and the rhyme scheme of the limerick are so
familiar that it is almost impossible to imagine putting the form to
straight-faced use.

Similarly, the **sonnet** has come to have structural conventions
which are so nearly fixed that to depart from them is to imply some
attitude toward poetic tradition. The sonnet form originated in Italy,
where it was brought to a high degree of excellence by Francesco
Petrarca, for whom the **Petrarchan sonnet** is named. Like all sonnets,
the Petrarchan consists of fourteen lines, usually in iambic pentame-
ter. The rhyme scheme echoes the poem's tendency to fall into two
divisions; it is rhymed *abbaabba cdcdcd*. The last six lines may also
be rhymed *cdedec*, or *ccdccd*, or in any other scheme that does not
end in a couplet.

J. K. Stephen [1859–1892]

A SONNET

Two voices are there: one is of the deep;
It learns the storm-cloud's thunderous melody,
Now roars, now murmurs with the changing sea,
Now bird-like pipes, now closes soft in sleep:
And one is of an old half-witted sheep   5
Which bleats articulate monotony,
And indicates that two and one are three,
That grass is green, lakes damp, and mountains steep:
And, Wordsworth, both are thine: at certain times
Forth from the heart of thy melodious rhymes,   10
The form and pressure of high thoughts will burst:
At other times—good Lord! I'd rather be
Quite unacquainted with the ABC
Than write such hopeless rubbish as thy worst.

The first eight lines, the octave, contain two rhymes, patterned
into two envelope quatrains. The last six lines, the sestet, fall into
two tercets. The structure of the poem follows the divisions suggested
by the rhyme scheme. The first quatrain introduces the proposition
that there are two voices, and characterizes one of them; the second
quatrain characterizes the second voice.

Then between the octave and the sestet there comes a **turn**, a change in attitude or, as here, a surprising revelation: both voices belong to Wordsworth. The speaker's reaction to the two voices falls into two parts, the two tercets. So the movement characteristic of the Petrarchan sonnet is the introduction and elaboration of a problem or situation in the octave, and the resolution of the problem, or some other relaxation of the octave's pressure, in the sestet.

The **Elizabethan** or **Shakespearean sonnet,** on the other hand, falls into three quatrains and a couplet; it is rhymed *abab cdcd efef gg,* with the turn called for between the third quatrain and the couplet. In many cases, however, the Elizabethan sonnet retains the eight-six division of the Petrarchan sonnet; the final couplet sums up the resolution begun in the third quatrain, rather than the entire twelve lines preceding it. It is hard to find an Elizabethan sonnet which adheres strictly to the twelve-two division, because this structure requires great compression in the couplet; there have been twelve lines instead of eight in which to build a situation to its turning point.

Michael Drayton [1563–1631]

Since there's no help, come let us kiss and part;
Nay, I have done, you get no more of me,
And I am glad, yea glad with all my heart
That thus so cleanly I myself can free;
Shake hands forever, cancel all our vows,   5
And when we meet at any time again,
Be it not seen in either of our brows
That we one jot of former love retain.
Now at the last gasp of love's latest breath,
When, his pulse failing, passion speechless lies,
When faith is kneeling by his bed of death,   10
And innocence is closing up his eyes,
   Now if thou wouldst, when all have given him over,
   From death to life thou mightst him yet recover.

The basic turn here does fall between the third quatrain and the final couplet, since each quatrain carries forward the notion of an affair's dissolution, and the couplet suddenly introduces the possibility of reopening it. However, as happens in many Elizabethan sonnets, the effect of the older Petrarchan convention can be felt between the second quatrain and the third: having spoken in a literal, almost businesslike way for eight lines, the speaker suddenly launches into high-sounding personifications of love, passion, faith, and innocence, thereby intensifying a feeling of loss, and perhaps foreshadowing the final declaration that all traces of love are not lost.

---

1. The following three poems are examples of **French forms**, so called because they evolved among the medieval French troubadors. Each of them—triolet, villanelle, and ballade—has rules requiring the repetition, at specified intervals, of certain lines; the term for a regularly repeating line is **refrain**. The rules also require that the rhyme scheme *and* the rhyme-sounds remain constant from stanza to stanza. In the ballade, for example, this means that there must be fourteen *b* rhymes. Each form has a fixed number of lines. Unlike the sonnet, however, these forms need not be written in a particular meter; the rules demand only that the meter, whatever it is, remains constant throughout the poem. With these general principles as a guide, try to determine the specific rules for each of the following three poems.

---

a. Triolet
Austin Dobson [1840–1921]

A KISS

Rose kissed me today,
  Will she kiss me tomorrow?
Let it be as it may,
Rose kissed me today.
But the picture gives way   5
  To a savor of sorrow;—
Rose kissed me today,—
  Will she kiss me tomorrow?

b. Villanelle
Dylan Thomas [1914–1953]

DO NOT GO GENTLE INTO THAT GOOD NIGHT

Do not go gentle into that good night,
Old age should burn and rave at close of day;
Rage, rage against the dying of the light.

Though wise men at their end know dark is right,
Because their words had forked no lightning they   5
Do not go gentle into that good night.

Good men, the last wave by, crying how bright
Their frail deeds might have danced in a green bay,
Rage, rage against the dying of the light.

Wild men who caught and sang the sun in flight,   *10*
And learn, too late, they grieved it on its way,
Do not go gentle into that good night.

Grave men, near death, who see with blinding sight
Blind eyes could blaze like meteors and be gay,
Rage, rage against the dying of the light.   *15*

And you, my father, there on the sad height,
Curse, bless, me now with your fierce tears, I pray.
Do not go gentle into that good night.
Rage, rage against the dying of the light.

c. Ballade
William Ernest Henley [1849–1903]

BALLADE OF DEAD ACTORS

Where are the passions they essayed,
    And where the tears they made to flow?
Where the wild humors they portrayed
    For laughing worlds to see and know?
    Othello's wrath and Juliet's woe?   *5*
Sir Peter's whims and Timon's gall?
    And Millamant and Romeo?
Into the night go one and all.

Where are the braveries, fresh or frayed?
    The plumes, the armours—friend and foe? *10*
The cloth of gold, the rare brocade,
    The mantles glittering to and fro?
    The pomp, the pride, the royal show?
The cries of youth and festival?
    The youth, the grace, the charm, the glow? *15*
Into the night go one and all.

The curtain falls, the play is played:
    The Beggar packs beside the Beau;
The Monarch troops, and troops the maid;
    The Thunder huddles with the Snow.   *20*
    Where are the revellers high and low?

The clashing swords? The lover's call?
    The dancers gleaming row on row?
Into the night go one and all.

Envoy

    Prince, in one common overthrow   ²⁵
The Hero tumbles with the Thrall;
    As dust that drives, as straws that blow,
Into the night go one and all.

An **envoy** is a somewhat conventionalized concluding stanza, sometimes addressed
to an eminent public figure or to the poet's patron. The word derives from the French
verb meaning *to send*; hence, the action of sending forth a poem.

---

2. Turn to page 141 and read "Hallelujah: A Sestina."

A sestina is another French form, but it differs from the three
above in that it employs neither rhyme nor refrain. It is based in-
stead on a principle of end-word repetition. The rules are as follows:

a. Meter is optional, but is usually iambic pentameter in English
examples.

b. The length of the poem is thirty-nine lines, divided into six
stanzas of six lines each, and a concluding stanza, or envoy, of three
lines.

c. The six end words of the first stanza are used as end words in
the next five stanzas; in the envoy, two of the end words appear in
each line—one at the end, and one somewhere earlier in the line.

d. The order in which the end words appear is formally deter-
mined. To discover the formal principle, we first number each of the
end words according to the order of their appearance in the first
stanza: 1, *Hallelujah*; 2, *boy*; 3, *hair*; 4, *praise*; 5, *father*; 6, *Ebenezer*.
Then in the second stanza we see that the order of the words is 6 1 5
2 4 3—last, first, next to last, second, third from last, third. The third
stanza's word order is based on the second stanza in the same way;
and so the order runs through the sixth stanza. The order in which
the end words appear in the envoy is also prescribed. Using the num-
bers assigned to the words in the first stanza, the order for the envoy
is: 5 3 1 at the ends of the lines, and 2 4 6 elsewhere in the lines. (If
the seventh stanza were six lines, with an end-word order deter-
mined by the sixth stanza, what would the order in the seventh
stanza be? Does this suggest a reason for the development of the
shortened conclusion?)

The incredible complexity of this form raises some questions.
Why would anyone try it? Does it seem appropriate to a certain logi-
cal structure, as the form of the sonnet does? If not, perhaps the poet

attempts a sestina for the sheer challenge of it. As Robert Francis has said, "If you drape thirty-nine iron chains over your arms and shoulders and then do a dance, the whole point of the dance will be to seem light and effortless."

A useful and instructive exercise is to attempt a poem in some fixed form. This may be to write from the surface toward the center, but the exercise demonstrates that form can sometimes help you think of ways of saying a thing which you might not have thought of if you were writing free verse.

3. Tom Clark's "Sonnet" (p. 166) is fourteen lines long. What other devices of the sonnet does it employ? Many traditional sonnets have dealt with love; how does this poem treat the subject? Is there any connection between the poem's stance toward the sonnet tradition and its uses of the sonnet's formal elements?

4. Examine John Peale Bishop's "A Recollection" (p. 315). Once you have established its prose sense and assimilated the information in the notes to the poem, read the poem through aloud and try to get a sense of its deftness and grace. Then, look up the word *acrostic* in a dictionary, and apply your knowledge of the word to Bishop's poem. The unusual discovery you make poses a serious artistic question: how can you reconcile your fresh discovery with your previous experience of the poem?

5. Examine David Wagoner's "Song to Accompany the Bearer of Bad News" (p. 213). Can you devise rules for composing a poem in this form?

6
The Process
of Revision

Henry Taylor [b. 1942]

THE HUGHESVILLE SCYTHE

The hills where I grew up had learned to hide
Destructions from each other long before
Hughesville saw destruction take its store,
And still the Hughesville legend has not died:

How once the storekeeper unlocked the door   5
To find he had been robbed. One clue, beside
The hearth, a swallow's nest on the stone floor,
Told him how the burglar had got inside.

The old man took a scythe-blade from his store
And fixed it in the chimney, across the fine-   10
Edged dark, where it would split a man who tried
To come that way again and steal his gold.

No burglar ever came. Now those designs
Are choked in honeysuckle, and the old
Insistent rituals of decay unfold;   15
Yet in my brain that unused blade still shines,

And when I try to walk through dark I hold
My hand before me, touching solid signs,
Thinking how a man can seek for gold
And lie in pieces in the raging vines.   20

Throughout these pages, the reader has been urged to try and see
what a poem wants to do, on the well-established grounds that we
cannot know what the poet was trying to do. Even if the poet decides

to tell all he knows about one of his poems, he cannot account for everything in it.

The following exhibit bears out this statement. I have arranged in chronological order the drafts of one of my own poems; each draft is followed by some remarks on the circumstances under which it was written, and on some of the technical problems I was concerned with at the time. In the process of composition, my own intentions seem to have become subordinated to those of the poem.

I.

The open country around the farm
Where I grew up and learned the way
A clean green hill can come between
A serene observer and an act of purest violence,
That country once was called a town.
The core of town consisted of a church, some houses,
And a country store. That store was closed
Years before I was born, but legends
Which had sprung from long nights spent there
By bored farmers away from their women,
Those legends hang about my old home still.
Once, it was broken into, that store, and robbed
Of every penny hidden in the till.
After a long investigation, it was found
That the culprit had come down through
The chimney. The storekeeper found a clean
Scythe-blade, put a ladder up the spacious chimney,
Climbed up, and with mortar and trowel
Fixed the scythe in place where it would
Split a man if he came down in dark
To steal his riches all away.
That blade gleams still, though the store
Is gone. It lies collapsed in honeysuckle,
Yielding up no sign of any life.
But when I walk through dark
I keep my hand before me, thinking
Of the way a man can seek for gold
And lie in pieces in the raging vines.

This version was written at top speed under unusual circumstances. Another poet, James Seay, and I had been giving joint readings in Virginia for a year or so, and had evolved a set procedure for the program: each of us would read for twenty minutes, then each of us would come back for a shorter ten-minute set. We would flip a coin to decide who would read first. Before a particular reading in

May of 1968, I gave Jim a hard time about his habit of exceeding his allotted time; he promised to hold himself within the limits of each set.

The toss of the coin gave me the first set. When I had finished, I sat down in the chair onstage which had been provided for me, and, as I knew Jim's poems almost by heart after all the readings we had given, I let my mind wander. I thought of the story of the Hughesville scythe, which my grandfather had told me years before, and for a few moments I thought of telling it, when I got up again, as if it were a poem I had already written. I realized soon enough that my interest and excitement should not be wasted that way: I was in my usual first-draft frame of mind, and I thought I had better get it down. I borrowed Jim's pen during one of his pauses between poems, and started scribbling. I hadn't finished by the end of his carefully watched time limit, so I asked him to read another poem. He read a very short one, so I asked for another, which he read in some consternation while I finished the draft.

I made no changes at all before I read it, right there, and I had to do a lot of vocal covering-up. The draft contains several gestures of the mindless hand; repeated words show up at points where I wanted to keep my hand moving while I thought of the next thing I wanted to say. One line, "To steal his riches all away," is lifted almost verbatim from James Wright's poem "An Offering for Mr. Bluehart," one of several poems which I know by heart. My memory sometimes gives me trouble by disguising itself as my imagination.

After the reading, Jim advised me to keep the poem tight; he thought it should be a Petrarchan sonnet. His advice had an influence on my revisions, as versions III and IV show.

II. THE SCYTHE IN THE CHIMNEY

The county around the farm where I grew up
To learn the way a still green field could rise
Between the casual eyewitness and an act
Of violence, that country had a town's name once:

A church, some houses, and a country store
That closed years before I was born, yet stood
Empty, for fifty years feeding only legends
Which had sprung from long nights spent there

By bored farmers away from their women.
Those legends hang about the green fields still:
Once, at night, the store was robbed of all
The money hidden in the till. When they

Came the next morning, no broken lock, no
Window, gave away the burglar's work;
No clue but a chimney-swallow's nest, knocked
Into the hearth, and fresh flecks of soot,

Led the storekeeper to put a ladder up
The chimney, go up with mortar and trowel
And a new scythe-blade, to fix it in place
Across the dark, where it would split a man

If he came down to rob the store again.
He never did. The store is gone, but in
My mind the scythe-blade gleams in the chimney,
Though the chimney lies in honeysuckle now,

Yielding up no sign of life or death. But when
I walk through dark I keep my hand before me,
Thinking how a man who hunts for gold
Can lie in pieces in the raging vines.

This was written less than two weeks later, and submitted to my
creative writing class for criticism. The poem still suffers from slack-
ness, and from dependence on habitual phrases and images which
seem to write themselves in most of my poems whenever I stop think-
ing. For example, I had already written a poem which has a first line
very similar to the first line of this draft. My students corroborated
my suspicion that a stricter form was required, and so I let the poem
lie for a few months.

III.A

1   First 4 lines; violent country,
2   the town, the store
3
4
5   Second quatrain   the robbery of the store
6   and the clues
7
8
9   The scythe
10
11
12
13
14 Can lie in pieces in the raging vines

III.B

1	The quiet hills where I grew up could hide	store
2	Violence from its neighbor years before	door
3	Depression overtook the Hughesville store;	more
4	The Hughesville legend still has never died	before
	And yet the Hughesville legend has not died	swore
5	How once the storekeeper swung the door wide	side
6	To find his money gone, goods on the floor;	wide
	swallow's nest	ride

7	No broken window-lock no ~~broken~~ open door	decide	beside
8	Betrayed the way the burglar got inside.	deride	spied
		chide	died
		cried	subside

This and the rest of the versions up through IX were done over a month or six weeks in the fall of 1968; only one draft, VI, is dated: 6 October 1968. The version above, III, was my first real attempt to make the poem work as a sonnet. III.A is a structural outline only. The lists of rhyming words in the margin of III.B constitute the only kind of rhyming dictionary I like to use; my feeling is that a complete rhyming dictionary might seduce me into using an inappropriate word, to which I would be attracted simply because I did not think of it myself. I make these marginal lists as I go along, sometimes consulting the right-hand edges of rhymed poems by poets whose work I admire. Often, when one of the words I think of seems just right, I do not list it, but work it immediately into the end of a line.

IV.

The hills where I grew up knew how to hide	a
Destruction from its neighbor years before	b
Destruction overtook the Hughesville store;	b
And yet the Hughesville legend has not died:	a
How once the storekeeper unlocked the door	b
To find he had been robbed. (Lying) (One clue,) beside	a
~~Only a chimney~~ The hearth, a swallow's nest upon the floor,	b
Betrayed the way the burglar got inside.	a

1
2
3
4

```
5  Thinking how a man who hunts for gold
6  Can lie in pieces in the raging vines                              a   vines
                                                                       b   hold

   But          try to walk
   ~~Now~~, when I ~~travel~~ thru ~~the~~ dark I hold                 b   gold
   My hand before me, in search of solid signs                        a   signs
   Thinking how a man who looks for gold                              b
   Can lie in pieces in the raging vines.                             a
```

Here I am still trying to make a sonnet, as the line numbers for the sestet indicate; but I am visibly losing confidence that it can be done. The basic problem is that, though the real impact of the poem begins with the installation of the scythe, this act is incomprehensible without some background information. Such information makes fourteen lines too small a space for the poem. So I began to abandon the idea of a sonnet, and let the rhymes in the second quatrain shift from their original positions.

V.

The hills where I grew up knew how to hide
Destruction from its neighbor years before
Destruction overtook the Hughesville store,
And yet the Hughesville legend has not died:

How once the storekeeper unlocked the door
To find he had been robbed. One clue, beside
The hearth, a swallow's nest upon the floor,
Betrayed the way the burglar got inside.

```
The keeper took a scythe-blade from his store                        b'
And fixed it in the chimney, across the fine-                        c
Edged dark, where it would split a man who tried                     a
To come again and rob him of his gold.                               d'
```

```
No burglar came again. The old designs                         ines  c
Lie in honeysuckle now, and I behold                           old   d
The dreary ritual of decay unfold;                             old   d
Yet in my mind that unused blade still shines,                 ines  c
and
~~Now~~ when I try to walk through dark I hold                        d
                      touching
                      ~~searching~~
My hand before me, ~~thinking~~ of solid signs,                      c
```

Thinking how a man who seeks for gold   d
Can lie in pieces in the raging vines.   c

In this version the poem's final form is beginning to evolve. I decided that, since I had failed with the principle of asymmetry which underlies the Petrarchan sonnet, I should try a principle of symmetry and balance. I first switched the rhyme scheme of the last two stanzas so they would move from an envelope to an alternating scheme, as do the first two stanzas. I still had the problem of getting the scythe into place, which I took care of in the middle stanza. To back up a bit, here are the steps I went through to get the middle stanza to the point where it stands above.

STEP 1:

1
2
3   split a man who tried
4 To come again and rob him of his gold

The stanza began to develop almost like a crossword puzzle. I had rhymes for *tried* in the stanzas above this one; I first thought of changing *gold*, since it was not a rhyme, but an exact repetition, from the stanzas below. But then I thought: Here I have a rhyme from above and a repetition from below. Maybe I could complete the scheme with a rhyme from below and a repetition from above, which would make the middle stanza pivotal in a formal as well as a narrative sense. The repetition from above was fairly easy:

STEP 2:

1 The keeper took a scythe-blade from his store
2
3   split a man who tried
4 To come again and rob him of his gold

Now all I needed was the rhyme from below and the words to go with it. In one of my verse-writing classes, we had been discussing the principle that broken words at the ends of lines were as justifiable in poetry as they are in prose, since they are caused by different types of the same phenomenon: arrival at the end of a line before arrival at the end of a word. (For an example of this technique, see Hopkins's "The Windhover," p. 142.) I did not think of this immediately; I merely began filling in the blank spaces, in the hope that something would suggest itself:

STEP 3:

1 The keeper took a scythe-blade from his store
2 And fixed it in the chimney, across
3 The dark, where it would split a man who tried
4 To come again and rob him of his gold.

Almost, almost. Then, as I was looking over a list I had made of words which rhyme with *vine*, the solution presented itself: I scratched out *The* in line 3, replaced it with *Edged*, and then in line 2 I followed *across* with *the fine-*. I had the stanza as it stands in version V. I made a fair copy of the whole poem, then immediately changed the first line of the fourth stanza, substituting *ever came* for *came again*, because *again* appeared already in the line immediately above.

VI.

No burglar ever came. The old designs
Lie in honeysuckle now; I watch the old
Insistent ritual of decay unfold;

No burglar ever came. Now those designs
Are wrapped in honeysuckle, and the old
Insistent rituals of decay unfold;

Here I was fiddling around to get rid of *behold*; its slightly archaic flavor had been bothering me ever since I had written it down. It took a couple of tries, because I couldn't think of everything at once—for example, the problem of repeating *old* in the first set of lines above had escaped my notice until I started to work with my resistance to claiming that I had watched decay taking place.

VII.

No burglar ever came. Now those designs
Are wrapped in honeysuckle, and the old (choked?)

Insistent rituals of decay unfold;
Yet in my brain that unused blade still shines,

And when I try to walk through dark I hold
My hand before me, touching solid signs,
Thinking how a man *(who)* seek*(s)* for gold *(can)*
(Can) lie in pieces in the raging vines. *(and)*

The marginal notes here suggest that I sometimes prefer a cliché to a slack substitute for one. And the changes in the last two lines have to do with my feeling that the *who* made the story too specific, limited to one person. I wanted to say, more clearly, that anyone can seek—for gold or anything else—and that all of us have to be careful.

VIII.

To find he had been robbed. One clue, beside
The hearth, a swallow's nest *on the stone* floor
Told him how the burglar *had* got inside.

Told him hòw the búrglar had gót insíde.

The *old man* took a scythe-blade from his store

Here there were three small matters scattered through the poem which I needed to fix. The change in the second line above reflects my aversion to the word *upon* when it appears merely as an iambic substitute for *on*. I was also happy to relieve the monotony of the meter by changing the last two iambs of that line to a pyrrhus and a spondee. In the next line, I was worried by the internal rhyme in the phrase *Betrayed the way;* internal rhyme can often be effective, but it is an obtrusive device which in this instance too heavily underscored the melodramatic quality of the poem. Finally, in the ninth line, I felt that *keeper* was too obviously a metrical abbreviation for *storekeeper;* so he became an *old man*.

IX.

The hills where I grew up had learned to hide
Destruction from its neighbor years before
Hughesville saw destruction take its store,
And yet the Hughesville legend has not died:

In the first line above, I wanted to make the hills' having learned seem farther in the past than was suggested by *knew how*. The third line shifts the positions of *Hughesville* and *destruction*, so that the two words alternate in the stanza instead of coming in pairs.

X.

The hills where I grew up had learned to hide
Destructions from *each other long* before
Hughesville saw destruction take its store,
And *still* the Hughesville legend has not died:

Neighbor seemed an awkward way of saying what I meant. *Long* and *still* sounded better than *years* and *yet*; besides *yet* already worked well enough in the last line of the fourth stanza.

At this point, the poem had reached a version which remained untouched from late 1968 until late 1972. While typing the poem up for a book manuscript, I was made suddenly uncomfortable by the last line of the third stanza: "To come again and rob him of his gold." "Rob him of" had not bothered me before, but now it did; it seemed willfully suited to the meter, somehow indirect. I changed the line:

XI.

To come that way again and steal his gold.

It may surprise some readers more than it does me that I would make a change after so long a time. In an earlier version of this chapter (even textbooks go through revision), before this change, I had written, "I cannot bring myself to think the poem is finished." That is still true. However, working on one poem makes others come to mind, and one has to go on to those eventually; as the French poet Paul Valéry (1871–1945) has said, poems are never finished; they are merely abandoned.

Anthology

1
The Dailiness
of Life

Boredom and
Survival

Randall Jarrell [1914–1965]

WELL WATER

What a girl called 'the dailiness of life'
(Adding an errand to your errand. Saying,
'Since you're up. . .' Making you a means to
A means to a means to) is well water
Pumped from an old well at the bottom of the world.   5
The pump you pump the water from is rusty
And hard to move and absurd, a squirrel-wheel
A sick squirrel turns slowly, through the sunny
Inexorable hours. And yet sometimes
The wheel turns of its own weight, the rusty   10
Pump pumps over your sweating face the clear
Water, cold, so cold! you cup your hands
And gulp from them the dailiness of life.

NEXT DAY

Moving from Cheer to Joy, from Joy to All,
I take a box
And add it to my wild rice, my Cornish game hens.
The slacked or shorted, basketed, identical
Food-gathering flocks   5
Are selves I overlook. Wisdom, said William James,

Is learning what to overlook. And I am wise
If that is wisdom.
Yet somehow, as I buy All from these shelves
And the boy takes it to my station wagon,   10
What I've become
Troubles me even if I shut my eyes.

When I was young and miserable and pretty
And poor, I'd wish
What all girls wish: to have a husband,   15
A house and children. Now that I'm old, my wish
Is womanish:
That the boy putting groceries in my car

See me. It bewilders me he doesn't see me.
For so many years   20
I was good enough to eat: the world looked at me
And its mouth watered. How often they have undressed me,
The eyes of strangers!
And, holding their flesh within my flesh, their vile

Imaginings within my imagining,   25
I too have taken
The chance of life. Now the boy pats my dog
And we start home. Now I am good.
The last mistaken,
Ecstatic, accidental bliss, the blind   30

Happiness that, bursting, leaves upon the palm
Some soap and water—
It was so long ago, back in some Gay
Twenties, Nineties, I don't know . . . Today I miss
My lovely daughter   35
Away at school, my sons away at school,

My husband away at work—I wish for them.
The dog, the maid,
And I go through the sure unvarying days
At home in them. As I look at my life,   40
I am afraid
Only that it will change, as I am changing:

I am afraid, this morning, of my face.
It looks at me
From the rear-view mirror, with the eyes I hate,   45
The smile I hate. Its plain, lined look
Of gray discovery
Repeats to me: "You're old." That's all, I'm old.

And yet I'm afraid, as I was at the funeral
I went to yesterday.   50
My friend's cold made-up face, granite among its flowers,

Her undressed, operated-on, dressed body
Were my face and body.
As I think of her I hear her telling me

How young I seem; I am exceptional;   55
I think of all I have.
But really no one is exceptional,
No one has anything. I'm anybody,
I stand beside my grave
Confused with my life, that is commonplace and solitary.   60

1, *Cheer, Joy, All:* brand names of washing detergents.

John Berryman [1914–1972]

DREAM SONG #14

Life, friends, is boring. We must not say so.
After all, the sky flashes, the great sea yearns,
we ourselves flash and yearn,
and moreover my mother told me as a boy
(repeatedly) 'Ever to confess you're bored   5
means you have no

Inner Resources.' I conclude now I have no
inner resources, because I am heavy bored.
Peoples bore me,
literature bores me, especially great literature,   10
Henry bores me, with his plights & gripes
as bad as achilles,

who loves people and valiant art, which bores me.
And the tranquil hills, & gin, look like a drag
and somehow a dog   15
has taken itself & its tail considerably away
into mountains or sea or sky, leaving
behind: me, wag.

Francis Bacon [1561–1626]

THE WORLD

The world's a bubble, and the Life of Man
  Less than a span:
In his conception wretched, from the womb,
  So to the tomb;

Curst from his cradle, and brought up to years   5
    With cares and fears.
Who then to frail mortality shall trust,
But limns on water, or but writes in dust.

Yet whilst with sorrow here we live opprest,
    What life is best?   10
Courts are but only superficial schools
    To dandle fools:
The rural parts are turned into a den
    Of savage men:
And where's a city from foul vice so free,   15
But may be term'd the worst of all the three?

Domestic cares afflict the husband's bed,
    Or pains his head:
Those that live single, take it for a curse,
    Or do things worse: 20
Some would have children: those that have them, moan,
    Or wish them gone:
What is it, then, to have or have no wife,
But single thraldom, or a double strife?

Our own affection still at home to please   25
    Is a disease:
To cross the seas to any foreign soil,
    Peril and toil:
Wars with their noise affright us; when they cease,
    We are worse in peace;—   30
What then remains, but that we still should cry
For being born, or, being born, to die?

Geoffrey Chaucer [1340?–1400]

THE COMPLAINT OF CHAUCER TO HIS PURSE

To yow, my purse, and to noon other wight
Complayne I, for ye be my lady dere!
I am so sory, now that ye been lyght;
For certes, but ye make me hevy chere,
Me were as leef be layd upon my bere;   5
For which unto your mercy thus I crye:
Beth hevy ageyn, or elles moote I dye!

Now voucheth sauf this day, or yt be nyght,
That I of yow the blisful soun may here,
Or see your colour lyk the sonne bryght,   *10*
That of yelownesse hadde never pere.
Ye be my lyf, ye be myn hertes stere,
Quene of comfort and of good companye:
Beth hevy ageyn, or elles moote I dye!

Now purse, that ben to me my lyves lyght   *15*
And saveour, as doun in this world here,
Out of this toune helpe me thurgh your myght,
Syn that ye wole nat ben my tresorere;
For I am shave as nye as any frere.
But yet I pray unto your curtesye: *20*
Beth hevy ageyn, or elles moote I dye!

Lenvoy de Chaucer:
O conquerour of Brutes Albyon,
Which that by lyne and free eleccion
Been verray king, this song to yow I sende;
And ye, that mowen alle oure harmes amende,   *25*
Have mynde upon my supplicacion!

The evidence we have indicates that Chaucer sent this poem to Henry IV, who granted the poet a raise in salary.

1, *wight*: person. 4, *certes*: certainly; *but*: unless. 8, *voucheth sauf*: vouchsafe; *or*: ere, before. 12, *myn hertes stere*: my heart's rudder. 16, *as*: while. 19, "For I am shaved as close as any friar": I am shorn of money, close as a friar's head. *Lenvoy de Chaucer*: In the ballade, the French form Chaucer has adapted here, the last stanza is called the *envoy*, and is conventionally addressed to a prince or a king. 22, *Brutes Albyon*: a name for England, based on the legend that Brutus, great-grandson of Aeneas, founded Britain; *Albion*: "the white land"; the term comes from the white cliffs of Dover.

Sir Walter Ralegh [1551?–1618]

WHAT IS OUR LIFE?

What is our life? A play of passion,
Our mirth the music of division;
Our mothers' wombs the tiring houses be,
Where we are dressed for this short comedy.
Heaven the judicious, sharp spectator is   *5*
That sits and marks still who doth act amiss.
Our graves that hide us from the searching sun
Are like drawn curtains when the day is done.

Thus march we playing to our latest rest,
Only we die in earnest, that's no jest.   *10*

2, *music of division*: musical passage of quickened tempo in contrast to the estab-
lished theme of the piece. 3, *tiring houses*: dressing rooms in an Elizabethan theater.
6, *still*: continually.

The above version of this poem has for many years been generally accepted as the
version Ralegh wrote. However, Michael Rudick has pointed out that there are good
reasons for considering two very early manuscripts, one in the British Museum and
the other in Archbishop Marsh's Library in Dublin, as Ralegh's versions. Professor
Rudick's conflation of those manuscripts results in the following version; in it, as in
the one above, spelling has been modernized. Which version seems least self-contra-
dictory?

What is our life? It is a play of passion.
What is our mirth? The music of division.
Our mothers, they the tiring houses be,
Where we are dressed for time's short tragedy;
Earth is the stage, heaven the spectator is,
Who doth behold whoe'er doth act amiss.
The graves which hide us from the parching sun
Are as drawn curtains till the play be done.

William Wordsworth [1770–1850]

THE WORLD IS TOO MUCH WITH US

The world is too much with us; late and soon,
Getting and spending, we lay waste our powers;
Little we see in Nature that is ours;
We have given our hearts away, a sordid boon!
The Sea that bares her bosom to the moon;   *5*
The winds that will be howling at all hours,
And are up-gathered now like sleeping flowers;
For this, for everything, we are out of tune;
It moves us not. — Great God! I'd rather be
A Pagan suckled in a creed outworn;   *10*
So might I, standing on this pleasant lea,
Have glimpses that would make me less forlorn;
Have sight of Proteus rising from the sea;
Or hear old Triton blow his wreathèd horn.

13, *Proteus*: In Greek mythology, an Old Man of the Sea who had the power to as-
sume whatever form he chose. 14, *Triton*: In Greek mythology, a sea-god, generally
represented as blowing a horn made from a shell.

Theodore Roethke [1908–1963]

DOLOR

I have known the inexorable sadness of pencils,
Neat in their boxes, dolor of pad and paper-weight,
All the misery of manilla folders and mucilage,
Desolation in immaculate public places,
Lonely reception room, lavatory, switchboard,   5
The unalterable pathos of basin and pitcher,
Ritual of multigraph, paper-clip, comma,
Endless duplication of lives and objects.
And I have seen dust from the walls of institutions,
Finer than flour, alive, more dangerous than silica,   10
Sift, almost invisible, through long afternoons of tedium,
Dropping a fine film on nails and delicate eyebrows,
Glazing the pale hair, the duplicate grey standard faces.

Howard Nemerov [b. 1920]

SEPTEMBER, THE FIRST DAY OF SCHOOL

I

My child and I hold hands on the way to school,
And when I leave him at the first-grade door
He cries a little but is brave; he does
Let go. My selfish tears remind me how
I cried before that door a life ago.   5
I may have had a hard time letting go.

Each fall the children must endure together
What every child also endures alone:
Learning the alphabet, the integers,
Three dozen bits and pieces of a stuff   10
So arbitrary, so peremptory,
That worlds invisible and visible

Bow down before it, as in Joseph's dream
The sheaves bowed down and then the stars bowed down
Before the dreaming of a little boy.   15
That dream got him such hatred of his brothers
As cost the greater part of life to mend,
And yet great kindness came of it in the end.

II

A school is where they grind the grain of thought,
And grind the children who must kind the thought.   20
It may be those two grindings are but one,

As from the alphabet come Shakespeare's Plays,
As from the integers comes Euler's Law,
As from the whole, inseparably, the lives,

The shrunken lives that have not been set free   25
By law or by poetic phantasy.
But may they be. My child has disappeared
Behind the schoolroom door. And should I live
To see his coming forth, a life away,
I know my hope, but do not know its form   30

Nor hope to know it. May the fathers he finds
Among his teachers have a care of him
More than his father could. How that will look
I do not know, I do not need to know.
Even our tears belong to ritual.   35
But may great kindness come of it in the end.

13, *Joseph's dream*: see Genesis, Chapter 37. 23, *Euler's Law*: any of several mathematical laws developed by Leonhard Euler (1707–1783), a Swiss mathematician. His last name is pronounced *oiler.*

Thomas Campion [1567–1620]

NOW WINTER NIGHTS ENLARGE

Now winter nights enlarge
The number of their hours,
And clouds their storms discharge
Upon the airy towers.
Let now the chimneys blaze   5
And cups o'erflow with wine;
Let well-tuned words amaze
With harmony divine!
Now yellow waxen lights
Shall wait on honey love   10
While youthful revels, masques and Courtly sights,
Sleep's leaden spells remove.

This time doth well dispense
With lovers' long discourse;
Much speech hath some defence,   15
Though beauty no remorse.
All do not all things well;
Some measures comely tread,

Some knotted riddles tell,
Some poems smoothly read.
The summer hath his joys,
And winter his delights;
Though love and all his pleasures are but toys,
They shorten tedious nights.

William Stafford [b. 1914]

THINKING FOR BERKY

In the late night listening from bed
I have joined the ambulance or the patrol
screaming toward some drama, the kind of end
that Berky must have some day, if she isn't dead.

The wildest of all, her father and mother cruel,   *5*
farming out there beyond the old stone quarry
where highschool lovers parked their lurching cars,
Berky learned to love in that dark school.

Early her face was turned away from home
toward any hardworking place; but still her soul,   *10*
with terrible things to do, was alive, looking out
for the rescue that—surely, some day—would have to come.

Windiest nights, Berky, I have thought for you,
and no matter how lucky I've been I've touched wood.
There are things not solved in our town though tomorrow came: *15*
there are things time passing can never make come true.

We live in an occupied country, misunderstood;
justice will take us millions of intricate moves.
Sirens will hunt down Berky, you survivors in your beds,
while in the night you lie, so far and good.   *20*

James Wright [b. 1927]

AUTUMN BEGINS IN MARTIN'S FERRY, OHIO

In the Shreve High football stadium,
I think of Polacks nursing long beers in Tiltonsville,
And gray faces of Negroes in the blast furnace at Benwood,
And the ruptured night watchman of Wheeling Steel,
Dreaming of heroes.   *5*

Thinking For Berky [79]

All the proud fathers are ashamed to go home.
Their women cluck like starved pullets,
Dying for love.

Therefore,
Their sons grow suicidally beautiful   10
At the beginning of October,
And gallop terribly against each other's bodies.

Lucille Clifton [b. 1936]

FOR DE LAWD

people say they have a hard time
understanding how I
go on about my business
playing my Ray Charles
hollering at the kids—   5
seem like my Afro
cut off in some old image
would show I got a long memory
and I come from a line
of black and going on women   10
who got used to making it through murdered sons
and who grief kept on pushing
who fried chicken
ironed
swept off the back steps   15
who grief kept
for their still alive sons
for their sons coming
for their sons gone
just pushing   20

John Haines [b. 1924]

DENALI ROAD

By the Denali road, facing
north, a battered chair
in which nothing but the wind
was sitting.

          And farther on
toward evening, an old man

with a vague smile,
his rifle rusting in his arms.

The *Denali Road* runs southward from Fairbanks, Alaska, to the town of Denali.
Haines spent about fifteen years as a homesteader in Alaska.

Edwin Arlington Robinson [1869–1935]

MR. FLOOD'S PARTY

Old Eben Flood, climbing alone one night
Over the hill between the town below
And the forsaken upland hermitage
That held as much as he should ever know
On earth again of home, paused warily.   5
The road was his with not a native near;
And Eben, having leisure, said aloud,
For no man else in Tilbury Town to hear:

"Well, Mr. Flood, we have the harvest moon
Again, and we may not have many more;   10
The bird is on the wing, the poet says,
And you and I have said it here before.
Drink to the bird." He raised up to the light
The jug that he had gone so far to fill,
And answered huskily: "Well, Mr. Flood,   15
Since you propose it, I believe I will."

Alone, as if enduring to the end
A valiant armor of scarred hopes outworn,
He stood there in the middle of the road
Like Roland's ghost winding a silent horn.   20
Below him, in the town among the trees,
Where friends of other days had honored him,
A phantom salutation of the dead
Rang thinly till old Eben's eyes were dim.

Then, as a mother lays her sleeping child   25
Down tenderly, fearing it may awake,
He set the jug down slowly at his feet
With trembling care, knowing that most things break;
And only when assured that on firm earth
It stood, as the uncertain lives of men   30

Assuredly did not, he paced away,
And with his hand extended paused again:

"Well, Mr. Flood, we have not met like this
In 'a long time; and many a change has come
To both of us, I fear, since last it was   35
We had a drop together. Welcome home!"
Convivially returning with himself,
Again he raised the jug up to the light;
And with an acquiescent quaver said:
"Well, Mr. Flood, if you insist, I might.   40

"Only a very little, Mr. Flood—
For auld lang syne. No more, sir; that will do."
So, for the time, apparently it did,
And Eben evidently thought so too;
For soon amid the silver loneliness   45
Of night he lifted up his voice and sang,
Secure, with only two moons listening,
Until the whole harmonious landscape rang—

"For auld lang syne." The weary throat gave out,
The last word wavered; and the song being done,   50
He raised again the jug regretfully
And shook his head, and was again alone.
There was not much that was ahead of him,
And there was nothing in the town below—
Where strangers would have shut the many doors   55
That many friends had opened long ago.

8, *Tilbury Town*: an imaginary town, based partly on Gardiner, Maine; many of
Robinson's poems are set here. 11, the *poet* Edward Fitzgerald, the author of "The
Rubaiyat of Omar Khayyam," in which these lines appear: "The Bird of Time has but
a little way / To flutter—and the Bird is on the Wing." 20, *Roland*: Roland, the most
celebrated of Charlemagne's knights, was overwhelmed in a pass in the Pyrenees; he
blew his horn so that Charlemagne would return and pay the dead heroes their right-
ful honors.

Dan Johnson [b. 1952]

STRAY THINGS

Beside a row of gates
Children scrape the air,
Their bicycles firmly beneath them.
The road, in smooth relief
Like a lake surface   rises   5

To tires flashing in tight circles.
A glass tide   stretching into foam
Douses the dark air   sweet
In summer, dancing on a warm night
Through black shrubbery, closing   10
Quickly on the arch   to suck a leaf
Along, then pull itself inside.

And the wind, hushed like a worn
Or grateful thing, takes a long
Rolling step over gravel   15
To touch the sacred places.
It marks the stones with sayings
That linger, though broken and torn
In the darkness by a song:
"I was there when you were born —   20
Remember the good times? I am strong
In you tonight; the flowers in your hand
Are mine. I own your graceful faces
And your thoughts — they are stray things."

Clarice Short [b. 1910]

TAKING LEAVE OF THE OLD

Taking leave of the old poses particular problems.
One cannot say,
"I'll see you. Wait for me," when it might be so much trouble
To them to stay.
And that strange turning away   5
To pull at some grass in a border or poke at the fire
Might be only a subterfuge to make bearable
The unbearable moment, or something lower or higher:
Evidence of a state transcending the foolishness
Of affections and obligations — remote concerns —   10
Centered now on important objects, the moment's needs
Of the bowels, or the bones, or the fingers ahunger for weeds.

Thomas Gray [1716–1771]

ELEGY WRITTEN IN A COUNTRY CHURCHYARD

The curfew tolls the knell of parting day,
  The lowing herd wind slowly o'er the lea,
The plowman homeward plods his weary way,
  And leaves the world to darkness and to me.

Now fades the glimmering landscape on the sight,   5
    And all the air a solemn stillness holds,
Save where the beetle wheels his droning flight,
    And drowsy tinklings lull the distant folds:

Save that from yonder ivy-mantled tow'r
    The moping owl does to the moon complain   10
Of such, as wand'ring near her secret bow'r,
    Molest her ancient solitary reign.

Beneath those rugged elms, that yew tree's shade,
    Where heaves the turf in many a mold'ring heap,
Each in his narrow cell forever laid,   15
    The rude forefathers of the hamlet sleep.

The breezy call of incense-breathing morn,
    The swallow twitt'ring from the straw-built shed,
The cock's shrill clarion, or the echoing horn,
    No more shall rouse them from their lowly bed.   20

For them no more the blazing hearth shall burn,
    Or busy housewife ply her evening care;
No children run to lisp their sire's return,
    Or climb his knees the envied kiss to share.

Oft did the harvest to their sickle yield,   25
    Their furrow oft the stubborn glebe has broke;
How jocund did they drive their team afield!
    How bowed the woods beneath their sturdy stroke!

Let not Ambition mock their useful toil,
    Their homely joys, and destiny obscure;   30
Nor Grandeur hear with a disdainful smile
    The short and simple annals of the poor.

The boast of heraldry, the pomp of pow'r,
    And all that beauty, all that wealth e'er gave,
Awaits alike th' inevitable hour.   35
    The paths of glory lead but to the grave.

Nor you, ye proud, impute to these the fault,
    If Mem'ry o'er their tomb no trophies raise,
Where through the long-drawn aisle and fretted vault
    The pealing anthem swells the note of praise.   40

Can storied urn or animated bust

Back to its mansion call the fleeting breath?
Can Honor's voice provoke the silent dust,
  Or Flatt'ry soothe the dull cold ear of Death?

Perhaps in this neglected spot is laid   45
  Some heart once pregnant with celestial fire;
Hands that the rod of empire might have swayed,
  Or waked to ecstasy the living lyre.

But knowledge to their eyes her ample page
  Rich with the spoils of time did ne'er unroll;   50
Chill Penury repressed their noble rage,
  And froze the genial current of the soul.

Full many a gem of purest ray serene,
  The dark unfathomed caves of ocean bear:
Full many a flower is born to blush unseen,   55
  And waste its sweetness on the desert air.

Some village Hampden, that with dauntless breast
  The little tyrant of his fields withstood;
Some mute inglorious Milton here may rest,
  Some Cromwell guiltless of his country's blood.   60

Th' applause of list'ning senates to command,
  The threats of pain and ruin to despise,
To scatter plenty o'er a smiling land,
  And read their hist'ry in a nation's eyes,

Their lot forbade: nor circumscribed alone   65
  Their growing virtues, but their crimes confined;
Forbade to wade through slaughter to a throne,
  And shut the gates of mercy on mankind,

The struggling pangs of conscious truth to hide,
  To quench the blushes of ingenuous shame,   70
Or heap the shrine of Luxury and Pride
  With incense kindled at the Muse's flame.

Far from the madding crowd's ignoble strife,
  Their sober wishes never learned to stray;
Along the cool sequestered vale of life   75
  They kept the noiseless tenor of their way.

Yet ev'n these bones from insult to protect
  Some frail memorial still erected nigh,

Elegy Written In A Country Churchyard   [85]

With uncouth rhymes and shapeless sculpture decked,
   Implores the passing tribute of a sigh.   *80*

Their name, their years, spelt by th' unlettered Muse,
   The place of fame and elegy supply:
And many a holy text around she strews,
   That teach the rustic moralist to die.

For who to dumb Forgetfulness a prey,   *85*
   This pleasing anxious being e'er resigned,
Left the warm precincts of the cheerful day,
   Nor cast one longing ling'ring look behind?

On some fond breast the parting soul relies,
   Some pious drops the closing eye requires;   *90*
Ev'n from the tomb the voice of Nature cries,
   Ev'n in our ashes live their wonted fires.

For thee, who mindful of th' unhonored dead
   Dost in these lines their artless tale relate;
If chance, by lonely contemplation led,   *95*
   Some kindred spirit shall inquire thy fate,

Haply some hoary-headed swain may say,
   "Oft have we seen him at the peep of dawn
Brushing with hasty steps the dews away
   To meet the sun upon the upland lawn.   *100*

"There at the foot of yonder nodding beech
   That wreathes its old fantastic roots so high,
His listless length at noontide would he stretch,
   And pore upon the brook that babbles by.

"Hard by yon wood, now smiling as in scorn,   *105*
   Mutt'ring his wayward fancies he would rove,
Now drooping, woeful wan, like one forlorn,
   Or crazed with care, or crossed in hopeless love.

"One morn I missed him on the customed hill,
   Along the heath and near his fav'rite tree;   *110*
Another came; nor yet beside the rill,
   Nor up the lawn, nor at the wood was he;

"The next with dirges due in sad array
   Slow through the churchway path we saw him borne.

Approach and read (for thou canst read) the lay,
    Graved on the stone beneath yon aged thorn."

The Epitaph

Here rests his head upon the lap of Earth
    A youth to Fortune and to Fame unknown.
Fair Science frowned not on his humble birth,
    And Melancholy marked him for her own.

Large was his bounty, and his soul sincere,
    Heav'n did a recompense as largely send:
He gave to Mis'ry all he had, a tear,
    He gained from Heav'n ('twas all he wished) a friend.

No farther seek his merits to disclose,
    Or draw his frailties from their dread abode,
(There they alike in trembling hope repose),
    The bosom of his Father and his God.

115

120

125

16, *rude:* unlettered. 19, *horn:* the huntsman's horn. 26, *glebe:* plot; here, turf. 33, *heraldry:* noble birth. 35, *Awaits:* the subject of this verb is *hour;* the objects of the verb are contained in the preceding two lines. 38, *trophies:* emblems of the deceased's achievements. 39, *fretted:* carved. 41, *storied urn:* funeral urn bearing an epitaph; *animated:* lifelike. 43, *provoke:* bring to life. 57–60: the references here are to John Hampden (1594–1643), who defended the people's rights against the tyrannies of Charles I; John Milton (see pages 140, 144, and 204); Oliver Cromwell, Lord Protector during the Commonwealth Interregnum (1653–58). 100, *upland lawn:* mountain pasture (see "Lycidas," p. 144, line 25 and note). 119, *Science:* knowledge.

William Carlos Williams [1883–1963]

TRACT

I will teach you my townspeople
how to perform a funeral —
for you have it over a troop
of artists —
unless one should scour the world —
you have the ground sense necessary.

See! the hearse leads.
I begin with a design for a hearse.
For Christ's sake not black —
nor white either — and not polished!

5

10

Let it be weathered—like a farm wagon—
with gilt wheels (this could be
applied fresh at small expense)
or no wheels at all:
a rough dray to drag over the ground.   15

Knock the glass out!
My God—glass, my townspeople!
For what purpose? Is it for the dead
to look out or for us to see
how well he is housed or to see   20
the flowers or the lack of them—
or what?
To keep the rain and snow from him?
He will have a heavier rain soon:
pebbles and dirt and what not.   25
Let there be no glass—
and no upholstery phew!
and no little brass rollers
and small easy wheels on the bottom—
my townspeople what are you thinking of?   30

A rough plain hearse then
with gilt wheels and no top at all.
On this the coffin lies
by its own weight.

                        No wreaths please—
especially no hot house flowers.   35
Some common memento is better,
something he prized and is known by:
his old clothes—a few books perhaps—
God knows what! You realize
how we are about these things   40
my townspeople—
something will be found—anything
even flowers if he had come to that.
So much for the hearse.

For heaven's sake though see to the driver!   45
Take off the silk hat! In fact
that's no place at all for him—
up there unceremoniously
dragging our friend out to his own dignity!
Bring him down—bring him down!   50

Low and inconspicuous! I'd not have him ride
on the wagon at all — damn him —
the undertaker's understrapper!
Let him hold the reins
and walk at the side   55
and inconspicuously too!

Then briefly as to yourselves:
Walk behind — as they do in France,
seventh class, or if you ride
Hell take curtains! Go with some show   60
of inconvenience; sit openly —
to the weather as to grief.
Or do you think you can shut grief in?
What — from us? We who have perhaps
nothing to lose? Share with us   65
share with us — it will be money
in your pockets.
          Go now
I think you are ready.

Trumbull Stickney [1874–1904]

SIX O'CLOCK

Now burst above the city's cold twilight
The piercing whistles and the tower-clocks:
For day is done. Along the frozen docks
The workmen set their ragged shirts aright.
Thro' factory doors a stream of dingy light   5
Follows the scrimmage as it quickly flocks
To hut and home among the snow's gray blocks. —
I love you, human labourers. Good-night!
Good-night to all the blackened arms that ache!
Good-night to every sick and sweated brow,   10
To the poor girl that strength and love forsake,
To the poor boy who can no more! I vow
The victim soon shall shudder at the stake
And fall in blood: we bring him even now.

2

A Musical
but
Melancholy
Chime

Nature and
Ecology

William Cullen Bryant [1794–1878]

INSCRIPTION FOR THE ENTRANCE TO A WOOD

Stranger, if thou hast learned a truth which
    needs
No school of long experience, that the world
Is full of guilt and misery, and hast seen
Enough of all its sorrows, crimes, and cares,
To tire thee of it, enter this wild wood   5
And view the haunts of Nature. The calm shade
Shall bring a kindred calm, and the sweet breeze
That makes the green leaves dance, shall waft a balm
To thy sick heart. Thou wilt find nothing here
Of all that pained thee in the haunts of men,   10
And made thee loathe thy life. The primal curse
Fell, it is true, upon the unsinning earth,
But not in vengeance. God hath yoked to guilt
Her pale tormentor, misery. Hence, these shades
Are still the abodes of gladness; the thick roof   15
Of green and stirring branches is alive
And musical with birds, that sing and sport
In wantonness of spirit; while below
The squirrel, with raised paws and form erect,
Chirps merrily. Throngs of insects in the shade   20
Try their thin wings and dance in the warm beam
That waked them into life. Even the green trees
Partake the deep contentment; as they bend
To the soft winds, the sun from the blue sky

Looks in and sheds a blessing on the scene.   25
Scarce less the cleft-born wild-flower seems to enjoy
Existence, than the winged plunderer
That sucks its sweets. The mossy rocks themselves,
And the old and ponderous trunks of prostrate trees
That lead from knoll to knoll a causey rude   30
Or bridge the sunken brook, and their dark roots,
With all their earth upon them, twisting high,
Breathe fixed tranquillity. The rivulet
Sends forth glad sounds, and tripping o'er its bed
Of pebbly sands, or leaping down the rocks,   35
Seems, with continuous laughter, to rejoice
In its own being. Softly tread the marge,
Lest from her midway perch thou scare the wren
That dips her bill in water. The cool wind,
That stirs the stream in play, shall come to thee,   40
Like one that loves thee nor will let thee pass
Ungreeted, and shall give its light embrace.

30, *causey*: causeway, raised road over wet ground or shallow water. 37, *marge*:
margin, edge.

Ralph Waldo Emerson [1803–1882]

THE SNOW-STORM

Announced by all the trumpets of the sky,
Arrives the snow, and, driving o'er the fields,
Seems nowhere to alight: the whited air
Hides hills and woods, the river, and the heaven,
And veils the farm-house at the garden's end.   5
The sled and traveller stopped, the courier's feet
Delayed, all friends shut out, the housemates sit
Around the radiant fireplace, enclosed
In a tumultuous privacy of storm.

  Come see the north wind's masonry.   10
Out of an unseen quarry evermore
Furnished with tile, the fierce artificer
Curves his white bastions with projected roof
Round every windward stake, or tree, or door.
Speeding, the myriad-handed, his wild work   15
So fanciful, so savage, nought cares he
For number or proportion. Mockingly,
On coop or kennel he hangs Parian wreaths;

A swan-like form invests the hidden thorn;
Fills up the farmer's lane from wall to wall,   20
Maugre the farmer's sighs; and at the gate
A tapering turret overtops the work.
And when his hours are numbered, and the world
Is all his own, retiring, as he were not,
Leaves, when the sun appears, astonished Art   25
To mimic in slow structures, stone by stone,
Built in an age, the mad wind's night-work,
The frolic architecture of the snow.

18, *Parian:* Paros, an island off the mainland of Greece, is known for its fine white
marble. 21, *Maugre:* from the French *malgré*, despite.

John Keats [1795–1821]

TO AUTUMN

Season of mists and mellow fruitfulness,
    Close bosom-friend of the maturing sun;
Conspiring with him how to load and bless
    With fruit the vines that round the thatch-eaves run;
To bend with apples the mossed cottage-trees,   5
    And fill all fruit with ripeness to the core;
        To swell the gourd, and plump the hazel shells
    With a sweet kernel; to set budding more,
And still more, later flowers for the bees,
Until they think warm days will never cease,   10
        For Summer has o'er-brimmed their clammy cells.

Who hath not seen thee oft amid thy store?
    Sometimes whoever seeks abroad may find
Thee sitting careless on a granary floor,
    Thy hair soft-lifted by the winnowing wind;   15
Or on a half-reaped furrow sound asleep,
    Drowsed with the fume of poppies, while thy hook
        Spares the next swath and all its twinèd flowers:
And sometimes like a gleaner thou dost keep
    Steady thy laden head across a brook;   20
    Or by a cider-press, with patient look,
        Thou watchest the last oozings hours by hours.

Where are the songs of Spring? Aye, where are they?
    Think not of them, thou hast thy music too —

While barrèd clouds bloom the soft-dying day,   25
    And touch the stubble-plains with rosy hue;
Then in a wailful choir the small gnats mourn
    Among the river sallows, borne aloft
        Or sinking as the light wind dives or dies;
And full-grown lambs loud bleat from hilly bourn;   30
    Hedge crickets sing; and now with treble soft
    The redbreast whistles from a garden-croft;
        And gathering swallows twitter in the skies.

17, *hook*: reaping-hook, sickle. 11, *clammy*: sweet, oozing; does not carry the un-
favorable connotations now associated with it. 28, *sallows*: willow trees. 30, *bourn*:
area, region. 32, *croft*: small plot.

A. E. Housman [1859–1936]

LOVELIEST OF TREES, THE CHERRY NOW

Loveliest of trees, the cherry now
Is hung with bloom along the bough,
And stands about the woodland ride
Wearing white for Eastertide.

Now, of my threescore years and ten,   5
Twenty will not come again,
And take from seventy springs a score,
It only leaves me fifty more.

And since to look at things in bloom
Fifty springs are little room,   10
About the woodlands I will go
To see the cherry hung with snow.

3, *ride*: path, wooded road.

Gerard Manley Hopkins [1844–1889]

PIED BEAUTY

Glory be to God for dappled things—
    For skies of couple-colour as a brinded cow;
        For rose-moles all in stipple upon trout that swim;
Fresh-firecoal chestnut-falls; finches' wings;
    Landscape plotted and pieced—fold, fallow, and plough;   5

And áll trádes, their gear and tackle and trim.
All things counter, original, spare, strange;
  Whatever is fickle, freckled (who knows how?)
    With swift, slow; sweet, sour; adazzle, dim;
He fathers-forth whose beauty is past change: 10
                    Praise him.

  Pied: spotted. 2, brinded: brindle—dark streaks on a tan background. 6, trim: as
noun, equipment; as adjective, well-ordered. 7, counter: opposing; spare: rare.

Howard Moss [b. 1922]

GOING TO SLEEP IN THE COUNTRY

The terraces rise and fall
As the light strides up and rides over
The hill I see from my window.
The spring in the dogwood now,
Enlarging its small preconceptions,   5
Puts itself away for the night.
The mountains do nothing but sit,
Waiting for something to happen—
Perhaps for the sky to open.

In the distance, a waterfall,   10
More sound than vision from here,
Is weighing itself again,
A sound you can hardly hear.
The birds of the day disappear,
As if the darkness were final.   15
The harder it is to see,
The louder the waterfall.

And then the whippoorwill
Begins its tireless, cool,
Calm, and precise lament—   20
Again and again and again—
Its love replying in kind,
Or blindly sung to itself,
Waiting for something to happen.

In that rain-prickle of song,   25
The waterfall stays its sound,
Diminishing like a gong
Struck by the weakening hand

Of a walker walking away,
Who is farther away each time,   *30*

Until it is finally dumb.
Each star, at a different depth,
Shines down. The moon shines down.
The night comes into its own,
Waiting for nothing to happen.   *35*

Andrew Marvell [1621–1678]

THE GARDEN

How vainly men themselves amaze
To win the palm, the oak, or bays,
And their incessant labors see
Crowned from some single herb, or tree,
Whose short and narrow-vergèd shade   *5*
Does prudently their toils upbraid;
While all flowers and all trees do close
To weave the garlands of repose!

Fair Quiet, have I found thee here,
And Innocence, thy sister dear?   *10*
Mistaken long, I sought you then
In busy companies of men.
Your sacred plants, if here below,
Only among the plants will grow;
Society is all but rude   *15*
To this delicious solitude.

No white nor red was ever seen
So amorous as this lovely green.
Fond lovers, cruel as their flame,
Cut in these trees their mistress' name: *20*
Little, alas, they know or heed
How far these beauties hers exceed!
Fair trees, wheresoe'er your barks I wound,
No name shall but your own be found.

When we have run our passion's heat,   *25*
Love hither makes his best retreat.
The gods, that mortal beauty chase,
Still in a tree did end their race:
Apollo hunted Daphne so,
Only that she might laurel grow;   *30*

And Pan did after Syrinx speed,
Not as a nymph, but for a reed.

   What wondrous life is this I lead!
Ripe apples drop about my head;
The luscious clusters of the vine   35
Upon my mouth do crush their wine;
The nectarine and curious peach
Into my hands themselves do reach;
Stumbling on melons, as I pass,
Insnared with flowers, I fall on grass.   40

   Meanwhile the mind, from pleasure less,
Withdraws into its happiness;
The mind, that ocean where each kind
Does straight its own resemblance find;
Yet it creates, transcending these,   45
Far other worlds and other seas,
Annihilating all that's made
To a green thought in a green shade.

   Here at the fountain's sliding foot,
Or at some fruit tree's mossy root,   50
Casting the body's vest aside,
My soul into the boughs does glide:
There, like a bird, it sits and sings,
Then whets and combs its silver wings,
And, till prepared for longer flight,   55
Waves in its plumes the various light.

   Such was that happy garden-state,
While man there walked without a mate:
After a place so pure and sweet,
What other help could yet be meet!   60
But 'twas beyond a mortal's share
To wander solitary there:
Two paradises 'twere in one
To live in paradise alone.

   How well the skillful gardener drew   65
Of flowers and herbs this dial new,
Where, from above, the milder sun
Does through a fragrant zodiac run;
And as it works, th' industrious bee
Computes its time as well as we!   70

How could such sweet and wholesome hours
Be reckoned but with herbs and flowers?

1. *amaze*: puzzle. 2, *palm, oak, bays*: wreaths symbolic of victory in games, war, and poetic competitions. 3. *uncessant*: incessant. 5, *short*: short-lived. 17, *white nor red*: colors of the lily and the rose, both flowers associated with love. 29, *Apollo, Daphne*: The greek god Apollo (see page 196) pursued Daphne, and the gods saved her by turning her into a laurel tree. Similarly, 31, *Pan, Syrinx*: Pan, the Greek god of shepherds and huntsmen, pursued Syrinx, who threw herself into a river and became a reed. Pan made his pipes from the reeds. 51, *body's vest*: the flesh. 57, *garden-state*: Eden. 60, *meet*: suitable. 65–67: flowers and greenery have been planted in the shape of a sundial's face, decorated with the signs of the zodiac.

William Jay Smith [b. 1918]

MORELS

A wet gray day—rain falling slowly, mist over the valley, mountains
  dark circumflex smudges in the distance—

Apple blossoms just gone by, the branches feathery still as if flutter-
  ing with half-visible antennae—

A day in May like so many in these green mountains, and I went out
  just as I had last year

At the same time, and found them there under the big maples—by
  the bend in the road—right where they had stood

Last year and the year before that, risen from the dark duff of the
  woods, emerging at odd angles   5

From spores hidden by curled and matted leaves, a fringe of rain on
  the grass around them,

Beads of rain on the mounded leaves and mosses round them,

Not in a ring themselves but ringed by jack-in-the-pulpits with deep
  eggplant-colored stripes;

Not ringed but rare, not gilled but polyp-like, having sprung up over-
  night—

These mushrooms of the gods, resembling human organs uprooted,
  rooted only on the air,   10

Looking like lungs wrenched from the human body, lungs reversed,
  not breathing internally

But being the externalization of breath itself, these spicy, twisted
  cones,

These perforated brown-white asparagus tips — these morels, smell-
    ing of wet graham crackers mixed with maple leaves;

And, reaching down by the pale green fern shoots, I nipped their
    pulpy stems at the base

And dropped them into a paper bag — a damp brown bag (their color)
    — and carried   15

Them (weighing absolutely nothing) down the hill and into the
    house; you held them

Under cold bubbling water and sliced them with a surgeon's stroke
    clean through,

And sautéed them over a low flame, butter-brown; and we ate them
    then and there —

Tasting of the sweet damp woods and of the rain one inch above the
    meadow:

It was like feasting upon air.   20

Julia Randall [b. 1923]

THE WRITER INDULGES A HOBBY

We searched the wood again
for mushrooms, after the last rain. In a mile or so
found only a few. Then, coming back,
saw dozens sprung beside our very track,
like leaves, like nuts, like chips of shale,   5
pale as a sunpatch, dark
as a waterstain, and all before unseen.

To the eye grown quiet on its spot,
fields open out their greens,
and every green his shape,   10
and every shape his shadow moving slow,
a nothing, a steeple-head in the sun's eye,
an ant on the steeple-bush, and in his jaw
a grain, and in that grain a cell. . .
It is only to tell   15
over again, how much we overpass,
walkers on dust, walkers on grass.

To tell the salamander from the leaf,
look out the stages of the Emperor's life,
to hear the vireo where we have sought her   20
is like walking on water.

John Hall Wheelock [b. 1886]

THE DIVINE INSECT

Already it's late summer. Sun-bathers go
Earlier now. Except for those who lie
Dazed between sea-music and radio
The beach is bare as the blue bowl of the sky,
Where a cloud floats, solitary and slow.   5

And up the beach, where at mid-summer's height
One gull with occasional lurch and pause would steer
Onward his leisurely loose-winged casual flight,
Gull wings weave patterns, their noise floods the ear
Like a fugue, cry answering cry in hoarse delight.   10

Now on the beach there also may be found,
Straddled in mimic flight, with arching wing
Spread either way, some gull swift death has downed
There, like a tumbled kite whose severed string
Kept it in heaven by binding it to the ground.   15

Inland, when the slant evening sun-beams touch
Leaves, long obscured in tunnelled shade, to flame,
The divine insect, for I called him such,
Begins his high thin music. To my shame
I never learned what he was, who owe him so much.   20

Listening to his frail song, so pure, so dim,
I made my poems, he was mystery's decoy,
Something far and lost, just over the rim
Of being, or so I felt, and as a boy
I wove fantastic notions about him.   25

Throughout long evenings and hushed midnights when
Grasshoppers shrilled, his barely perceptible note
Wound on like a thread of time, while my pen
Made its own scratchy music as I wrote.
The divine insect and I were comrades then.   30

That high hypnotic note opened some door
On a world seemingly come upon by chance,
But a world, surely, I had known before.
Deeper I sank into a timeless trance —
Strange thoughts and fancies troubled me more and more.   35

I could pass through that minuscule sound, it seemed to me,

As through a fine tube, getting smaller and still more small,
Until I was smaller than nothing—then, suddenly,
Come to the other end of the tube, and crawl
Out, into glittering immensity.   40

For, if by travelling west you shall come east
Or, as Einstein has it, the continuum
Curves on itself, may we not through the least
Come to the largest, and so finally come
Back where we were, undiminished and unincreased?   45

Since then, I have tried to put this into verse,
But language limits the sense it often mars—
I still believe, for better or for worse,
We look through one atom into all the stars,
In the note of one insect hear the universe.   50

These few green acres where so many a day
Has found me, acres I have loved so long,
Have the whole galaxy for crown, and stay
Unspoiled by that. Here in some thrush's song
I have heard things that took my breath away.   55

It is a country out of the world's ken,
Time has no power upon it. Year on year,
Summer unfolds her pageant here again—
I have looked deep into all being here
Through one loved place far from the storms of men.   60

Here often, day and night, there will be heard
The sea's grave rhythm, a dark undertone
Beneath the song of insect or of bird—
Sea-voices by sea-breezes landward blown,
And shudder of leaves by the soft sea-wind stirred.   65

In the jade light and gloom of woodland walks
The spider lily and slender shinleaf stand,
The catbird from his treetop pulpit talks
The morning up, and in the meadowland
The velvet mullein lift their woolly stalks.   70

The world grows old. Ageless and undefiled
These stay, meadow and thicket, wood and hill:
The green fly wears her golden dress, the wild
Grape is in bloom, the fork-tailed swallow still
Veers on the wind as when I was a child.   75

And in mid-August, when the sun has set
And the first star out of the west shows through,
The divine insect, as I call him yet,
Begins his high thin note, so pure, so true,
Putting me ever deeper in his debt.

80

The old enchantment takes me as before,
I listen, half in dream, hearing by chance
The soft lapse of the sea along the shore,
And sink again into that timeless trance,
Deeper and deeper now, and more and more.

85

42–43, *Einstein, continuum*: Albert Einstein (1879–1955) postulated a space which curved in the presence of large masses, curving on itself. He also developed the notion that space and time are dimensions of a continuum, a continuous universe.

Edward Newman [fl. 1850]

from THE INSECT HUNTERS

Take thy hat, my little Laura,
Fix it by the loop elastic;
Let us go to Haddo Villas,
Passing by the church and churchyard,
Now so bright with shortlived flowers,

5

Apt mementoes of the buried;
Passing hand in hand together,
Passing, old and young together,
Gravely walking, gaily tripping,
Through the shady lane of lovers,

10

Where the railtrain rattles under,
And so on to Haddo Villas.

Let us take a stroll, my Laura,
Down Farm Lane and to the sedge pond,
Where thy father often fishes

15

For the pretty water beetles,
Graperi and branchiatus,
Hubneri and marginalis,
Agilis and punctulatus,
Ater, Sturmii and fuscus,

20

Pretty Colymbetes fuscus . . .
. . . .
Laura, let us go to Plumstead,
By the well-known North Kent Railway,
Starting from the Blackheath Station,

Passing through the Charlton tunnel,
Through that damp and darksome tunnel,
By the sandy pits at Charlton,
Through the warlike town of Woolwich . . .
In this large tin case, containing
A few slips of blotting paper,   30
And a little mass of wadding,
Slightly damped with benzine colas,
Stupefying fumes exhaling;

In this case we will imprison
All the two-winged flies we capture.
· ·

First of walkers come the Earwigs,
Earwigs or FORFICULINA;
At the tail we find a weapon
Very like a pair of pincers,
And with this 'tis said the Earwigs   40
Open and fold up the hind wings;
You may watch them and observe it;
I have never had that pleasure.

The names of town and places are British and require no specific explanation.
17–21: the generic names of certain water beetles. 32, *benzine colas*: extracts of benzine, a petroleum derivative.

J. V. Cunningham [b. 1911]

MONTANA PASTORAL

I am no shepherd of a child's surmises.
I have seen fear where the coiled serpent rises,

Thirst where the grasses burn in early May
And thistle, mustard, and the wild oat stay.

There is dust in this air. I saw in the heat   5
Grasshoppers busy in the threshing wheat.

So to this hour. Through the warm dusk I drove
To blizzards sifting on the hissing stove,

And found no images of pastoral will,
But fear, thirst, hunger, and this huddled chill.   10

James Seay [b. 1939]

NO MAN'S GOOD BULL

No man's good bull grazes wet clover
And leaves the pasture as he came.
My uncle's prize Angus was bloated
And breathing hard by afternoon
On the day he got into our clover pasture   5
Before the sun could burn the dew away.
He bellowed death from the field
As we grappled to hold his legs and head;
Our vet inserted a trocar between his ribs,
           let the whelming gas escape,   10
And to show us the nature of that gas
Put a match to the valve . . . a blue flame caught
      and the animal bolted from us,
Heading into the woods along the river bottom,
Turning only to test the new fire   15
          of his black side.

Each night we see his flame, blue and soft
              beside the river,
As he steals in before dawn
To plunge his head into wet clover,   20
Graze his fill,
     blaze up,
And answer that which lows to him in heat.
We watch him burn—
         hoof, hide, and bone.   25

9, *trocar*: a sharp, pointed tube, like an oversized hypodermic needle; when the sharp point is withdrawn, a small valve is left in the animal's side to let the bloat-gas out. Bloat is a phenomenon occurring mainly in ruminant animals.

Frederick Goddard Tuckerman [1821–1873]

from SONNETS, First Series

XXVIII

Not the round natural world, not the deep mind,
The reconcilement holds: the blue abyss
Collects it not; our arrows sink amiss
And but in Him may we our import find.

The agony to know, the grief, the bliss   5
Of toil, is vain and vain: clots of the sod
Gathered in heat and haste and flung behind
To blind ourselves and others, what but this
Still grasping dust and sowing toward the wind?
No more thy meaning seek, thine anguish plead,   10
But leaving straining thought and stammering word,
Across the barren azure pass to God:
Shooting the void in silence like a bird,
A bird that shuts his wings for better speed.

Ralph Hodgson [1871–1962]

THE BELLS OF HEAVEN

'Twould ring the bells of Heaven
The wildest peal for years,
If Parson lost his senses
And people came to theirs,
And he and they together   5
Knelt down with angry prayers
For tamed and shabby tigers,
And dancing dogs and bears,
And wretched, blind pit ponies,
And little hunted hares.   10

9, *pit ponies:* ponies used to pull carts loaded with coal; they were often blinded to minimize the danger of their becoming frightened in the mine tunnels.

William Wordsworth [1770–1850]

MUTABILITY

From low to high doth dissolution climb,
And sink from high to low, along a scale
Of awful notes, whose concord shall not fail;
A musical but melancholy chime,
Which they can hear who meddle not with crime,   5
Nor avarice, nor over-anxious care.
Truth fails not; but her outward forms that bear
The longest date do melt like frosty rime,
That in the morning whitened hill and plain
And is no more; drop like the tower sublime   10
Of yesterday, which royally did wear
His crown of weeds, but could not even sustain

Some casual shout that broke the silent air,
Or the unimaginable touch of Time.

8, *rime:* frost.

Samuel Taylor Coleridge [1772–1834]

THE RIME OF THE ANCIENT MARINER

Part 1

*An ancient Mariner
meeteth three Gallants
bidden to a wedding-
feast, and detaineth one.*

It is an ancient Mariner
And he stoppeth one of three.
"By thy long gray beard and glittering eye,
Now wherefore stopp'st thou me?

The Bridegroom's doors are opened wide,   *5*
And I am next of kin;
The guests are met, the feast is set:
May'st hear the merry din."

He holds him with his skinny hand,
"There was a ship," quoth he.   *10*
"Hold off! unhand me, gray-beard loon!"
Eftsoons his hand dropt he.

*The Wedding-Guest is
spellbound by the eye
of the old sea-faring
man, and constrained to
hear his tale.*

He holds him with his glittering eye—
The Wedding-Guest stood still,
And listens like a three years' child: *15*
The Mariner hath his will.

The Wedding-Guest sat on a stone:
He cannot choose but hear;
And thus spake on that ancient man,
The bright-eyed Mariner.   *20*

"The ship was cheered, the harbor cleared,
Merrily did we drop
Below the kirk, below the hill,
Below the lighthouse top.

*The Mariner tells how
the ship sailed south-
ward with a good wind
and fair weather, till it
reached the Line.*

The Sun came up upon the left,   *25*
Out of the sea came he!
And he shone bright, and on the right
Went down into the sea.

Higher and higher every day,
Till over the mast at noon—"   30
The Wedding-Guest here beat his breast,
For he heard the loud bassoon.

The bride hath paced into the hall,
Red as a rose is she;
Nodding their heads before her goes   35
The merry minstrelsy.

The Wedding-Guest he beat his breast,
Yet he cannot choose but hear;
And thus spake on that ancient man,
The bright-eyed Mariner.   40

"And now the storm-blast came, and he
Was tyrannous and strong:
He struck with his o'ertaking wings,
And chased us south along.

With sloping masts and dipping prow,   45
As who pursued with yell and blow
Still treads the shadow of his foe,
And forward bends his head,
The ship drove fast, loud roared the blast,
And southward aye we fled.   50

And now there came both mist and snow,
And it grew wondrous cold:
And ice, mast-high, came floating by,
As green as emerald.

And through the drifts the snowy clifts   55
Did send a dismal sheen:
Nor shapes of men nor beast we ken—
The ice was all between.

The ice was here, the ice was there,
The ice was all around: 60
It cracked.and growled, and roared and howled,
Like noises in a swound!

At length did cross an Albatross,
Thorough the fog it came;

came through the snow-
fog, and was received
with great joy and hos-
pitality.

As if it had been a Christian soul,   65
We hailed it in God's name.

It ate the food it ne'er had eat,
And round and round it flew.
The ice did split with a thunder-fit;
The helmsman steered us through!   70

And lo! the Albatross
proveth a bird of good
omen, and followeth the
ship as it returned north-
ward through fog and
floating ice.

And a good south wind sprung up behind;
The Albatross did follow,
And every day, for food or play,
Came to the mariners' hollo!

In mist or cloud, on mast or shroud,   75
It perched for vespers nine;
Whiles all the night, through fog-smoke white,
Glimmered the white moon-shine."

The ancient Mariner in-
hospitably killeth the
pious bird of good omen.

"God save thee, ancient Mariner!
From the fiends, that plague thee thus! —   80
Why look'st thou so?" — "With my crossbow
I shot the Albatross."

Part II

"The Sun now rose upon the right:
Out of the sea came he,
Still hid in mist, and on the left   85
Went down into the sea.

And the good south wind still blew behind
But no sweet bird did follow,
Nor any day for food or play
Came to the mariners' hollo!   90

His shipmates cry out
against the ancient
Mariner, for killing the
bird of good luck.

And I had done a hellish thing,
And it would work 'em woe:
For all averred, I had killed the bird
That made the breeze to blow.
'Ah wretch!' said they, 'the bird to slay,   95
That made the breeze to blow!'

But when the fog cleared
off, they justify the same.

Nor dim nor red, like God's own head,
The glorious Sun uprist:

and thus make them-
selves accomplices in
the crime.

Then all averred, I had killed the bird
That brought the fog and mist.   *100*
''Twas right,' said they, 'such birds to slay,
That bring the fog and mist.'

The fair breeze con-
tinues; the ship enters
the Pacific Ocean, and
sails northward, even
till it reaches the Line.
The ship hath been sud-
denly becalmed.

The fair breeze blew, the white foam flew,
The furrow followed free;
We were the first that ever burst   *105*
Into that silent sea.

Down dropt the breeze, the sails dropt down,
'Twas sad as sad could be;
And we did speak only to break
The silence of the sea!   *110*

All in a hot and copper sky,
The bloody Sun, at noon,
Right up above the mast did stand,
No bigger than the Moon.

Day after day, day after day,   *115*
We stuck, nor breath nor motion;
As idle as a painted ship
Upon a painted ocean.

And the Albatross begins
to be avenged.

Water, water, everywhere,
And all the boards did shrink;   *120*
Water, water, everywhere
Nor any drop to drink.

The very deep did rot: O Christ!
That ever this should be!
Yea, slimy things did crawl with legs   *125*
Upon the slimy sea.

A Spirit had followed
them; one of the invis-
ible inhabitants of this
planet, neither departed
souls nor angels; con-
cerning whom the
learned Jew, Josephus,
and the Platonic Con-
stantinopolitan, Michael
Psellus, may be con-
sulted. They are very
numerous, and there is
no climate or element
without one or more.

About, about, in reel and rout
The death-fires danced at night;
The water, like a witch's oils,
Burnt green, and blue, and white.   *130*

And some in dreams assurèd were
Of the Spirit that plagued us so:
Nine fathom deep he had followed us
From the land of mist and snow.

And every tongue, through utter drought,   *135*
Was withered at the root;

We could not speak, no more than if
We had been choked with soot.

Ah! well a-day! what evil looks
Had I from old and young!   *140*
Instead of the cross, the Albatross
About my neck was hung."

Part III

"There passed a weary time. Each throat
Was parched, and glazed each eye.
A weary time! a weary time!   *145*
How glazed each weary eye,
When looking westward, I beheld
A something in the sky.

At first it seemed a little speck,
And then it seemed a mist;   *150*
It moved and moved, and took at last
A certain shape, I wist.

A speck, a mist, a shape, I wist!
And still it neared and neared:
As if it dodged a water-sprite,   *155*
It plunged and tacked and veered.

With throats unslaked, with black lips baked,
We could nor laugh nor wail;
Through utter drought all dumb we stood!
I bit my arm, I sucked the blood,   *160*
And cried, 'A sail! a sail!'

With throats unslaked, with black lips baked,
Agape they heard me call;
Gramercy! they for joy did grin,
And all at once their breath drew in,   *165*
As they were drinking all.

'See! see! (I cried) she tacks no more!
Hither to work us weal;
Without a breeze, without a tide,
She steadies with upright keel!'   *170*

The western wave was all a-flame;
The day was well nigh done!

Almost upon the western wave
Rested the broad bright Sun;
When that strange shape drove suddenly   *175*
Betwixt us and the Sun.

And straight the Sun was flecked with bars
(Heaven's Mother send us grace!)
As if through a dungeon-grate he peered
With broad and burning face.   *180*

Alas! (thought I, and my heart beat loud)
How fast she nears and nears!
Are those her sails that glance in the Sun,
Like restless gossameres?

Are those her ribs through which the Sun   *185*
Did peer, as through a grate?
And is that Woman all her crew?
Is that a Death? and are there two?
Is Death that woman's mate?

Her lips were red, her looks were free,   *190*
Her locks were yellow as gold:
Her skin was as white as leprosy,
The nightmare Life-in-Death was she,
Who thicks man's blood with cold.

The naked hulk alongside came,   *195*
And the twain were casting dice;
'The game is done! I've won! I've won!'
Quoth she, and whistles thrice.

The Sun's rim dips; the stars rush out:
At one stride comes the dark;   *200*
With far-heard whisper, o'er the sea,
Off shot the spectre-bark.

We listened and looked sideways up!
Fear at my heart, as at a cup,
My life-blood seemed to sip!   *205*
The stars were dim, and thick the night,
The steersman's face by his lamp gleamed white;
From the sails the dew did drip—
Till clomb above the eastern bar
The hornèd Moon, with one bright star   *210*
Within the nether tip.

One after one, by the star-dogged Moon,
Too quick for groan or sigh,
Each turned his face with a ghastly pang,
And cursed me with his eye.   215

Four times fifty living men
(And I heard nor sigh nor groan)
With heavy thump, a lifeless lump,
They dropped down one by one.

The souls did from their bodies fly —   220
They fled to bliss or woe!
And every soul, it passed me by,
Like the whizz of my cross-bow!"

Part IV

"I fear thee, ancient Mariner!
I fear thy skinny hand!   225
And thou art long, and lank, and brown,
As is the ribbed sea-sand.

I fear thee and thy glittering eye,
And thy skinny hand, so brown." —
"Fear not, fear not, thou Wedding-Guest!   230
This body dropt not down.

Alone, alone, all, all alone,
Alone on a wide, wide sea!
And never a saint took pity on
My soul in agony.   235

The many men, so beautiful!
And they all dead did lie:
And a thousand thousand slimy things
Lived on; and so did I.

I looked upon the rotting sea,   240
And drew my eyes away;
I looked upon the rotting deck,
And there the dead men lay.

I looked to heaven, and tried to pray;
But or ever a prayer had gusht,   245
A wicked whisper came, and made
My heart as dry as dust.

I closed my lids, and kept them close,
And the balls like pulses beat;
For the sky and the sea, and the sea and the
    sky   *250*
Lay like a load on my weary eye,
And the dead were at my feet.

But the curse liveth for
him in the eye of the
dead men.

The cold sweat melted from their limbs,
Nor rot nor reek did they:
The look with which they looked on me   *255*
Had never passed away.

An orphan's curse would drag to hell
A spirit from on high;
But oh! more horrible than that
Is the curse in a dead man's eye!   *260*
Seven days, seven nights, I saw that curse,
And yet I could not die.

In his loneliness and
fixedness he yearneth
toward the journeying
Moon, and the stars that
still sojourn, yet still
move onward; and every-
where the blue sky be-
longs to them, and is
their appointed rest, and
their native country and
their own natural homes,
which they enter unan-
nounced, as lords that
are certainly expected
and yet there is a silent
joy at their arrival.

The moving Moon went up the sky,
And nowhere did abide:
Softly she was going up,   *265*
And a star or two beside —

Her beams bemocked the sultry main,
Like April hoar-frost spread;
But where the ship's huge shadow lay,
The charmed water burnt alway   *270*
A still and awful red.

Beyond the shadow of the ship,
I watched the water-snakes:
They moved in tracks of shining white,
And when they reared, the elfish light   *275*
Fell off in hoary flakes.

Within the shadow of the ship
I watched their rich attire:

By the light of the Moon
he beholdeth God's
creatures of the great
calm.

Blue, glossy green, and velvet black,
They coiled and swam; and every track   *280*
Was a flash of golden fire.

Their beauty and their
happiness.

O happy living things! no tongue
Their beauty might declare:

He blesseth them in
his heart.

A spring of love gushed from my heart,
And I blessed them unaware: *285*

Sure my kind saint took pity on me,
And I blessed them unaware.

The spell begins to break.

The selfsame moment I could pray;
And from my neck so free
The Albatross fell off, and sank   *290*
Like lead into the sea."

Part V

"Oh, sleep! it is a gentle thing,
Beloved from pole to pole!
To Mary Queen the praise be given!
She sent the gentle sleep from Heaven,   *295*
That slid into my soul.

By grace of the holy Mother, the ancient Mariner is refreshed with rain.

The silly buckets on the deck,
That had so long remained,
I dreamt that they were filled with dew;
And when I awoke, it rained.   *300*

My lips were wet, my throat was cold,
My garments all were dank;
Sure I had drunken in my dreams,
And still my body drank.

I moved, and could not feel my limbs;   *305*
I was so light—almost
I thought that I had died in sleep,
And was a blessed ghost.

He heareth sounds and seeth strange sights and commotions in the sky and the element.

And soon I heard a roaring wind:
It did not come anear;   *310*
But with its sound it shook the sails,
That were so thin and sere.

The upper air burst into life!
And a hundred fire-flags sheen,
To and fro they were hurried about!   *315*
And to and fro, and in and out,
The wan stars danced between.

And the coming wind did roar more loud,
And sails did sigh like sedge;
And the rain poured down from one black
    cloud;   *320*
The moon was at its edge.

The thick black cloud was cleft, and still
The Moon was at its side:
Like waters shot from some high crag,
The lightning fell with never a jag,   *325*
A river steep and wide.

The loud wind never reached the ship,
Yet now the ship moved on!
Beneath the lightning and the Moon
The dead men gave a groan.   *330*

The bodies of the ship's crew are inspired and the ship moves on;

They groaned, they stirred, they all uprose,
Nor spake, nor moved their eyes;
It had been strange, even in a dream,
To have seen those dead men rise.

The helmsman steered, the ship moved on;   *335*
Yet never a breeze up blew;
The mariners all 'gan work the ropes,
Where they were wont to do;
They raised their limbs like lifeless tools —
We were a ghastly crew.   *340*

The body of my brother's son
Stood by me, knee to knee:
The body and I pulled at one rope
But he said nought to me."

But not by the souls of the men, nor by daemons of earth or middle air, but by a blessed troop of angelic spirits, sent down by the invocation of the guardian saint.

"I fear thee, ancient Mariner!"   *345*
"Be calm, thou Wedding-Guest!
'Twas not those souls that fled in pain,
Which to their corses came again,
But a troop of spirits blest:

For when it dawned — they dropped their
    arms,   *350*
And clustered round the mast;
Sweet sounds rose slowly through their mouths,
And from their bodies passed.

Around, around, flew each sweet sound,
Then darted to the Sun;   *355*
Slowly the sounds came back again,
Now mixed, now one by one.

Sometimes a-dropping from the sky
I heard the sky-lark sing;
Sometimes all little birds that are,   360
How they seemed to fill the sea and air
With their sweet jargoning!

And now 'twas like all instruments,
Now like a lonely flute;
And now it is an angel's song,   365
That makes the heavens be mute.

It ceased; yet still the sails made on
A pleasant noise till noon,
A noise like of a hidden brook
In the leafy month of June,   370
That to the sleeping woods all night
Singeth a quiet tune.

Till noon we quietly sailed on,
Yet never a breeze did breathe:
Slowly and smoothly went the ship   375
Moved onward from beneath.

*The lonesome Spirit
from the south pole
carries on the ship as
far as the Line, in
obedience to the angelic
troop, but still re-
quireth vengeance.*

Under the keel nine fathom deep,
From the land of mist and snow,
The Spirit slid: and it was he
That made the ship to go.   380
The sails at noon left off their tune,
And the ship stood still also.

The Sun, right up above the mast,
Had fixed her to the ocean:
But in a minute she 'gan stir,   385
With a short uneasy motion—
Backwards and forwards half her length
With a short uneasy motion.

Then like a pawing horse let go,
She made a sudden bound: 390
It flung the blood into my head,
And I fell down in a swound.

*The Polar Spirit's
fellow-daemons, the*

How long in that same fit I lay,
I have not to declare;

*invisible inhabitants of
the element, take part
in his wrong; and two
of them relate one to the
other, that penance long
and heavy for the
ancient Mariner hath
been accorded to the
Polar Spirit, who return-
eth southward.*

But ere my living life returned,   395
I heard and in my soul discerned
Two voices in the air.

'Is it he?' quoth one, 'Is this the man?
By Him who died on cross,
With his cruel bow he laid full low   400
The harmless Albatross.

The Spirit who bideth by himself
In the land of mist and snow,
He loved the bird that loved the man   405
Who shot him with his bow.'

The other was a softer voice,
As soft as honey-dew:
Quoth he, 'The man hath penance done,
And penance more will do.'''   410

Part VI

First Voice

"'But tell me, tell me! speak again,
Thy soft response renewing—
What makes that ship drive on so fast?
What is the ocean doing?'

Second Voice

'Still as a slave before his lord,   415
The ocean hath no blast;
His great bright eye most silently
Up to the Moon is cast—

If he may know which way to go;
For she guides him smooth or grim.   420
See, brother, see! how graciously
She looketh down on him.'

First Voice

'But why drives on that ship so fast,
Without or wave or wind?'

*The Mariner hath been
cast into a trance; for
the angelic power
causeth the vessel to
drive northward faster
than human life could
endure.*

Second Voice

'The air is cut away before,   425
And closes from behind.

Fly, brother, fly! more high, more high!
Or we shall be belated:
For slow and slow that ship will go,
When the Mariner's trance is abated.'   430

*The supernatural
motion is retarded; the
Mariner awakes, and
his penance begins anew.*
I woke, and we were sailing on
As in a gentle weather:
'Twas night, calm night, the Moon was high,
The dead men stood together.

All stood together on the deck,   435
For a charnel-dungeon fitter:
All fixed on me their stony eyes,
That in the Moon did glitter.

The pang, the curse, with which they died,
Had never passed away: 440
I could not draw my eyes from theirs,
Nor turn them up to pray.

*The curse is finally
expiated.*
And now this spell was snapt: once more
I viewed the ocean green,
And looked far forth, yet little saw   445
Of what had else been seen—

Like one, that on a lonesome road
Doth walk in fear and dread,
And having once turned round walks on,
And turns no more his head;   450
Because he knows a frightful fiend
Doth close behind him tread.

But soon there breathed a wind on me,
Nor sound nor motion made:
Its path was not upon the sea,   455
In ripple or in shade.

It raised my hair, it fanned my cheek
Like a meadow-gale of spring—
It mingled strangely with my fears,
Yet it felt like a welcoming.   460

Swiftly, swiftly flew the ship,
Yet she sailed softly too:

Sweetly, sweetly blew the breeze—
On me alone it blew.

Oh! dream of joy! is this indeed   465
The light-house top I see?
Is this the hill? is this the kirk?
Is this mine own countree?

We drifted o'er the harbor-bar,
And I with sobs did pray—   470
O let me be awake, my God!
Or let me sleep alway.

The harbor-bay was clear as glass,
So smoothly it was strewn!
And on the bay the moonlight lay,   475
And the shadow of the Moon.

The rock shone bright, the kirk no less,
That stands above the rock:
The moonlight steeped in silentness
The steady weathercock.   480

And the bay was white with silent light
Till rising from the same,
Full many shapes, that shadows were,
In crimson colors came.

A little distance from the prow   485
Those crimson shadows were:
I turned my eyes upon the deck—
Oh, Christ, what saw I there!

Each corse lay flat, lifeless and flat,
And, by the holy rood!   490
A man all light, a seraph-man,
On every corse there stood.

This seraph-band, each waved his hand;
It was a heavenly sight!
They stood as signals to the land   495
Each one a lovely light;

This seraph-band, each waved his hand,
No voice did they impart—

No voice; but oh! the silence sank
Like music on my heart.   500

But soon I heard the dash of oars,
I heard the Pilot's cheer;
My head was turned perforce away,
And I saw a boat appear.

The Pilot and the Pilot's boy,   505
I heard them coming fast:
Dear Lord in Heaven! it was a joy
The dead men could not blast.

I saw a third—I heard his voice:
It is the Hermit good!   510
He singeth loud his godly hymns
That he makes in the wood.
He'll shrieve my soul; he'll wash away
The Albatross's blood."

Part VII

The Hermit of the
Wood,

"This Hermit good lives in that wood   515
Which slopes down to the sea.
How loudly his sweet voice he rears!
He loves to talk with marineres
That come from a far countree.

He kneels at morn, and noon, and eve—   520
He hath a cushion plump:
It is the moss that wholly hides
The rotted old oak-stump.

The skiff-boat neared: I heard them talk,
'Why, this is strange, I trow!   525
Where are those lights so many and fair,
That signal made but now?'

Approacheth the ship
with wonder.

'Strange, by my faith!' the Hermit said—
'And they answered not our cheer!
The planks look warped! and see those sails,   530
How thin they are and sere!
I never saw aught like to them,
Unless perchance it were

Brown skeletons of leaves that lag
My forest-brook along;   535

The Rime of the Ancient Mariner   [**119**]

When the ivy-tod is heavy with snow,
And the owlet whoops to the wolf below,
That eats the she-wolf's young.'

'Dear Lord! it hath a fiendish look—
(The Pilot made reply)   540
I am a-feared'—'Push on, push on!'
Said the Hermit cheerily.

The boat came closer to the ship,
But I nor spake nor stirred;
The boat came close beneath the ship,   545
And straight a sound was heard.

The ship suddenly
sinketh.

Under the water it rumbled on,
Still louder and more dread:
It reached the ship, it split the bay;
The ship went down like lead.   550

The ancient Mariner
is saved in the Pilot's
boat.

Stunned by that loud and dreadful sound,
Which sky and ocean smote,
Like one that hath been seven days drowned
My body lay afloat;
But swift as dreams, myself I found   555
Within the Pilot's boat.

Upon the whirl, where sank the ship,
The boat spun round and round;
And all was still, save that the hill
Was telling of the sound.   560

I moved my lips—the Pilot shrieked
And fell down in a fit;
The holy Hermit raised his eyes,
And prayed where he did sit.

I took the oars: the Pilot's boy,   565
Who now doth crazy go,
Laughed loud and long, and all the while
His eyes went to and fro.
'Ha! ha!' quoth he, 'full plain I see,
The Devil knows how to row.'   570

And now, all in my own countree,
I stood on the firm land!

The Hermit stepped forth from the boat,
And scarcely he could stand.

The ancient Mariner
earnestly entreateth
the Hermit to shrieve
him; and the penance
of life falls on him.

'O shrieve me, shrieve me, holy man!'   575
The Hermit crossed his brow.
'Say quick,' quoth he, 'I bid thee say —
What manner of man art thou?'

Forthwith this frame of mine was wrenched
With a woful agony,   580
Which forced me to begin my tale;
And then it left me free.

And ever and anon
throughout his future
life an agony con-
straineth him to
travel from land to
land,

Since then, at an uncertain hour,
That agony returns:
And till my ghastly tale is told,   585
This heart within me burns.

I pass, like night, from land to land;
I have strange power of speech;
That moment that his face I see,
I know the man that must hear me: 590
To him my tale I teach.

What loud uproar bursts from that door!
The wedding-guests are there:
But in the garden-bower the bride
And bride-maids singing are: 595
And hark the little vesper bell
Which biddeth me to prayer!

O Wedding-Guest! this soul hath been
Alone on a wide, wide sea;
So lonely 'twas, that God himself   600
Scarce seemèd there to be.

O sweeter than the marriage-feast,
'Tis sweeter far to me,
To walk together to the kirk
With a goodly company! —   605

To walk together to the kirk,
And all together pray,
While each to his great Father bends,

Old men, and babes, and loving friends,   *610*
And youths and maidens gay!

And to teach, by his
own example, love and
reverence to all
things that God made
and loveth.

Farewell, farewell! but this I tell
To thee, thou Wedding-Guest!
He prayeth well, who loveth well
Both man and bird and beast.   *615*

He prayeth best, who loveth best
All things both great and small;
For the dear God who loveth us,
He made and loveth all."

The Mariner, whose eye is bright,   *620*
Whose beard with age is hoar,
Is gone: and now the Wedding-Guest
Turned from the Bridegroom's door.

He went like one that hath been stunned,
And is of sense forlorn: *625*
A sadder and a wiser man,
He rose the morrow morn.

12, *Eftsoons:* immediately. 23, *kirk:* church. 55, *clifts:* cliffs. 62, *swound:* swoon, faint. 76, *vespers:* the hour of evening worship. 128, *death-fires:* St. Elmo's fire, a portent of disaster in sailors' superstitions. 152, *wist:* knew. 164, *Gramercy:* many thanks. 168, *weal:* happiness, benefit. 184, *gossameres:* spider webs. 188, *a Death:* a death's head, a skeleton. 209, *clomb:* climbed. 210–211, *the horned Moon* is a crescent moon; it is of course impossible for a star to appear between the tips of the crescent; the omen here is therefore an evil one. 275, *elfish:* bewitched. 297, *silly:* see page 35. 314, *fire-flags:* Southern Lights. 325, *jag:* zig-zag. 348, *corses:* corpses. 362, *jargoning,* chirping, singing. 436, *charnel-dungeon:* a pit for bones which have been removed from graveyards to make room for fresh corpses. 490, *rood:* cross, crucifix, 491, *seraph:* an angel, 513, *shrieve:* to grant absolution after hearing confession, 536, *tod:* bush.

John Haines [b. 1924]

THE LEGEND OF PAPER PLATES

They trace their ancestry
back to the forest.
There all the family stood,
proud, bushy and strong.

Until hard times,
when from fire and drought
the patriarchs crashed.   5

The land was taken for taxes,
the young people cut down
and sold to the mills.   10

Their manhood and womanhood
was crushed, bleached
with bitter acids,
their fibres dispersed
as sawdust   15
among ten million offspring.

You see them at any picnic,
at ballgames, at home,
and at state occasions.

They are thin and pliable,   20
porous and identical.
They are made to be thrown away.

Brewster Ghiselin [b. 1903]

VANTAGE

I
All over the blue
Ocean the trees of the whales' breath:
All over the ocean,
Around the steeps of the headland
Falling westward and northward,   5
Punta Banda, and southward toward the turn of the land, three
   hundred miles,
Toward the lagoons, the pools of calm on the coast of deserts:
The fountains of the breath of the beasts
Whitening and leaning in the wind
On the ocean curve of the world,   10
Floating and misting,
Into mist
         into distance
                   into light.

The time is not yet
Of the continent-cities
And the forests cut.   15

When our age of glass is no more
Than glitter in dunes
Of detritus
The clouds will be here
In season, the water   20
Always.

The regret will be gone.

II

Ocean and air will lift
Shoring combers pluming
Over their leaning green   25
In landwind wings of spume.

If creatures astir on the cliffs
Have then the gift of light, let it
Be larger than ours, that lost
The world and took the moon.   30

_____

6, *Punta Banda:* a point of land on the western coast of Baja California.

3
Shadow in
the Deepening
Shade

Personal
Interpretations
of Tradition

William Wordsworth [1770–1850]

ODE

Intimations of Immortality from Recollections of Early Childhood

> *The Child is father of the Man;*
> *And I could wish my days to be*
> *Bound each to each by natural piety.*

I

There was a time when meadow, grove, and stream,
The earth, and every common sight,
      To me did seem
     Apparelled in celestial light,
The glory and the freshness of a dream.   *5*
It is not now as it hath been of yore;—
     Turn wheresoe'er I may,
     By night or day,
The things which I have seen I now can see no more.

II

     The Rainbow comes and goes,   *10*
     And lovely is the Rose,
     The Moon doth with delight
Look round her when the heavens are bare;
     Waters on a starry night
     Are beautiful and fair;   *15*
  The sunshine is a glorious birth;
  But yet I know, where'er I go,
That there hath past away a glory from the earth.

III

Now, while the birds thus sing a joyous song,
   And while the young lambs bound   *20*
      As to the tabor's sound,
To me alone there came a thought of grief:
A timely utterance gave that thought relief,
      And I again am strong:
The cataracts blow their trumpets from the steep;   *25*
No more shall grief of mine the season wrong;
I hear the Echoes through the mountains throng,
The Winds come to me from the fields of sleep,
      And all the earth is gay;
          Land and sea   *30*
     Give themselves up to jollity,
      And with the heart of May
     Doth every Beast keep holiday;—
      Thou Child of Joy,
Shout round me, let me hear thy shouts, thou happy Shepherd-boy!   *35*

IV

Ye blessèd Creatures, I have heard the call
  Ye to each other make; I see
The heavens laugh with you in your jubilee;
  My heart is at your festival,
     My head hath its coronal,   *40*
The fulness of your bliss, I feel—I feel it all.
     Oh evil day! if I were sullen
     While Earth herself is adorning,
      This sweet May-morning,
     And the Children are culling   *45*
      On every side,
    In a thousand valleys far and wide,
    Fresh flowers; while the sun shines warm,
And the Babe leaps up on his Mother's arm:—
     I hear, I hear, with joy I hear!   *50*
     —But there's a Tree, of many, one,
A single Field which I have looked upon,
Both of them speak of something that is gone:
     The Pansy at my feet
     Doth the same tale repeat: *55*
Whither is fled the visionary gleam?
Where is it now, the glory and the dream?

V

Our birth is but a sleep and a forgetting:
The Soul that rises with us, our life's Star,
     Hath had elsewhere its setting,   *60*

And cometh from afar:
    Not in entire forgetfulness,
    And not in utter nakedness,
But trailing clouds of glory do we come
    From God, who is our home: 65
Heaven lies about us in our infancy!
Shades of the prison-house begin to close
    Upon the growing Boy,
        But He
Beholds the light, and whence it flows,   70
    He sees it in his joy;
The Youth, who daily farther from the east
    Must travel, still is Nature's Priest,
    And by the vision splendid
    Is on his way attended;   75
At length the Man perceives it die away,
And fade into the light of common day.

VI

Earth fills her lap with pleasures of her own;
Yearnings she hath in her own natural kind,
And, even with something of a Mother's mind,   80
    And no unworthy aim,
    The homely Nurse doth all she can
To make her Foster-child, her Inmate Man,
    Forget the glories he hath known,
And that imperial palace whence he came.   85

VII

Behold the Child among his new-born blisses,
A six years' Darling of a pigmy size!
See, where 'mid work of his own hand he lies,
Frettied by sallies of his mother's kisses,
With light upon him from his father's eyes!   90
See, at his feet, some little plan or chart,
Some fragment from his dream of human life,
Shaped by himself with newly-learned art;
    A wedding or a festival,
    A mourning or a funeral;   95
    And this hath now his heart,
    And unto this he frames his song:
    Then will he fit his tongue
To dialogues of business, love, or strife;
    But it will not be long   100
    Ere this be thrown aside,
    And with new joy and pride
The little Actor cons another part;

Filling from time to time his "humorous stage"
With all the Persons, down to palsied Age,   *105*
That Life brings with her in her equipage;
      As if his whole vocation
      Were endless imitation.

VIII

Thou, whose exterior semblance doth belie
      Thy Soul's immensity;   *110*
Thou best Philosopher, who yet dost keep
Thy heritage, thou Eye among the blind,
That, deaf and silent, read'st the eternal deep,
Haunted for ever by the eternal mind,—
      Mighty Prophet! Seer blest!   *115*
      On whom those truths do rest,
Which we are toiling all our lives to find,
In darkness lost, the darkness of the grave;
Thou, over whom thy Immortality
Broods like the Day, a Master o'er a Slave,   *120*
A Presence which is not to be put by;
Thou little Child, yet glorious in the might
Of heaven-born freedom on thy being's height,
Why with such earnest pains dost thou provoke
The years to bring the inevitable yoke,   *125*
Thus blindly with thy blessedness at strife?
Full soon thy Soul shall have her earthly freight,
And custom lie upon thee with a weight,
Heavy as frost, and deep almost as life!

IX

      O joy! that in our embers   *130*
      Is something that doth live,
      That nature yet remembers
      What was so fugitive!
The thought of our past years in me doth breed
Perpetual benediction: not indeed   *135*
For that which is most worthy to be blest;
Delight and liberty, the simple creed
Of Childhood, whether busy or at rest,
With new-fledged hope still fluttering in his breast:—
      Not for these I raise   *140*
      The song of thanks and praise;
     But for those obstinate questionings
     Of sense and outward things,
     Fallings from us, vanishings;
     Blank misgivings of a Creature   *145*
Moving about in worlds not realised,
High instincts before which our mortal Nature

Did tremble like a guilty Thing surprised:
  But for those first affections,
  Those shadowy recollections,   *150*
 Which, be they what they may,
Are yet the fountain light of all our day,
Are yet a master light of all our seeing;
  Uphold us, cherish, and have power to make
Our noisy years seem moments in the being   *155*
Of the eternal Silence: truths that wake,
  To perish never;
Which neither listlessness, nor mad endeavour,
  Nor Man nor Boy,
Nor all that is at enmity with joy,   *160*
Can utterly abolish or destroy!
  Hence in a season of calm weather
  Though inland far we be,
Our Souls have sight of that immortal sea
  Which brought us hither,   *165*
 Can in a moment travel thither,
And see the Children sport upon the shore,
And hear the mighty waters rolling evermore.

X

Then sing, ye Birds, sing, sing a joyous song!
  And let the young Lambs bound   *170*
  As to the tabor's sound!
We in thought will join your throng,
  Ye that pipe and ye that play,
  Ye that through your hearts to-day
  Feel the gladness of the May!   *175*
What though the radiance which was once so bright
Be now for ever taken from my sight,
  Though nothing can bring back the hour
Of splendour in the grass, of glory in the flower;
  We will grieve not, rather find   *180*
  Strength in what remains behind;
  In the primal sympathy
  Which having been must ever be;
  In the soothing thoughts that spring
  Out of human suffering;   *185*
  In the faith that looks through death,
In years that bring the philosophic mind.

XI

And O, ye Fountains, Meadows, Hills, and Groves,
Forebode not any severing of our loves!
Yet in my heart of hearts I feel your might;   *190*
I only have relinquished one delight

To live beneath your more habitual sway.
I love the Brooks which down their channels fret,
Even more than when I tripped lightly as they;
The innocent brightness of a new-born Day   *195*
        Is lovely yet;
The Clouds that gather round the setting sun
Do take a sober colouring from an eye
That hath kept watch o'er man's mortality;
Another race hath been, and other palms are won.   *200*
Thanks to the human heart by which we live,
Thanks to its tenderness, its joys, and fears,
To me the meanest flower that blows can give
Thoughts that do often lie too deep for tears.

Ode: a lyric poem of irregularly rhymed and metered stanzas, characterized by loftiness of theme and diction. Originally, odes were those stanzaic portions of Greek tragedies sung by the chorus. 21, *tabor:* a small drum used to beat time in country rounds and dances. 40, *coronal:* a crown of flowers worn by shepherds celebrating the joys of spring. 59, *our life's Star:* the sun. 89, *Fretted by sallies:* covered over with profusions (of kisses). 103, *cons:* memorizes. 104, *"humorous stage":* the phrase comes from a sonnet by the Elizabethan poet Samuel Daniel (1562–1619), who meant by "humorous" the various kinds of temperaments ("humors") represented on the dramatic stage. 146, *realised:* here, to seem real. 193, *fret:* ripple. 200, *palms:* prize wreaths; see Marvell's "The Garden," line 2, page 95, and note, page 97.

Fred Bornhauser [b. 1925]

THE WISHBONE

It used to be said that love is a bird,
And I am willing to consider that.
All flight and feathers each affair,
And when the dead flesh is interred
In the mausoleum of the air,   *5*
There the broken bones before the cat.

We used to break the breast of fowl.
We would plunge to the bone the silver dirk
And capture the sling-shot, heart's whole fort,
Then sit like cats with mystic scowl,   *10*
Tormenting destiny for its report,
Occult and devilish innocents at work.

No bone I dare break now. I am afraid
To crack the body in which love is said to rest.

I eat the flesh and flourish on the dish —
For that is destiny's last word obeyed —
And sometimes utter subtle terms of wish,
But never desecrate the relic in the breast.

Paul Laurence Dunbar [1872–1906]

WE WEAR THE MASK

We wear the mask that grins and lies,
It hides our cheeks and shades our eyes —
This debt we pay to human guile;
With torn and bleeding hearts we smile,
And mouth with myriad subtleties.   5
Why should the world be over-wise,
In counting all our tears and sighs?
Nay, let them only see us, while
    We wear the mask.

We smile, but, O great Christ, our cries   10
To thee from tortured souls arise.
We sing, but oh the clay is vile
Beneath our feet, and long the mile;
But let the world dream otherwise,
    We wear the mask!   15

William Stafford [b. 1914]

PRAIRIE TOWN

There was a river under First and Main:
the salt mines honeycombed farther down.
A wealth of sun and wind ever so strong
converged on that home town, long gone.

At the north edge there were the sandhills.   5
I used to stare for hours at prairie dogs,
which had their town, and folded their little paws
to stare beyond their fence where I was.

River rolling in secret, salt mines with care
holding your crystals and stillness, north prairie — 10
what kind of trip can I make, with what old friend,
ever to find a town so widely rich again?

Pioneers, for whom history was walking through dead grass,
and the main things that happened were miles and the time of day —
you built that town, and I have let it pass.   15
Little folded paws, judge me: I came away.

John Hall Wheelock [b. 1886]

BONAC

Du bist Orplid, mein Land, das ferne leuchtet

—Mörike

I

This is enchanted country, lies under a spell,
Bird-haunted, ocean-haunted — land of youth,
Land of first love, land of death also, perhaps,
And desired return. Sea-tang and honeysuckle
Perfume the air, where the old house looks out   5
Across mild lowlands, meadows of scrub and pine,
A shell echoing the sea's monotone
That haunts these shores. And here, all summer through,
From dawn to dusk, there will be other music,
Threading the sea's music: at rise of sun,   10
With jubilation half-awakened birds
Salute his coming again, the lord of life,
His ambulatory footstep over the earth,
Who draws after him all that tide of song —
Salute the oncoming day, while from the edges   15
Of darkness, westward, fading voices call,
Night's superseded voices, the whip-poor-will's
Lamentation and farewell. Morning and noon
And afternoon and evening, the singing of birds
Lies on this country like an incantation: 20
Robin and wren, catbird, phoebe and chat,
Song-sparrow's music-box tune, and from the slender
Arches of inmost shade, the woodland's roof,
Where few winds come, flutelike adagio or
Wild syrinx-cry and high raving of the thrush,   25
Their clang and piercing pierce the spirit through —
Look off into blue heaven, you shall witness
Angelic motions, the volt and sidewise shift
Of the swallow in mid-air. Enchanted land,
Where time has died; old ocean-haunted land;   30

Land of first love, where grape and honeysuckle
Tangle their vines, where the beach-plum in spring
Snows all the inland dunes; bird-haunted land,
Where youth still dwells forever, your long day
Draws to its close, bringing for evening-star   35
Venus, a bud of fire in the pale west,
Bringing dusk and the whip-poor-will again,
And the owl's tremolo and the firefly,
And gradual darkness. Silently the bat,
Over still lawns that listen to the sea,   40
Weaves the preoccupation of his flight.
The arch of heaven soars upward with all its stars.

II

Summer fades soon here, autumn in this country
Comes early and exalted. Where the wild land,
With its sparse bayberry and huckleberry,   45
Slopes seaward, where the seaward dunes go down,
Echoing, to the sea; over the beaches,
Over the shore-line stretching east and west,
The ineffable slant light of autumn lingers.
The roof of heaven is higher now, the clouds   50
That drag, trailing, along the enormous vault,
Hang higher, the wide ways are wider now.
Sea-hawks wander the ocean solitudes,
Sea-winds walk there, the waters grow turbulent,
And inland also a new restlessness   55
Walks the world, remembering something lost,
Seeking something remembered: wheeling wings
And songless woods herald the great departure,
Cattle stray, swallows gather in flocks,
The cloud-travelling moon through gusty cloud   60
Looks down on the first pilgrims going over,
And hungers in the blood are whispering, "Flee!
Seek otherwhere, here is no lasting home."
Now bird-song fails us, now an older music
Is vibrant in the land—the drowsy cry   65
Of grasshopper and cricket, earth's low cry
Of sleepy love, her inarticulate cry,
Calling life downward, promising release
From these vague longings, these immortal torments.
The drowsy voice drones on—oh, siren voice: 70
Aeons of night, millenniums of repose,
Soundless oblivion, divine surcease,
Dark intermingling with the primal darkness,
Oh, not to be, to slough this separate being,

Flow home at last! The alert spirit listens,   *75*
Hearing, meanwhile, far off, along the coast,
Rumors of the rhythm of some wakeful thing,
Reverberations, oceanic tremors,
The multitudinous motions of the sea,
With all its waters, all its warring waves.   *80*

Bonac: a local name for the northern end of Long Island. The epigraph is from a
poem by Eduard Mörike (1804–1875), and may be translated "Thou art Orplid, my
country, that shineth from afar." Orplid was an imaginary land invented by Mörike.

Dylan Thomas [1914–1953]

FERN HILL

Now as I was young and easy under the apple boughs
About the lilting house and happy as the grass was green,
    The night above the dingle starry,
        Time let me hail and climb
    Golden in the heydays of his eyes,   *5*
And honoured among wagons I was prince of the apple towns
And once below a time I lordly had the trees and leaves
        Trail with daisies and barley
    Down the rivers of the windfall light.

And as I was green and carefree, famous among the barns   *10*
About the happy yard and singing as the farm was home.
    In the sun that is young once only,
        Time let me play and be
    Golden in the mercy of his means,
And green and golden I was huntsman and herdsman, the calves   *15*
Sang to my horn, the foxes on the hills barked clear and cold,
        And the sabbath rang slowly
    In the pebbles of the holy streams.

All the sun long it was running, it was lovely, the hay
Fields high as the house, the tunes from the chimneys, it was air   *20*
    And playing, lovely and watery
        And fire green as grass.
    And nightly under the simple stars
As I rode to sleep the owls were bearing the farm away,
All the moon long I heard, blessed among stables, the night-jars   *25*
    Flying with the ricks, and the horses
        Flashing into the dark.

And then to awake, and the farm, like a wanderer white
With the dew, come back, the cock on his shoulder: it was all
      Shining, it was Adam and maiden,   30
         The sky gathered again
      And the sun grew round that very day.
So it must have been after the birth of the simple light
In the first, spinning place, the spellbound horses walking warm
      Out of the whinnying green stable   35
         On to the fields of praise.

And honoured among foxes and pheasants by the gay house
Under the new made clouds and happy as the heart was long,
      In the sun born over and over,
         I ran my heedless ways,   40
      My wishes raced through the house high hay
And nothing I cared, at my sky blue trades, that time allows
In all his tuneful turning so few and such morning songs
      Before the children green and golden
         Follow him out of grace,   45

Nothing I cared, in the lamb white days, that time would take me
Up to the swallow thronged loft by the shadow of my hand,
      In the moon that is always rising,
         Nor that riding to sleep
I should hear him fly with the high fields   50
And wake to the farm forever fled from the childless land.
Oh as I was young and easy in the mercy of his means,
        Time held me green and dying
      Though I sang in my chains like the sea.

Anthony Hecht [b. 1923]

LIZARDS AND SNAKES

On the summer road that ran by our front porch
  Lizards and snakes came out to sun.
It was hot as a stove out there, enough to scorch
  A buzzard's foot. Still, it was fun   5
To lie in the dust and spy on them. Near but remote,
  They snoozed in the carriage ruts, a smile
In the set of the jaw, a fierce pulse in the throat
Working away like Jack Doyle's after he'd run the mile.

Aunt Martha had an unfair prejudice
  Against them (as well as being cold   10
Toward bats.) She was pretty inflexible in this,

Being a spinster and all, and old.
So we used to slip them into her knitting box.
   In the evening she'd bring in things to mend
And a nice surprise would slide out from under the socks.   15
It broadened her life, as Joe said. Joe was my friend.

But we never did it again after the day
   Of the big wind when you could hear the trees
Creak like rockingchairs. She was looking away
   Off, and kept saying, "Sweet Jesus, please   20
Don't let him near me. He's as like as twins.
   He can crack us like lice with his fingernail.
I can see him plain as a pikestaff. Look how he grins
And swinges the scaly horror of his folded tail."

_____

   24: Taken from "On the Morning of Christ's Nativity," by John Milton. The woman
speaking at the end of the poem has assimilated both Biblical and Miltonic language.

John Alexander Allen [b. 1922]

A WORD TO A FATHER, DEAD

Whatever it was that went wrong—the stove aflame
In the kitchen with a sudden rage to burn
The house down; or the shower madly bent
On flooding us out, when stubbornly the drain
Backed up and nothing you did could shut the water   5
Off—whatever it was, it worried you;
And though your faith was perfect, in your hand
Buckets wickedly would turn to seives.

I believe you were ready to call it quits
When something in your heart, a part of you not   10
To be gotten along without, went wrong. I believe
You were ready then, when all was said and done,
For death, unsent-for though it was, to come;
Willing, as anyone might have been, for someone
Different, in event of fire and flood,   15
To be on hand, to do the worrying.

Familiar now with death, whatever it is,
You will have forgotten the old bizarre concoction

Of the kitchen, the old routine of plumbing's
Comic imperfection. Still, I've not   20
Forgotten how you told me, in a dream,
"I'm sorry, sorry," and I knew your flesh
Had only pity for its own, and held
Itself alone accountable for grief.

But no. I've kept my hand in, in the kitchen;   25
Being a tenant, needn't worry my head,
Though a rusty pool appear beside the grumbling
Water heater. What's a landlord for?
Whatever it is that's happened since we met,
You're used to it. I'm getting the hang of time   30
In time for what comes next. Whatever it is,
Don't worry. Don't, whatever it is, be sorry.

Theodore Roethke [1908–1963]

IN A DARK TIME

In a dark time, the eye begins to see,
I meet my shadow in the deepening shade;
I hear my echo in the echoing wood—
A lord of nature weeping to a tree.
I live between the heron and the wren,   5
Beasts of the hill and serpents of the den.

What's madness but nobility of soul
At odds with circumstance? The day's on fire!
I know the purity of pure despair,
My shadow pinned against a sweating wall.   10
That place among the rocks—is it a cave,
Or winding path? The edge is what I have.

A steady storm of correspondences!
A night flowing with birds, a ragged moon,
And in broad day the midnight come again!   15
A man goes far to find out what he is—
Death of the self in a long, tearless night,
All natural shapes blazing unnatural light.

Dark, dark my light, and darker my desire.
My soul, like some heat-maddened summer fly,   20
Keeps buzzing at the sill. Which I is I?

A fallen man, I climb out of my fear.
The mind enters itself, and God the mind,
And one is One, free in the tearing wind.

13, *correspondences:* interrelationships. The French symbolist poet Charles Bau-
delaire (1821–1867), in a sonnet entitled "Correspondances," developed the notion
that sounds, colors, and smells could be sensed in terms of one another's qualities.

May Miller [b. 1900]

BELL AT MIDNIGHT

Under the bronze-lipped Jesus bell
Midnight answers old, flesh-wise.
All that was red, tipping heaven at noon,
Left no wild thing to stir the calm
Except a hollow crone coaxing her cat,   5
Calling down the alley-ways,
"Here, Sue! Here, Sue! Here, Sue!"
Above stairs, a girl sleeps
In an old man's bed, quiet, free;
And they who rage and pray sleep too,   10
Their tongues impotent to revive a legend.

George Herbert [1593–1633]

THE COLLAR

I struck the board, and cried, No more.
          I will abroad.
  What? shall I ever sigh and pine?
My lines and life are free; free as the road,
  Loose as the wind, as large as store.   5
       Shall I be still in suit?
Have I no harvest but a thorn
To let me blood, and not restore
What I have lost with cordial fruit?
       Sure there was wine   10
Before my sighs did dry it: there was corn
      Before my tears did drown it.
Is the year only lost to me?
      Have I no bays to crown it?

No flowers, no garlands gay? all blasted?
        All wasted?
  Not so, my heart: but there is fruit,
        And thou hast hands.
  Recover all thy sigh-blown age
On double pleasures: leave thy cold dispute   20
Of what is fit, and not. Forsake thy cage,
        Thy rope of sands,
Which petty thoughts have made, and made to thee
  Good cable, to enforce and draw,
        And be thy law,   25
  While thou didst wink and wouldst not see.
        Away; take heed:
        I will abroad.
Call in thy death's head there: tie up thy fears.
        He that forbears   30
    To suit and serve his need,
        Deserves his load.
But as I raved and grew more fierce and wild
        At every word,
  Methought I heard one calling,*Child!*   35
        And I replied, *My Lord.*

1, *board:* table. 6, *in suit:* awaiting a favor. 9, *cordial:* spiritually restorative. 14, *bays:* a wreath, traditionally awarded to winners of poetic competitions; here, it is used in a more generally festive sense. 22, *rope of sands:* Christian doctrine, which the speaker sees as having been made too restrictive by believers who have too easily accepted it. 29, *death's head:* skull which reminds the believer that his death is approaching.

John Donne [1572–1631]

HOLY SONNET XIV

Batter my heart, three-personed God; for You
As yet but knock, breathe, shine, and seek to mend;
That I may rise and stand, o'erthrow me, and bend
Your force to break, blow, burn, and make me new.
I, like an usurped town, to another due,   5
Labor to admit You, but O, to no end;
Reason, Your Viceroy in me, me should defend,
But is captived, and proves weak or untrue.
Yet dearly I love You, and would be loved fain,
But am betrothed unto Your enemy.   10
Divorce me, untie or break that knot again;

Take me to You, imprison me, for I,
Except You enthrall me, never shall be free,
Nor ever chaste, except You ravish me.

1, *three-personed God*: a reference to God as the Trinity.

John Milton [1608–1674]

WHEN I CONSIDER HOW MY LIGHT IS SPENT

When I consider how my light is spent
  Ere half my days, in this dark world and wide,
  And that one talent which is death to hide
  Lodged with me useless, though my soul more bent
To serve therewith my Maker, and present   *5*
  My true account, lest he returning chide;
  "Doth God exact day-labor, light denied?"
  I fondly ask; but Patience to prevent
That murmur, soon replies, "God doth not need
  Either man's work or his own gifts; who best   *10*
  Bear his mild yoke, they serve him best. His state
Is kingly. Thousands at his bidding speed
  And post o'er land and ocean without rest:
  They also serve who only stand and wait."

Milton had become blind by the time he was forty-three.

8, *fondly*: foolishly.

John Greenleaf Whittier [1807–1892]

FIRST-DAY THOUGHTS

In calm and cool and silence, once again
  I find my old accustomed place among
  My brethren, where, perchance, no human tongue
  Shall utter words; where never hymn is sung,
  Nor deep-toned organ blown, nor censer swung,   *5*
Nor dim light falling through the pictured pane!
There, syllabled by silence, let me hear
The still small voice which reached the prophet's ear;
Read in my heart a still diviner law
Than Israel's leader on his tables saw!   *10*
There let me strive with each besetting sin,

Recall my wandering fancies, and restrain
The sore disquiet of a restless brain;
And, as the path of duty is made plain,
May grace be given that I may walk therein, 15
Not like the hireling, for his selfish gain,
With backward glances and reluctant tread,
Making a merit of his coward dread,
But, cheerful, in the light around me thrown,
Walking as one to pleasant service led; 20
Doing God's will as if it were my own,
Yet trusting not in mine, but in his strength alone!

First-Day: Sunday, in Quaker usage. The poem begins with a description of the traditional Friends' Meeting for Worship. 10, *Israel's leader:* Moses; *tables:* tablets on which were carved the Ten Commandments.

Robert Francis [b. 1901]

HALLELUJAH: A SESTINA

A wind's word, the Hebrew Hallelujah.
I wonder they never give it to a boy
(Hal for short) boy with wind-wild hair.
It means Praise God, as well it should since praise
Is what God's for. Why didn't they call my father 5
Hallelujah instead of Ebenezer?

Eben, of course, but christened Ebenezer,
Product of Nova Scotia (hallelujah).
Daniel, a country doctor, was his father
And my father his tenth and final boy. 10
A baby and last, he had a baby's praise:
Red petticoat, red cheeks, and crow-black hair.

A boy has little to say about his hair
And little about a name like Ebenezer
Except that he can shorten either. Praise 15
God for that, for that shout Hallelujah.
Shout Hallelujah for everything a boy
Can be that is not his father or grandfather.

But then, before you know it, he is a father
Too and passing on his brand of hair 20
To one more perfectly defenseless boy,

Dubbing him John or James or Ebenezer
But never, so far as I know, Hallelujah,
As if God didn't need quite that much praise.

But what I'm coming to—Could I ever praise   25
My father half enough for being a father
Who let me be myself? Sing Hallelujah.
Preacher he was with a prophet's head of hair
And what but a prophet's name was Ebenezer,
However little I guessed it as a boy?   30

Outlandish names of course are never a boy's
Choice. And it takes time to learn to praise.
Stone of Help is the meaning of Ebenezer.
Stone of Help—what fitter name for my father?
Always the Stone of Help however his hair   35
Might graduate from black to hallelujah.

Such is the old drama of boy and father.
Praise from a graybeard now with thinning hair.
Sing Ebenezer, Robert, sing Hallelujah!

Gerard Manley Hopkins [1844–1889]

THE WINDHOVER:

To Christ our Lord

I caught this morning morning's minion, king-
   dom of daylight's dauphin, dapple-dawn-drawn Falcon, in his
     riding
   Of the rolling level underneath him steady air, and striding
High there, how he rung upon the rein of a wimpling wing
In his ecstasy! then off, off forth on swing,   5
   As a skate's heel sweeps smooth on a bow-bend: the hurl and
     gliding
   Rebuffed the big wind. My heart in hiding
Stirred for a bird,—the achieve of, the mastery of the thing!

Brute beauty and valour and act, oh, air, pride, plume here
   Buckle! AND the fire that breaks from thee then, a billion   10
Times told lovelier, more dangerous, O my chevalier!

No wonder of it: shéer plód makes plough down sillion
Shine, and blue-bleak embers, ah my dear,
Fall, gall themselves, and gash gold-vermilion.

---

windhover: small hawk, kestrel; 1, *minion:* subordinate, favorite; 2, *dauphin:* heir
to a throne; 4, *wimpling:* rippling; 9, *Buckle:* here, both "to join" and "to give way"
could be meant; 12, *sillion:* furrow.

William Butler Yeats [1865–1939]

THE SECOND COMING

Turning and turning in the widening gyre
The falcon cannot hear the falconer;
Things fall apart; the centre cannot hold;
Mere anarchy is loosed upon the world,
The blood-dimmed tide is loosed, and everywhere   5
The ceremony of innocence is drowned;
The best lack all conviction, while the worst
Are full of passionate intensity.

Surely some revelation is at hand;
Surely the Second Coming is at hand.   10
The Second Coming! Hardly are those words out
When a vast image out of *Spiritus Mundi*
Troubles my sight: somewhere in sands of the desert
A shape with lion body and the head of a man,
A gaze blank and pitiless as the sun,   15
Is moving its slow thighs, while all about it
Reel shadows of the indignant desert birds.
The darkness drops again; but now I know
That twenty centuries of stony sleep
Were vexed to nightmare by a rocking cradle,   20
And what rough beast, its hour come round at last,
Slouches towards Bethlehem to be born?

This poem arises from Yeats's vision of history as a 2000-year cycle, each cycle
announced by a momentous event.

1, *gyre:* spiral. 12, *Spiritus Mundi:* the Soul of the World, source of dreams and
racial memories.

John Milton [1608–1674]

LYCIDAS

In this monody the author bewails a learned friend, unfortunately drowned in his passage from Chester on the Irish Seas, 1637. And by occasion foretells the ruin of our corrupted clergy, then in their height.

Yet once more, O ye laurels, and once more,
Ye myrtles brown, with ivy never sere,
I come to pluck your berries harsh and crude,
And with forced fingers rude
Shatter your leaves before the mellowing year.   5
Bitter constraint and sad occasion dear
Compels me to disturb your season due;
For Lycidas is dead, dead ere his prime,
Young Lycidas, and hath not left his peer.
Who would not sing for Lycidas? he knew   10
Himself to sing, and build the lofty rhyme.
He must not float upon his wat'ry bier
Unwept, and welter to the parching wind,
Without the meed of some melodious tear.
   Begin, then, Sisters of the Sacred Well   15
That from beneath the seat of Jove doth spring,
Begin, and somewhat loudly sweep the string.
Hence with denial vain and coy excuse:
So may some gentle Muse
With lucky words favor my destined urn,   20
And, as he passes, turn
And bid fair peace be to my sable shroud!
For we were nursed upon the self-same hill,
Fed the same flocks, by fountain, shade, and rill;
   Together both, ere the high lawns appeared   25
Under the opening eyelids of the Morn,
We drove a-field, and both together heard
What time the gray-fly winds her sultry horn,
Battening our flocks with the fresh dews of night,
Oft till the star that rose at evening bright   30
Towards Heaven's descent had sloped his westering wheel.
Meanwhile the rural ditties were not mute,
Tempered to the oaten flute,
Rough Satyrs danced, and Fauns with cloven heel
From the glad sound would not be absent long;   35
And old Damætas loved to hear our song.
   But, O the heavy change, now thou art gone,
Now thou art gone, and never must return!
Thee, Shepherd, thee the woods and desert caves,

With wild thyme and the gadding vine o'ergrown,   40
And all their echoes mourn.
The willows, and the hazel copses green,
Shall now no more be seen
Fanning their joyous leaves to thy soft lays.
As killing as the canker to the rose.   45
Or taint-worm to the weanling herds that graze,
Or frost to flowers, that their gay wardrobe wear
When first the white thorn blows;
Such, Lycidas, thy loss to shepherd's ear.
    Where were ye. Nymphs, when the remorseless deep   50
Closed o'er the head of your loved Lycidas?
For neither were ye playing on the steep
Where your old bards, the famous druids, lie,
Nor yet on the shaggy top of Mona high,
Nor yet where Deva spreads her wizard stream.   55
Ay me! I fondly dream
"Had ye been there" . . . for what could that have done?
What could the Muse herself that Orpheus bore,
The Muse herself, for her enchanting son,
Whom universal Nature did lament,   60
When, by the rout that made the hideous roar,
His gory visage down the stream was sent,
Down the swift Hebrus to the Lesbian shore?
    Alas! what boots it with uncessant care
To tend the homely, slighted, shepherd's trade,   65
And strictly meditate the thankless Muse?
Were it not better done, as others use,
To sport with Amaryllis in the shade,
Or with the tangles of Neæra's hair?
Fame is the spur that the clear spirit doth raise   70
(That last infirmity of noble mind)
To scorn delights and live laborious days;
But the fair guerdon when we hope to find,
And think to burst out into sudden blaze,
Comes the blind Fury with the abhorred shears,   75
And slits the thin-spun life. "But not the praise,"
Phœbus replied, and touched my trembling ears:
"Fame is no plant that grows on mortal soil,
Nor in the glistering foil.
Set off to the world, nor in broad rumor lies,   80
But lives and spreads aloft by those pure eyes
And perfect witness of all-judging Jove;
As he pronounces lastly on each deed,
Of so much fame in Heav'n expect thy meed."
    O fountain Arethuse, and thou honored flood,   85

Smooth-sliding Mincius, crowned with vocal reeds,
That strain I heard was of a higher mood:
But now my oat proceeds,
And listens to the Herald of the Sea,
That came in Neptune's plea.   90
He asked the waves, and asked the felon winds,
What hard mishap hath doomed this gentle swain?
And questioned every gust of rugged wings
That blows from off each beakèd promontory:
They knew not of his story;   95
And sage Hippotadés their answer brings,
That not a blast was from his dungeon strayed:
The air was calm, and on the level brine
Sleek Panopé with all her sisters played.
It was the fatal and perfidious bark,   100
Built in the eclipse, and rigged with curses dark,
That sunk so low that sacred head of thine.
    Next, Camus, reverend sire, went footing slow,
His mantle hairy, and his bonnet sedge,
Inwrought with figures dim, and on the edge   105
Like to that sanguine flower inscribed with woe.
"Ah! who hath reft," quoth he, "my dearest pledge?"
Last came, and last did go,
The pilot of the Galilean lake;
Two massy keys he bore of metals twain   110
(The golden opes, the iron shuts amain).
He shook his mitered locks, and stern bespake:—
"How well could I have spared for thee, young swain,
Enow of such, as for their bellies' sake,
Creep, and intrude, and climb into the fold!   115
Of other care they little reckoning make
Than how to scramble at the shearers' feast,
And shove away the worthy bidden guest.
Blind mouths! that scarce themselves know how to hold
A sheep-hook, or have learned aught else the least   120
That to the faithful herdsman's art belongs!
What recks it them? What need they? they are sped;
And, when they list, their lean and flashy songs
Grate on their scrannel pipes of wretched straw;
The hungry sheep look up, and are not fed,   125
But, swoll'n with wind and the rank mist they draw,
Rot inwardly, and foul contagion spread;
Besides what the grim wolf with privy paw
Daily devours apace, and nothing said;
But that two-handed engine at the door   130
Stands ready to smite once, and smite no more."

Return, Alphéus; the dread voice is past
That shrunk thy streams; return, Sicilian Muse,
And call the vales, and bid them hither cast
Their bells and flowerets of a thousand hues. 135
Ye valleys low, where the mild whispers use
Of shades, and wanton winds, and gushing brooks,
On whose fresh lap the swart star sparely looks,
Throw hither all your quaint enameled eyes,
That on the green turf suck the honied showers, 140
And purple all the ground with vernal flowers.
Bring the rathe primrose that forsaken dies,
The tufted crow-toe, and pale jessamine,
The white pink, and the pansy freaked with jet,
'The glowing violet, 145
The musk-rose, and the well-attired woodbine,
With cowslips wan that hang the pensive head,
And every flower that sad embroidery wears;
Bid Amaranthus all his beauty shed,
And daffadillies fill their cups with tears, 150
To strew the laureate hearse where Lycid lies.
For so, to interpose a little ease,
Let our frail thoughts dally with false surmise,
Ay me! whilst thee the shores and sounding seas
Wash far away, where'er thy bones are hurled; 155
Whether beyond the stormy Hebrides,
Where thou, perhaps, under the whelming tide
Visit'st the bottom of the monstrous world;
Or whether thou, to our moist vows denied,
Sleep'st by the fable of Bellerus old, 160
Where the great Vision of the guarded mount
Looks toward Namancos and Bayona's hold:
Look homeward, angel, now, and melt with ruth;
And, O ye Dolphins, waft the hapless youth.
    Weep no more, woeful shepherds, weep no more, 165
For Lycidas, your sorrow, is not dead,
Sunk though he be beneath the watery floor:
So sinks the day-star in the ocean bed,
And yet anon repairs his drooping head,
And tricks his beams, and with new-spangled ore 170
Flames in the forehead of the morning sky:
So Lycidas sunk low, but mounted high,
Through the dear might of Him that walked the waves,
Where, other groves and other streams along,
With nectar pure his oozy locks he laves, 175
And hears the unexpressive nuptial song,
In the blest kingdoms meek of Joy and Love.

There entertain him all the Saints above,
In solemn troops, and sweet societies,
That sing, and singing in their glory move,   *180*
And wipe the tears forever from his eyes.
Now, Lycidas, the shepherds weep no more;
Henceforth thou art the Genius of the shore,
In thy large recompense, and shalt be good
To all that wander in that perilous flood.   *185*

    Thus sang the uncouth swain to the oaks and rills,
While the still Morn went out with sandals gray;
He touched the tender stops of various quills,
With eager thought warbling his Doric lay:
And now the sun had stretched out all the hills,   *190*
And now was dropped into the western bay.
At last he rose, and twitched his mantle blue:
Tomorrow to fresh woods and pastures new.

Monody: song. *Learned friend:* Edward King, who was on his way to his new parish
in Ireland; Milton and King's schoolmates joined together to produce a volume of
poetry in King's memory. Milton's poem takes the form, and most of the conventions,
of the pastoral elegy: simple, virtuous shepherds with classical names, who recall
their dead friend's history, ask what destiny intends of him, form a procession of
mourners with flowers for the bier, and, finally, discover some consolation of grief.
1, *laurels:* a poet's wreath. 2, *myrtles:* wreath symbolic of love; *ivy:* associated with
Bacchus, god of wine and revelry; *sere:* yellowing with age. 3, *crude:* green, unripe.
6, *dear:* deeply moving. 14, *meed:* reward. 15, *sisters of the sacred well:* the nine
Muses, who dwelt near the sacred spring close to Mt. Helicon in central Greece. 25,
high lawns: mountain pastures. 29. *Battening:* fattening. 33, *oaten flute:* pan-pipes.
36, *Damoetas:* a name conventional in pastoral elegies; Milton may refer to a par-
ticular tutor known to himself and King. 40, *gadding:* scraggly. 45, *canker:* a worm
which infests roses. 48, *blows:* blooms. 50, *nymphs:* nature goddesses. 53, *Druids:*
ancient priests; the *steep*, or mountain, where they lie buried is in Wales. 54, *Mona:*
ancient name for the island of Anglesey, off Wales. 55, *Deva:* the river Dee, called
"wizard" because of the legend that its movements foretold the success or failure of
each season's harvest. 58–63: The "Muse" is Calliope, Muse of epic poetry; she was
the mother of Orpheus, a legendary poet, who was torn to pieces by a mob of Thracian
women. His head was thrown into the river Hebrus, which flows toward the island
of Lesbos in the Aegean sea. 64, *what boots it:* what use is it. 68–69: *Amaryllis* and
Neaera are conventional names for nymphs who might provide a moment's entertain-
ment for the shepherds. 73, *guerdon:* reward. 75, The *Fury* is what Milton calls one
of the three Fates; she cuts the thread of human life with the shears. 77, *Phoebus:*
Apollo, god of poetic inspiration, among other things. He touches his listener's ears
to remind him not to forget what he says. 79, *foil:* cheap metal used to make cheap
jewelry more glittering. 85, *Arethuse:* a fountain in Sicily. 86, *Mincius:* a river in
northern Italy. Arethusa was a nymph who went bathing in a river in Greece; when the
river-god pursued her, she went underground and came up as a fountain in Sicily. 88,
oat: pipe; here, song. 89, *herald of the sea:* Triton, a sea-god (see "The World is Too
Much With Us," page 76). He comes to "plead" his master's innocence in the death
of Lycidas (King). 96, *Hippotadés:* literally, "son of Hippotas," Aeolus, the god of the

winds. 99, *Panopé*: chief among the sea-nymphs. 101: It was considered bad luck to build anything during an eclipse. 103, *Camus*: the god of the river Cam, which flows by the University of Cambridge, where Milton and King were students. 109–110: St. Peter, who was a fisherman on Lake Tiberias in Galilee when he became Christ's disciple; his keys open and close the gates of heaven; *amain*: forcefully, forever. 111, *mitered locks*: St. Peter wears a miter, symbolic of his being a bishop. 114, *Enow*: enough. 120, *sheep-hook*: a bishop's staff is in the shape of a shepherd's crook. Line 122: i.e, "What is it to them? They have succeeded and have also written their own death warrants." 123, *list*: choose. 124, *scrannel*: harsh. 130, *two-handed engine*: critics have advanced several interpretations of the phrase; it may be a two-handed sword. Whatever it is, it is clearly a dread instrument of vengeance. 132, *Alphéus*: a river in Greece. This line begins a turn in the poem's mood. 136, *use*: are used to. 138, *swart star*: Sirius, the Dog Star, which was said to burn flowers black in late summer. 142, *rathe*: early. 144, *freaked*: streaked. 149, *amaranthus*: an imaginary flower which never wilts, except here. 151, *laureate hearse*: bier laden with laurels (see line 1). 153: i.e, "for a moment, let us console ourselves by forgetting that Lycidas is not really on the bier, but is in fact lost at sea." 156–163: The Hebrides are west of northern Scotland; Bellerus is a legendary giant supposedly buried at Land's End. These places mark the boundaries of the area where Lycidas drowned. The "guarded mount" is St. Michael's Mount in Cornwall, where the archangel Michael is viewed as looking toward Namancos, in Spain, and Bayona, also in Spain. *Ruth* is pity. 164: dolphins are legendary for their friendliness to men in danger at sea. 168, *day-star*: the sun. 170, *tricks*: trims, as of sails. 173: *him that walked the waves*: it's been years since that was done really well. 176, *unexpressive nuptial song*: inexpressibly beautiful song of joy sung in heaven. 183, *genius*: guardian spirit. 186, *uncouth swain*: illiterate shepherd. 188, *quills*: stalks of the pan-pipes. 189, *Doric*: originally a rustic dialect in Greek; hence, simple.

Robert Lowell [b. 1917]

THE QUAKER GRAVEYARD IN NANTUCKET

(For Warren Winslow, Dead at Sea)

Let man have dominion over the fishes of the sea and the
fowls of the air and the beasts and the whole earth, and
every creeping creature that moveth upon the earth.

I
A brackish reach of shoal off Madaket,—
The sea was still breaking violently and night
Had steamed into our North Atlantic Fleet,
When the drowned sailor clutched the drag-net. Light
Flashed from his matted head and marble feet,   5
He grappled at the net
With the coiled, hurdling muscles of his thighs:
The corpse was bloodless, a botch of reds and whites,
Its open staring eyes
Were lustreless dead-lights   10

Or cabin-windows on a stranded hulk
Heavy with sand. We weight the body, close
Its eyes and heave it seaward whence it came,
Where the heel-headed dogfish barks its nose
On Ahab's void and forehead; and the name   *15*
Is blocked in yellow chalk.
Sailors, who pitch this portent at the sea
Where dreadnaughts shall confess
Its hell-bent deity,
When you are powerless   *20*
To sand-bag this Atlantic bulwark, faced
By the earth-shaker, green, unwearied, chaste
In his steel scales: ask for no Orphean lute
To pluck life back. The guns of the steeled fleet
Recoil and then repeat   *25*
The hoarse salute.

II

Whenever winds are moving and their breath
Heaves at the roped-in bulwarks of this pier,
The terns and sea-gulls tremble at your death
In these home waters. Sailor, can you hear   *30*
The Pequod's sea wings, beating landward, fall
Headlong and break on our Atlantic wall
Off 'Sconset, where the yawing S-boats splash
The bellbuoy, with ballooning spinnakers,
As the entangled, screeching mainsheet clears   *35*
The blocks: off Madaket, where lubbers lash
The heavy surf and throw their long lead squids
For blue-fish? Sea-gulls blink their heavy lids
Seaward. The winds' wings beat upon the stones,
Cousin, and scream for you and the claws rush   *40*
At the sea's throat and wring it in the slush
Of this old Quaker graveyard where the bones
Cry out in the long night for the hurt beast
Bobbing by Ahab's whaleboats in the East.

III

All you recovered from Poseidon died   *45*
With you, my cousin, and the harrowed brine
Is fruitless on the blue beard of the god,
Stretching beyond us to the castles in Spain,
Nantucket's westward haven, To Cape Cod
Guns, cradled on the tide,   *50*
Blast the eelgrass about a waterclock
Of bilge and backwash, roil the salt and sand
Lashing earth's scaffold, rock

Our warships in the hand
Of the great God, where time's contrition blues   55
Whatever it was these Quaker sailors lost
In the mad scramble of their lives. They died
When time was open-eyed,
Wooden and childish; only bones abide
There, in the nowhere, where their boats were tossed   60
Sky-high, where mariners had fabled news
Of IS, the whited monster. What it cost
Them is their secret. In the sperm-whale's slick
I see the Quakers drown and hear their cry:
"If God himself had not been on our side,   65
If God himself had not been on our side,
When the Atlantic rose against us, why,
Then it had swallowed us up quick."

IV
This is the end of the whaleroad and the whale
Who spewed Nantucket bones on the thrashed swell   70
And stirred the troubled waters to whirlpools
To send the Pequod packing off to hell:
This is the end of them, three-quarters fools,
Snatching at straws to sail
Seaward and seaward on the turntail whale,   75
Spouting out blood and water as it rolls,
Sick as a dog to these Atlantic shoals:
Clamavimus, O depths. Let the sea-gulls wail

For water, for the deep where the high tide
Mutters to its hurt self, mutters and ebbs.   80
Waves wallow in their wash, go out and out.
Leave only the death-rattle of the crabs,
The beach increasing, its enormous snout
Sucking the ocean's side.
This is the end of running on the waves;   85
We are poured out like water. Who will dance
The mast-lashed master of Leviathans
Up from this field of Quakers in their unstoned graves?

V
When the whale's viscera go and the roll
Of its corruption overruns this world   90
Beyond tree-swept Nantucket and Wood's Hole
And Martha's Vineyard, Sailor, will your sword
Whistle and fall and sink into the fat?
In the great ash-pit of Jehoshaphat
The bones cry for the blood of the white whale,   95

The Quaker Graveyard in Nantucket [**151**]

The fat flukes arch and whack about its ears,
The death-lance churns into the sanctuary, tears
The gun-blue swingle, heaving like a flail,
And hacks the coiling life out: it works and drags
And rips the sperm-whale's midriff into rags,   100
Gobbets of blubber spill to wind and weather,
Sailor, and gulls go round the stoven timbers
Where the morning stars sing out together
And thunder shakes the white surf and dismembers
The red flag hammered in the mast-head. Hide,   105
Our steel, Jonas Messias, in Thy side.

VI. OUR LADY OF WALSINGHAM
There once the penitents took off their shoes
And then walked barefoot the remaining mile;
And the small trees, a stream and hedgerows file
Slowly along the munching English lane,   110
Like cows to the old shrine, until you lose
Track of your dragging pain.
The stream flows down under the druid tree,
Shiloah's whirlpools gurgle and make glad
The castle of God. Sailor, you were glad   115
And whistled Sion by that stream. But see:

Our Lady, too small for her canopy,
Sits near the altar. There's no comeliness
At all or charm in the expressionless
Face with its heavy eyelids. As before,   120
This face, for centuries a memory,
Non est species, neque decor,
Expressionless, expresses God: it goes
Past castled Sion. She knows what God knows,
Not Calvary's Cross nor crib at Bethlehem   125
Now, and the world shall come to Walsingham.

VII
The empty winds are creaking and the oak
Splatters and splatters on the cenotaph,
The boughs are trembling and a gaff
Bobs on the untimely stroke   130
Of the greased wash exploding on a shoal-bell
In the old mouth of the Atlantic. It's well;
Atlantic, you are fouled with the blue sailors,
Sea-monsters, upward angel, downward fish:
Unmarried and corroding, spare of flesh

Mart once of supercilious, wing'd clippers,
Atlantic, where your bell-trap guts its spoil
You could cut the brackish winds with a knife
Here in Nantucket, and cast up the time
When the Lord God formed man from the sea's slime 140
And breathed into his face the breath of life,
And blue-lung'd combers lumbered to the kill.
The Lord survives the rainbow of His will.

The epigraph comes from Genesis 1:26.

1, *Madaket:* a small town on Nantucket Island, Massachusetts. Lines 1–12 are based on a passage in the opening chapter of Henry David Thoreau's *Cape Cod.* 15, *Ahab:* Captain Ahab, the hero of Herman Melville's *Moby Dick.* 22, *earth-shaker:* Poseidon, Greek god of the sea. 23, *Orphean lute:* In Greek mythology, Orpheus retrieved his wife Eurydice from the underworld by charming the queen of Hades with his lute-playing. 31, *Pequod:* name of the ship on which Ahab sailed from Nantucket in search of the white whale. 33, *'Sconset:* Siasconsét, a small town on Nantucket. 40, *Cousin:* Warren Winslow, to whom the poem is dedicated. 62, *IS:* In *Robert Lowell: The First Twenty Years* (New York: Farrar, Straus & Giroux, 1962), Hugh B. Staples suggests that by calling the white whale IS, Lowell simultaneously refers to Christ (Iesus Salvator) to draw a parallel between the Quaker whalers and those who crucified Christ. 78, *Clamavimus:* "we have cried." Psalm 130 begins "Out of the depths have I cried unto thee, O Lord." 87, *Leviathans:* the Biblical name for great sea-beasts. 91: Wood's Hole is a town in Southern Massachusetts; it is north of the island of Martha's Vineyard, which lies west of Nantucket. 94, *Jehoshaphat:* "Let the heathen be wakened, and come up to the valley of Jehoshaphat: for there will I sit to judge all the heathen round about" (Joel 3:12). 105, *red flag:* In the last chapter of *Moby Dick,* as the *Pequod* sinks, the arm of a crew member nails a red flag to the mast. 106, *Jonas Messias:* among the Biblical passages linking Jonah and the Messiah is Matthew 12:40: "For as Jonas was three days and three nights in the whale's belly; so shall the Son of man be three days and three nights in the heart of the earth." *Our Lady of Walsingham:* a medieval English shrine to the Virgin Mary, destroyed during the Reformation but recently restored. 114, *Shiloah's whirlpools:* Shiloah or Shiloh was the holy place where Israel's tabernacle was located. A stream flowed near it, as a stream flows near Walsingham. Isaiah 8:5–7 prophesies a punishing turbulence in Shiloah's stream. 122: As Lowell translates in lines 118–119: "There's no comeliness/At all or charm." 124, *Sion:* Zion, the hill in Jerusalem where David dwelt. 126: English Catholics used to say, "When England goes to Walsingham, England will return to the Church." 134, *upward angel, downward fish:* In Book I of *Paradise Lost,* Milton describes Dagon the sea monster as "upward man/ And downward fish." 143, *rainbow:* In Genesis 9:13, God's symbol of his covenant with the earth.

Wallace Stevens [1879–1955]

SUNDAY MORNING

I

Complacencies of the peignoir, and late
Coffee and oranges in a sunny chair,
And the green freedom of a cockatoo

Upon a rug mingle to dissipate
The holy hush of ancient sacrifice.   5
She dreams a little, and she feels the dark
Encroachment of that old catastrophe,
As a calm darkens among water-lights.
The pungent oranges and bright, green wings
Seem things in some procession of the dead,   10
Winding across wide water, without sound.
The day is like wide water, without sound,
Stilled for the passing of her dreaming feet
Over the seas, to silent Palestine,
Dominion of the blood and sepulchre.   15

II

Why should she give her bounty to the dead?
What is divinity if it can come
Only in silent shadows and in dreams?
Shall she not find in comforts of the sun,
In pungent fruit and bright, green wings, or else   20
In any balm or beauty of the earth,
Things to be cherished like the thought of heaven?
Divinity must live within herself:
Passions of rain, or moods in falling snow;
Grievings in loneliness, or unsubdued   25
Elations when the forest blooms; gusty
Emotions on wet roads on autumn nights;
All pleasures and all pains, remembering
The bough of summer and the winter branch.
These are the measures destined for her soul.   30

III

Jove in the clouds had his inhuman birth.
No mother suckled him, no sweet land gave
Large-mannered motions to his mythy mind.
He moved among us, as a muttering king,
Magnificent, would move among his hinds,   35
Until our blood, commingling, virginal,
With heaven, brought such requital to desire
The very hinds discerned it, in a star.
Shall our blood fail? Or shall it come to be
The blood of paradise? And shall the earth   40
Seem all of paradise that we shall know?
The sky will be much friendlier then than now,
A part of labor and a part of pain,
And next in glory to enduring love,
Not this dividing and indifferent blue.   45

IV

She says, "I am content when wakened birds,
Before they fly, test the reality
Of misty fields, by their sweet questionings;
But when the birds are gone, and their warm fields
Return no more, where, then, is paradise?"   *50*
There is not any haunt of prophecy,
Nor any old chimera of the grave,
Neither the golden underground, nor isle
Melodious, where spirits gat them home,
Nor visionary south, nor cloudy palm   *55*
Remote on heaven's hill, that has endured
As April's green endures; or will endure
Like her remembrance of awakened birds,
Or her desire for June and evening, tipped
By the consummation of the swallow's wings.   *60*

V

She says, "But in contentment I still feel
The need of some imperishable bliss."
Death is the mother of beauty; hence from her,
Alone, shall come fulfilment to our dreams
And our desires. Although she strews the leaves   *65*
Of sure obliteration on our paths,
The path sick sorrow took, the many paths
Where triumph rang its brassy phrase, or love
Whispered a little out of tenderness,
She makes the willow shiver in the sun   *70*
For maidens who were wont to sit and gaze
Upon the grass, relinquished to their feet.
She causes boys to pile new plums and pears
On disregarded plate. The maidens taste
And stray impassioned in the littering leaves.   *75*

VI

Is there no change of death in paradise?
Does ripe fruit never fall? Or do the boughs
Hang always heavy in that perfect sky,
Unchanging, yet so like our perishing earth,
With rivers like our own that seek for seas   *80*
They never find, the same receding shores
That never touch with inarticulate pang?
Why set the pear upon those river-banks
Or spice the shores with odors of the plum?
Alas, that they should wear our colors there,   *85*
The silken weavings of our afternoons,

And pick the strings of our insipid lutes!
Death is the mother of beauty, mystical,
Within whose burning bosom we devise
Our earthly mothers waiting, sleeplessly.   *90*

VII

Supple and turbulent, a ring of men
Shall chant in orgy on a summer morn
Their boisterous devotion to the sun,
Not as a god, but as a god might be,
Naked among them, like a savage source.   *95*
Their chant shall be a chant of paradise,
Out of their blood, returning to the sky;
And in their chant shall enter, voice by voice,
The windy lake wherein their lord delights,
The trees, like serafin, and echoing hills,   *100*
That choir among themselves long afterward.
They shall know well the heavenly fellowship
Of men that perish and of summer morn.
And whence they came and whither they shall go
The dew upon their feet shall manifest.   *105*

VII

She hears, upon that water without sound,
A voice that cries, "The tomb in Palestine
Is not the porch of spirits lingering.
It is the grave of Jesus, where he lay."
We live in an old chaos of the sun,   *110*
Or old dependency of day and night,
Or island solitude, unsponsored, free,
Of that wide water, inescapable.
Deer walk upon our mountains, and the quail
Whistle about us their spontaneous cries;   *115*
Sweet berries ripen in the wilderness;
And, in the isolation of the sky,
At evening, casual flocks of pigeons make
Ambiguous undulations as they sink
Downward to darkness, on extended wings.   *120*

1, *peignoir*: dressing gown, negligée. 31, *Jove*: The Latin counterpart of Zeus, ruler of the gods. 100, *serafin*: angels. The usual form is *seraphim*.

4

A Bliss
in Proof

Love and Sex

Anonymous [fifteenth century]

WESTERN WIND

Western wind, when will thou blow,
  The small rain down can rain?
Christ, if my love were in my arms
  And I in my bed again!

Christopher Marlowe [1564–1593]

THE PASSIONATE SHEPHERD TO HIS LOVE

Come live with me and be my love,
And we will all the pleasures prove
That valleys, groves, hills, and fields,
Woods, or steepy mountain yields.

And we will sit upon the rocks,   5
Seeing the shepherds feed their flocks,
By shallow rivers to whose falls
Melodious birds sing madrigals.

And I will make thee beds of roses
And a thousand fragrant posies,   10
A cap of flowers, and a kirtle
Embroidered all with leaves of myrtle;

A gown made of the finest wool
Which from our pretty lambs we pull;
Fair-linèd slippers for the cold,   15
With buckles of the purest gold;

A belt of straw and ivy buds,
With coral clasps and amber studs:
And if these pleasures may thee move,
Come live with me, and be my love.   *20*

The shepherds' swains shall dance and sing
For thy delight each May morning:
If these delights thy mind may move,
Then live with me and be my love.

4, *steepy*: steep. 11, *kirtle*: skirt or dress.

Sir Walter Ralegh [1552?–1618]

THE NYMPH'S REPLY TO THE SHEPHERD

If all the world and love were young,
And truth in every shepherd's tongue,
These pretty pleasures might me move
To live with thee and be thy love.

Time drives the flocks from field to fold   *5*
When rivers rage and rocks grow cold,
And Philomel becometh dumb;
The rest complains of cares to come.

The flowers do fade, and wanton fields
To wayward winter reckoning yields;   *10*
A honey tongue, a heart of gall,
Is fancy's spring, but sorrow's fall.

Thy gowns, thy shoes, thy beds of roses,
Thy cap, thy kirtle, and thy posies
Soon break, soon wither, soon forgotten —   *15*
In folly ripe, in reason rotten.

Thy belt of straw and ivy buds,
Thy coral clasps and amber studs,
All these in me no means can move
To come to thee and be thy love.   *20*

But could youth last and love still breed,
Had joys no date nor age no need,

Then these delights my mind might move
To live with thee and be thy love.

7, *Philomel*: poetic name for the nightingale, so called because of the myth of Phil-
omela, the daughter of a king of Athens whom the gods changed into a nightingale.

Melvin DeBruhl [b. 1950]

BROWN CIRCLES

my woman
she look at me
so easy

the mirror
close its eyes   5
she still look

I climb
the stairs
she — brown
circles   10
on the roof
smile
when I touch

Diane Wakoski [b. 1937]

WHAT I WANT IN A HUSBAND BESIDES A MUSTACHE

Well, to begin with,
you might as well not apply for the job
if you don't have
a mustache (
        or any plans   5
        for growing
        one
)
and I tend to like men who are not too
tall,   10
say 5'8" or 9".
I like men with powerful shoulders
and prefer big hands;

no requirements for the size of your cock,
but you have to like to use it,   *15*
preferably just on — in me,
and be willing to fuck quite frequently
at least until we're 90.

That's another thing.
I want a man to be steady   *20*
To plan to be married to me
at least 50 or
60 years
with no sabbaticals.

I like men who read poetry,   *25*
and men who write turn me on even more (though I know that's
                              trouble
In fact it's such a dangerous line that I think I'll reverse it:
men who write "don't turn me on")
if they're good.
I also only like ambitious men,   *30*
men who will take their destinies in their hands
and try to shape them.

I want a man who is mechanical,
physical,
likes to build,   *35*
work with his hands,
perhaps even a sportsman,
but one who does all these things with intelligence
and preferably learned them from
books.   *40*
I like a man who has faith in books.
That means he'll also have faith in me.
I'm a very long and imaginative book.

I'd also like my man to be a simultaneous traveler
and homebody,   *45*
one who would be happy working at home
with me,
or equally happy
out wandering around
looking at new things with me;   *50*
one who found himself the key to the meaning of the world,
and who found me the key to the meaning of himself.

I like a man
with good manners,

one willing to respond to the world;
a man who likes music,
and who has a definite style.

One who could earn a living,
though I'd contribute a good deal;
one who wanted a real woman
and who loved her
for her womanly
accomplishments.

A man who reads.
A man who likes painting.
A man who likes to talk in bed.
A man who likes the sun but thrives in the cold.
One who loves to touch my body.
Who kisses often.
Who types his letters.

One who drinks bourbon.
Who can ride a motorcycle.
Who collects books.
Who has a big dog.
Who calls my name in his sleep.

So far, I've only met one man like this;
but if you think you qualify,
write in for the application forms.
Truthfully,
you don't have much of a chance against
this first candidate.
But I'm democratic
and want to give everyone a chance.

Include a photo of your mustache.
I have not yet finished my document
describing the exact kinds of mustaches I prefer.
But that is an area of connoisseurship
to me.
Believe me,
there are some mustaches
that just wouldn't qualify.

I am known for my
discrimination.

What I Want in a Husband Besides a Mustache [**161**]

Erica Jong [b. 1942]

HERE COMES

(a flip through Bride's)

The silver spoons
were warbling
their absurd musical names
when, drawing back
her veil (illusion),   5

she stepped into
the valentine-shaped bathtub,
& slid her perfect bubbles
in between
the perfect bubbles.   10

Oh brilliantly complex as
compound interest,
her diamond gleams
(Forever) on the edge
of a weddingcake-shaped bed.   15

What happens there
is merely icing since
a snakepit of dismembered
douchebag coils (all writhing)
awaits her on the tackier back pages.   20

Dearly beloved, let's hymn
her (& Daddy) down
the aisle with
epithalamions composed
for Ovulen ads: 25

"It's the right
of every (married) couple
to wait   to space   to wait"
— & antistrophes
appended by the Pope.   30

Good Grief — the groom!
Has she (or we)
entirely forgot?
She'll dream him whole.
American type with ushers   35

halfbacks headaches drawbacks backaches
& borrowed suit
stuffed in a borrowed face
(or was it the reverse?)
Oh well. Here's he: 40

part coy pajamas,
part mothered underwear
& of course
an enormous prick
full of money.   45

Anonymous [English Ballad (Child, No. 84A)]

BONNY BARBARA ALLAN

It was in and about the Martinmas time,
  When the green leaves were a-falling,
That Sir John Graeme, in the West Country,
  Fell in love with Barbara Allan.

He sent his man down through the town,   5
  To the place where she was dwelling:
"O haste and come to my master dear,
  Gin ye be Barbara Allan."

O hooly, hooly rose she up,
  To the place where he was lying,   10
And when she drew the curtain by:
  "Young man, I think you're dying."

"O it's I'm sick, and very, very sick,
  And 'tis a' for Barbara Allan."
"O the better for me ye s'never be,
  Though your heart's blood were a-spilling.

"O dinna ye mind, young man," said she,
  "When ye was in the tavern a-drinking,
That ye made the healths gae round and round,
  And slighted Barbara Allan?"   20

He turned his face unto the wall,
  And death was with him dealing:
"Adieu, adieu, my dear friends all,
  And be kind to Barbara Allan."

And slowly, slowly raise she up, 25
   And slowly, slowly left him,
And sighing said, she could not stay,
   Since death of life had reft him.

She had not gane a mile but twa,
   When she heard the dead-bell ringing, 30
And every jow that the dead-bell geid,
   It cried, "Woe to Barbara Allan."

"O mother, mother, make my bed!
   O make it saft and narrow!
Since my love died for me today, 35
   I'll die for him tomorrow."

Child, No. 84A: Ballad texts are often identified according to the number and letter given them in *English and Scottish Popular Ballads* (1892–98), edited by Francis James Child.

1, *Martinmas:* November 11, St. Martin's Day. 8, *Gin:* if. 9, *hooly:* slowly. 15, *ye s'never:* you shall never. 17, *dinna ye mind:* don't you remember. 19, *gae:* go. 25, *raise:* rose. 28, *reft:* bereft, deprived. 29, *gane:* gone; *twa:* two. 31, *jow:* stroke; *geid:* gave. 34, *saft:* soft.

Andrew Marvell [1621–1678]

TO HIS COY MISTRESS

Had we but world enough, and time,
This coyness, lady, were no crime.
We would sit down, and think which way
To walk, and pass our long love's day.
Thou by the Indian Ganges' side 5
Shouldst rubies find; I by the tide
Of Humber would complain. I would
Love you ten years before the flood,
And you should, if you please, refuse
Till the conversion of the Jews. 10
My vegetable love should grow
Vaster than empires and more slow;
An hundred years should go to praise
Thine eyes, and on thy forehead gaze;
Two hundred to adore each breast, 15
But thirty thousand to the rest;
An age at least to every part,
And the last age should show your heart.
For, lady, you deserve this state,

Nor would I love at lower rate.
 But at my back I always hear
Time's wingèd chariot hurrying near;
And yonder all before us lie
Deserts of vast eternity.
Thy beauty shall no more be found;
Nor, in thy marble vault, shall sound
My echoing song; then worms shall try
That long-preserved virginity,
And your quaint honor turn to dust,
And into ashes all my lust:
The grave's a fine and private place,
But none, I think, do there embrace.
 Now therefore, while the youthful hue
Sits on thy skin like morning glow,
And while thy willing soul transpires
At every pore with instant fires,
Now let us sport us while we may,
And now, like amorous birds of prey,
Rather at once our time devour
Than lanquish in his slow-chapped power.
Let us roll all our strength and all
Our sweetness up into one ball,
And tear our pleasures with rough strife
Thorough the iron gates of life:
Thus, though we cannot make our sun
Stand still, yet we will make him run.

20
25
30
35
40
45

7, *Humber:* a river in Marvell's native Yorkshire. 8, *flood:* the Flood. 10, traditionally, the Jews would convert at the end of human time. 11, *vegetable:* growing without conscious effort. 29, *quaint:* not only subtle, finicky, but also a pun on *queynte,* the Middle-English term for pudendum. 40, *slow-chapped:* slow-jawed. 44, *Thorough:* through.

Robert Frost [1874–1963]

THE SILKEN TENT

She is as in a field a silken tent
At midday when a sunny summer breeze
Has dried the dew and all its ropes relent,
So that in guys it gently sways at ease,
And its supporting central cedar pole,
That is its pinnacle to heavenward
And signifies the sureness of the soul,

5

Seems to owe naught to any single cord,
But strictly held by none, is loosely bound
By countless silken ties of love and thought   *10*
To everything on earth the compass round,
And only by one's going slightly taut
In the capriciousness of summer air
Is of the slightest bondage made aware.

4, *guys:* ropes, chains, or rods attached to something to steady or guide it.

William Shakespeare [1564–1616]

SONNET 130

My mistress' eyes are nothing like the sun;
Coral is far more red than her lips' red;
If snow be white, why then her breasts are dun;
If hairs be wires, black wires grow on her head.
I have seen roses damasked, red and white,   *5*
But no such roses see I in her cheeks;
And in some perfumes is there more delight
Than in the breath that from my mistress reeks.
I love to hear her speak, yet well I know
That music hath a far more pleasing sound;   *10*
I grant I never saw a goddess go;
My mistress, when she walks, treads on the ground.
    And yet, by heaven, I think my love as rare
    As any she belied with false compare.

This poem was written as a retort to many love poems of the period, in which women's beauties were exaggerated in far-fetched conceits (see page 26).

5, *damasked:* variegated. 11, *go:* walk.

Tom Clark [b. 1941]

SONNET

The orgasm completely
Takes the woman out of her
Self in a wave of ecstasy
That spreads through all of her body.
Her nervous, vascular and muscular   *5*
Systems participate in the act.

The muscles of the pelvis contract
And discharge a plug of mucus from the cervix
While the muscular sucking motions of the cervix
Facilitate the incoming of the semen.   10
At the same time the constriction of the pelvic
Muscles prevents the loss of the semen. The discharge
Makes the acid vaginal lubricant
Alkaline, so as not to destroy the spermatozoa.

Gregory Corso [b. 1930]

MARRIAGE

for Mr. and Mrs. Mike Goldberg

Should I get married? Should I be good?
Astound the girl next door
with my velvet suit and faustus hood?
Don't take her to movies but to cemeteries
tell all about werewolf bathtubs and forked clarinets   5
then desire her and kiss her and all the preliminaries
and she going just so far and I understanding why
not getting angry saying You must feel! It's beautiful to feel!
Instead take her in my arms
lean against an old crooked tombstone   10
and woo her the entire night the constellations in the sky—

When she introduces me to her parents
back straightened, hair finally combed, strangled by a tie,
should I sit knees together on their 3rd-degree sofa
and not ask Where's the bathroom?   15
How else to feel other than I am,
a young man who often thinks Flash Gordon soap—
O how terrible it must be for a young man
seated before a family and the family thinking
We never saw him before! He wants our Mary Lou!   20
After tea and homemade cookies they ask What do you do?
Should I tell them? Would they like me then?
Say All right get married, we're losing a daughter
but we're gaining a son—
And should I then ask Where's the bathroom?   25

O God, and the wedding! All her family and her friends
and only a handful of mine all scroungy and bearded
just waiting to get at the drinks and food—

And the priest! he looking at me as if I masturbated
asking me Do you take this woman   30
for your lawful wedded wife?
And I, trembling what to say, say Pie Glue!
I kiss the bride all those corny men slapping me on the back:
She's all yours, boy! Ha-ha-ha!
And in their eyes you could see   35
some obscene honeymoon going on—
Then all that absurd rice and clanky cans and shoes
Niagara Falls! Hordes of us! Husbands! Wives! Flowers!
All streaming into cozy hotels
All going to do the same thing tonight   40
The indifferent clerk he knowing what was going to happen
The lobby zombies they knowing what
The whistling elevator man he knowing
The winking bellboy knowing
Everybody knows! I'd be almost inclined not to do anything!   45
Stay up all night! Stare that hotel clerk in the eye!
Screaming: I deny honeymoon! I deny honeymoon!
running rampant into those almost climactic suites
yelling Radio belly! Cat shovel!
O I'd live in Niagara forever! in a dark cave beneath the Falls   50
I'd sit there the Mad Honeymooner
devising ways to break marriages, a scourge of bigamy
a saint of divorce—

But I should get married I should be good
How nice it'd be to come home to her   55
and sit by the fireplace and she in the kitchen
aproned young and lovely wanting my baby
and so happy about me she burns the roast beef
and comes crying to me and I get up from my big papa chair
saying Christmas teeth! Radiant brains! Apple deaf!   60
God what a husband I'd make! Yes, I should get married!
So much to do! like sneaking into Mr. Jones' house late at night
and cover his golf clubs with 1920 Norwegian books
Like hanging a picture of Rimbaud on the lawnmower
Like pasting Tannu Tuva postage stamps   65
all over the picket fence
Like when Mrs. Kindhead comes to collect
for the Community Chest
grab her and tell her There are unfavorable omens in the sky!
And when the mayor comes to get my vote tell him   70
When are you going to stop people killing whales!
And when the milkman comes leave him a note in the bottle
Penguin dust, bring me penguin dust, I want penguin dust—

Yet if I should get married and it's Connecticut and snow
and she gives birth to a child and I am sleepless, worn,   75
up for nights, head bowed against a quiet window,
the past behind me,
finding myself in the most common of situations
a trembling man
knowledged with responsibility not twig-smear   80
nor Roman coin soup—
O what would that be like!
Surely I'd give it for a nipple a rubber Tacitus
For a rattle a bag of broken Bach records
Tack Della Francesca all over its crib   85
Sew the Greek alphabet on its bib
And build for its playpen a roofless Parthenon—

No, I doubt I'd be that kind of father
not rural not snow no quiet window
but hot smelly tight New York City   90
seven flights up, roaches and rats in the walls
a fat Reichian wife screeching over potatoes Get a job!
And five nose-running brats in love with Batman
And the neighbors all toothless and dry haired
like those hag masses of the 18th century   95
all wanting to come in and watch TV
The landlord wants his rent
Grocery store Blue Cross Gas & Electric Knights of Columbus
Impossible to lie back and dream Telephone snow,
ghost parking—   100
No! I should not get married I should never get married!

But—imagine if I were married to a beautiful
sophisticated woman
tall and pale wearing an elegant black dress
and long black gloves   105
holding a cigarette holder in one hand
and a highball in the other
and we lived high up in a penthouse with a huge window
from which we could see all of New York
and even farther on clearer days   110
No, can't imagine myself married to that pleasant prison dream—

O but what about love? I forget love
not that I am incapable of love
it's just that I see love as odd as wearing shoes—
I never wanted to marry a girl who was like my mother   115
And Ingrid Bergman was always impossible

And there's maybe a girl now but she's already married
And I don't like men and —
but there's got to be somebody!
Because what if I'm 60 years old and not married,   120
all alone in a furnished room with pee stains on my underwear
and everybody else is married! All the universe married but me!

Ah, yet well I know that were a woman possible
as I am possible
then marriage would be possible —   125
Like SHE in her lonely alien gaud waiting her Egyptian lover
so I wait — bereft of 2,000 years and the bath of life.

64, *Rimbaud:* Arthur Rimbaud (1854–1891), French symbolist poet. 65, *Tannu
Tuva:* an autonomous region in the USSR, northwest of Mongolia. 83, *Tacitus:* Gaius
Cornelius Tacitus (ca. 55–117 A.D.), Roman historian. 85, *Della Francesca:* (1406–
1492), Italian painter. 93, *Reichian:* Germanic; specifically, of the Reich, the German
Republic; there are perhaps connotations of dictatorial conduct here. 126, *SHE:*
Ayesha, the principal character in *She*, a novel by H. Rider Haggard (1856–1925).
Ayesha is the queen of a remote region in Africa; she has been alive for over two thou-
sand years, preserved by a fire called the Pillar of Life; her "Egyptian lover" was her
husband, Kallikrates, whom she murdered; twenty centuries later, he returns to her
in the form of a British adventurer whose ancestry is Egyptian. When she tries to con-
vince him to enter the fire by doing so herself, it kills her.

John Donne [1572–1631]

SONG

Go and catch a falling star,
   Get with child a mandrake root,
Tell me where all past years are,
   Or who cleft the Devil's foot,
Teach me to hear mermaids singing,   5
Or to keep off envy's stinging,
      And find
      What wind
Serves to advance an honest mind.

If thou beest born to strange sights,   10
   Things invisible to see,
Ride ten thousand days and nights,
   Till age snow white hairs on thee.
Thou, when thou return'st, wilt tell me
All strange wonders that befell thee,   15
      And swear

Nowhere
Lives a woman true, and fair.

If thou find'st one, let me know,
  Such a pilgrimage were sweet; 20
Yet do not, I would not go,
  Though at next door we might meet;
Though she were true when you met her,
And last till you write your letter,
    Yet she 25
    Will be
False, ere I come, to two, or three.

2, *mandrake root*: the mandragora, a plant of the nightshade family, has a root formerly thought to resemble the human form; it was supposed to have medicinal qualities, including the power to promote conception.

John Keats [1795–1821]

LA BELLE DAME SANS MERCI

O, what can ail thee, knight-at-arms,
  Alone and palely loitering?
The sedge has wither'd from the lake,
  And no birds sing.

O, what can ail thee, knight-at-arms, 5
  So haggard and so woe-begone?
The squirrel's granary is full,
  And the harvest's done.

I see a lilly on thy brow,
  With anguish moist and fever dew; 10
And on thy cheeks a fading rose
  Fast withereth too.

I met a lady in the meads,
  Full beautiful—a faery's child,
Her hair was long, her foot was light, 15
  And her eyes were wild.

I made a garland for head,
  And bracelets too, and fragrant zone;
She look'd at me as she did love,
  And made sweet moan. 20

I set her on my pacing steed,
  And nothing else saw all day long;
For sidelong would she bend, and sing
  A faery's song.

She found me roots of relish sweet,   25
  And honey wild, and manna dew,
And sure in language strange she said—
  'I love thee true'.

She took me to her elfin grot,
  And there she wept and sigh'd full sore,   30
And there I shut her wild wild eyes
  With kisses four.

And there she lullèd me asleep
  And there I dream'd—Ah! woe betide!
The latest dream I ever dream'd   35
  On the cold hill side.

I saw pale kings and princes too,
  Pale warriors, death-pale were they all;
They cried—'La Belle Dame sans Merci
  Hath thee in thrall!'   40

I saw their starved lips in the gloam,
  With horrid warning gapèd wide,
And I awoke and found me here
  On the cold hill's side.

And this is why I sojourn here   45
  Alone and palely loitering,
Though the sedge has wither'd from the lake,
  And no birds sing.

La Belle Dame Sans Merci: The Beautiful Lady without Mercy. 13, meads: meadows. 18, zone: girdle. 26, manna dew: honeydew. 29 elfin grot: enchanted grotto. 35, latest: last. 41, gloam: twilight, gloaming.

William Butler Yeats [1865–1939]

LEDA AND THE SWAN

A sudden blow: the great wings beating still
Above the staggering girl, her thighs caressed

By the dark webs, her nape caught in his bill,
He holds her helpless breast upon his breast.

How can those terrified vague fingers push   5
The feathered glory from her loosening thighs?
And how can body, laid in that white rush,
But feel the strange heart beating where it lies?

A shudder in the loins engenders there
The broken wall, the burning roof and tower   10
And Agamemnon dead.
                        Being so caught up,
So mastered by the brute blood of the air,
Did she put on his knowledge with his power
Before the indifferent beak could let her drop?

According to Greek mythology, Leda, wife of the king of Sparta, was raped by Zeus,
who came to her in the form of a swan. The issue of this union was Helen of Troy.

11, *Agamemnon dead:* Agamemnon fought at Troy, returned home, and was killed
by his wife, Clytemnestra, and her lover, Aegisthus. Clytemnestra was also a daughter
of Leda, but not of Zeus.

Theo. Marzials [fl. 1873]

A TRAGEDY

     Death!
     Plop.
The barges down in the river flop.
     Flop, plop,
   Above, beneath.   5
From the slimy branches the grey drips drop,
As they scraggle black on the thin grey sky,
Where the black cloud rack-hackles drizzle and fly
To the oozy waters that lounge and flop
On the black scrag-piles, where the loose cords plop,   10
As the raw wind whines in the thin tree-top.
     Plop, plop.
   And scudding by
The boatmen call out hoy! and hey!
And all is running in water and sky,   15
     And my head shrieks—"Stop,"
     And my heart shrieks—"Die."

My thought is running out of my head;
My love is running out of my heart;
My soul runs after, and leaves me as dead,   *20*
For my life runs after to catch them — and fled
They are all every one! — and I stand, and start,
At the water that oozes up, plop and plop,
On the barges that flop
   And dizzy me dead.   *25*
I might reel and drop.
        Plop
        Dead.
And the shrill wind whines in the thin tree-top.
   Flop, plop.   *30*

A curse on him.
       Ugh! yet I knew — I knew —
If a woman is false can a friend be true?
It was only a lie from beginning to end —
   My Devil — my "Friend"   *35*
I had trusted the whole of my living to!
  Ugh! and I knew!
   Ugh!
  So what do I care,
And my head is as empty as air —   *40*
    I can do,
    I can dare
  (Plop, plop,
  The barges flop
  Drip, drop.)   *45*
    I can dare, I can dare!
And let myself all run away with my head,
And stop.
   Drop
   Dead.   *50*
  Flip, flop.
  Plop.

William Shakespeare [1564–1616]

SONNET 129

Th' expense of spirit in a waste of shame
Is lust in action; and till action, lust
Is perjured, murderous, bloody, full of blame,
Savage, extreme, rude, cruel, not to trust;

Enjoyed no sooner but despisèd straight: 5
Past reason hunted; and no sooner had,
Past reason hated, as a swallowed bait,
On purpose laid to make the taker mad:
Mad in pursuit, and in possession so;
Had, having, and in quest to have, extreme;   10
A bliss in proof, and proved, a very woe;
Before, a joy proposed; behind, a dream.
    All this the world well knows; yet none knows well
    To shun the heaven that leads men to this hell.

11, *in proof:* during the experience; *proved:* after the experience.

A. D. Hope [b. 1907]

CONQUISTADOR

I sing of the decline of Henry Clay
Who loved a white girl of uncommon size.
Although a small man in a little way,
He had in him some seed of enterprise.

Each day he caught the seven-thirty train   5
To work, watered his garden after tea,
Took an umbrella if it looked like rain
And was remarkably like you or me.

He had his hair cut once a fortnight, tried
Not to forget the birthday of his wife,   10
And might have lived unnoticed till he died
Had not ambition entered Henry's life.

He met her in the lounge of an hotel
—A most unusual place for him to go—
But there he was and there she was as well,   15
Sitting alone. He ordered beers for two.

She was so large a girl that when they came
He gave the waiter twice the usual tip.
She smiled without surprise, told him her name,
And as the name trembled on Henry's lip,   20

His parched soul, swelling like a desert root,
Broke out its delicate dream upon the air;

The mountains shook with earthquake under foot;
An angel seized him suddenly by the hair;

25

The sky was shrill with peril as he passed;
A hurricane crushed his senses with its din;
The wildfire crackled up his reeling mast;
The trumpet of a maelstrom sucked him in;

The desert shrivelled and burnt off his feet;
His bones and buttons an enormous snake
Vomited up; still in the shimmering heat
The pygmies showed him their forbidden lake

30

And then transfixed him with their poison darts;
He married six black virgins in a bunch,
Who, when they had drawn out his manly parts,
Stewed him and ate him lovingly for lunch.

35

Adventure opened wide its grisly jaws;
Henry looked in and knew the Hero's doom.
The huge white girl drank on without a pause
And, just at closing time, she asked him home.

40

The tram they took was full of Roaring Boys
Announcing the world's ruin and Judgment Day;
The sky blared with its grand orchestral voice
The Götterdämmerung of Henry Clay.

45

But in her quiet room they were alone.
There, towering over Henry by a head,
She stood and took her clothes off one by one,
And then she stretched herself upon the bed.

Her bulk of beauty, her stupendous grace
Challenged the lion heart in his puny dust.
Proudly his Moment looked him in the face:
He rose to meet it as a hero must;

50

Climbed the white mountain of unravished snow,
Planted his tiny flag upon the peak.
The smooth drifts, scarcely breathing, lay below.
She did not take the trouble to smile or speak.

55

And afterwards, it may have been in play,
The enormous girl rolled over and squashed him flat;

And, as she could not send him home that way,
Used him thereafter as a bedside mat.   60

Speaking at large, I will say this of her:
She did not spare expense to make him nice.
Tanned on both sides and neatly edged with fur,
The job would have been cheap at any price.
                                                                          65

And when, in winter, getting out of bed,
Her large soft feet pressed warmly on the skin,
The two glass eyes would sparkle in his head,
The jaws extend their papier-mâché grin.

Good people, for the soul of Henry Clay   70
Offer your prayers, and view his destiny!
He was the Hero of our Time. He may
With any luck, one day, be you or me.

Conquistador: Spanish; conqueror. 41, Roaring Boys: originally a sixteenth-century
term for riotous, noisy young playboys. 44, Götterdämmerung: German; twilight of the
gods; in Germanic mythology, the end of the world.

James Dickey [b. 1923]

ADULTERY

We have all been in rooms
We cannot die in, and they are odd places, and sad.
Often Indians are standing eagle-armed on hills

In the sunrise   open wide to the Great Spirit
Or gliding in canoes   or cattle are browsing on the walls   5
Far away   gazing down with the eyes of our children

Not far away   or there are men driving
The last railspike, which has turned
Gold in their hands. Gigantic forepleasure lives

Among such scenes, and we are alone with it   10
At last. There is always some weeping
Between us   and someone is always checking

A wrist watch by the bed to see how much
Longer we have left. Nothing can come
Of this   nothing can come   15

Of us: of me with my grim techniques
Or you who have sealed your womb
With a ring of convulsive rubber:

Although we come together,
Nothing will come of us. But we would not give 20
It up, for death is beaten

By praying Indians   by distant cows   historical
Hammers   by hazardous meetings that bridge
A continent. One could never die here

Never die   never die 25
While crying. My lover, my dear one
I will see you next week

When I'm in town. I will call you
If I can. Please get hold of   please don't
Oh God, Please don't any more I can't bear . . . Listen: 30

We have done it again   we are
Still living. Sit up and smile,
God bless you. Guilt is magical.

Gary Snyder [b. 1930]

TO HELL WITH YOUR FERTILITY CULT

To hell with your Fertility Cult, I
never did want to be fertile,
you think this world is just
a goddamn oversize cunt, don't you? Everything
crowding in and out of it like a railway 5
terminal   and isn't that nice?
all those people going on trips.
well this is what it feels like, she said,
—and knocked the hen off the nest, grabbed
an egg and threw it at him, right in the face, 10
the half-formed chick half clung, half slid
half-alive, down over his cheekbone, around
the corner of his mouth, part of it thick
yellow and faintly visible bones and it drippt
down his cheek and chin 15
—he had nothing to say.

Robert Browning [1812–1889]

MY LAST DUCHESS

Ferrara

That's my last duchess painted on the wall,
Looking as if she were alive. I call
That piece a wonder, now: Frà Pandolf's hands
Worked busily a day, and there she stands.
Will't please you sit and look at her? I said   5
"Frà Pandolf" by design, for never read
Strangers like you that pictured countenance,
The depth and passion of its earnest glance,
But to myself they turned (since none puts by
The curtain I have drawn for you, but I)   10
And seemed as they would ask me, if they durst,
How such a glance came there; so, not the first
Are you to turn and ask thus. Sir, 'twas not
Her husband's presence only, called that spot
Of joy into the Duchess' cheek: perhaps   15
Frà Pandolf chanced to say "Her mantle laps
"Over my lady's wrist too much," or "Paint
"Must never hope to reproduce the faint
"Half-flush that dies along her throat": such stuff
Was courtesy, she thought, and cause enough   20
For calling up that spot of joy. She had
A heart—how shall I say?—too soon made glad,
Too easily impressed; she liked whate'er
She looked on, and her looks went everywhere.
Sir, 'twas all one! My favor at her breast,   25
The dropping of the daylight in the West,
The bough of cherries some officious fool
Broke in the orchard for her, the white mule
She rode with round the terrace—all and each
Would draw from her alike the approving speech,   30
Or blush, at least. She thanked men—good! but thanked
Somehow—I know not how—as if she ranked
My gift of a nine-hundred-years-old name
With anybody's gift. Who'd stoop to blame
This sort of trifling? Even had you skill   35
In speech—which I have not—to make your will
Quite clear to such an one, and say, "Just this
"Or that in you disgusts me; here you miss,
"Or there exceed the mark"—and if she let
Herself be lessoned so, nor plainly set   40

Her wits to yours, forsooth, and made excuse,
—E'en then would be some stooping; and I choose
Never to stoop. Oh sir, she smiled, no doubt,
Whene'er I passed her; but who passed without
Much the same smile? This grew; I gave commands;   45
Then all smiles stopped together. There she stands
As if alive. Will't please you rise? We'll meet
The company below, then. I repeat,
The Count your master's known munificence
Is ample warrant that no just pretense   50
Of mine for dowry will be disallowed;
Though his fair daughter's self, as I avowed
At starting, is my object. Nay, we'll go
Together down, sir. Notice Neptune, though,
Taming a sea-horse, thought a rarity,   55
Which Claus of Innsbruck cast in bronze for me!

6, *Frà Pandolf:* an imaginary artist. 54, *Neptune:* the god of the ocean. 56, *Claus of Innsbruck:* an imaginary artist, from the city of Innsbruck in Austria.

George Garrett [b. 1929]

SALOME

I had a dream of purity.

From weight of flesh and cage of bone,
it was I who was set free
and that other me like a blown weed
was scattered by the wind. Frail bones
(They were so small and light to carry   5
so much hunger and fury.)
crumbled into finest dust
and the wind took that away too.
And last of all my mouth, my lips,
a red yawn, a taut shriek, my tongue   10
fluttered like a dead leaf and vanished.
And then it was I who was free,
flying lonely above the ruins,
the slight debris of all the fires
I had lived with, wholly consumed by.   15
All my dust was gone for good,
and that part of me, the breath of God,
glowed without burning, shone with dark light,

danced like fountains at the weightless peak
of pure delight and fell. . . .   20

I woke up gnashing my teeth.
—Is anything wrong? they asked.
—Did you have a bad dream?
—Do you have a fever?

—I have had a dream of purity, I said.   25
And then they all laughed
and my mouth stretched with laughter too,
red and white, obscene,
and my tongue was as sweet as a fresh plum again.
And I . . . I was on fire as before.   30

I have known other dreams,
the ordinary ones:
Myself naked,
riding bareback on a horse
across a country like the moon.   35
Something is chasing us
(or me anyway)
and my little whip sings
and the horse gnaws at the bit.
The wind is like ice water.   40
Then suddenly the horse is riding me!
I wake up screaming my name.

Another:
Myself with feathers and wings.
But I can't fly. I am caught.   45
They start to pluck me.
Now each feather is a single hair
yanked by the tender roots.
I try to cry but no sound comes.
My mouth is full of fur.   50
I wake up and find
I have fallen out of my cold bed.

I tell you all this
not for the pennies of your pity.
Save those coins to cover your eyes.   55
Nor for your eyebrows
to chevron my rank of shame.
Nor for you to whisper about me

behind your cupped palms.
But that you may know   60
what a thing it is to be chosen.

I had every right to love and hate holiness.

—What is flesh? you ask.
I have been called sweet,
a hive of dark honey,   65
worthy of worship
from roots of hair to toes.
I have been called cruel,
the tormentor of dreams,
a dancer of the abstract fancy.   70
All of which is a dirty lie.
The plain truth is
I was a creature that sweats,
excretes, sags, ages, wrinkles. . . .
My bones were weary of me.   75

The soul, then?
I think I dreamed it once.

—And the other dreams?
They weren't me. Not me! Not me!
I was not the one who was dreaming.   80

Bring on the wild man,
bearded like black sky before a storm,
eyes all alight like white water,
wrapped in rags,
skin and bones corrupted by neglect,   85
a mouth of ruined teeth and bitter breath,
a cripple cursing every dancer.

—How have you come from my dream?
I wanted to say. —Bless me!
I longed to kiss   90
but my lips spat for me.

Understand this:
I loved him as myself.
God must love His creatures so.

But I was caged.
My skin and bones hated me.
My thoughts hooded me like a wild bird.

The Dance?
Believe what you care to.
Picture it any way you want to.
All the world knows
truth is best revealed
by gradual deception.
It was a striptease pure and simple.

My tongue cried for his head.
But it was my mouth that kissed him
and was damned.

Then I was free and able to rejoice.

A bad marriage from the beginning,
you say, a complete mismatch.
Flesh and spirit wrestle
and we call it love.

We couple like dogs in heat.
We shudder and are sundered.
We pursue ourselves,
sniffing, nose to tail,
a comic parade of appetites.

That is the truth,
but not the whole truth.
Do me a little justice.
I had a dream of purity
and I have lived in the desert ever since.

The story of Salome may be found in Matthew, Chapter 14.

5
The Book
of Lies

Language Barriers
and Credibility Gaps

Carl Sandburg [1878–1967]

USELESS WORDS

So long as we speak the same language and never understand each
    other,
So long as the spirals of our words snarl and interlock
And clutch each other with the irreckonable gutturals,
Well . . .

Robert Creeley [b. 1926]

THE PATTERN

As soon as
I speak, I
speaks. It

wants to
be free but
impassive lies

in the direction
of its
words. Let

x equal x, x
also
equals x. I

speak to
hear myself
speak? I

had not thought
that some-
thing had such

undone. It
was an idea
of mine.

William Blake [1757–1827]

A POISON TREE

I was angry with my friend:
I told my wrath, my wrath did end.
I was angry with my foe:
I told it not, my wrath did grow.

And I water'd it in fears,
Night and morning with my tears;
And I sunnèd it with smiles,
And with soft deceitful wiles.

And it grew both day and night,
Till it bore an apple bright;
And my foe beheld it shine,
And he knew that it was mine,

And into my garden stole
When the night had veil'd the pole:
In the morning glad I see
My foe outstretch'd beneath the tree.

14: when night had covered the earth.

Steven Graves [b. 1947]

THE RENDEZVOUS

I, when exposed, will pass the letter on to you,
the slender man beneath the dripping tree.
Our meeting must resemble idleness.

I have been given our instructions.   They are
explicit:

You are to serve no limit.
You will move without true motion.
You must prove indifferent.

I will arrange the place. We will approach it
on gravel paths. When you hear my footsteps,   *10*
set your pace to mine. It will serve
as recognition. As we approach, you will nod,
but it will go without return. We then stop
and let the gravel suffice as our alarm.
If undiscovered, the letter will be yours,   *15*
and we may depart on avenues of sand.
It is yours to deliver to them,
the drifting multitudes hidden in the fog.
They will know you by your dampened hair.
They will welcome you as me.   *20*

Emily Dickinson [1830–1886]

HE PREACHED UPON "BREADTH"

He preached upon "Breadth" till it argued him narrow—
The Broad are too broad to define
And of "Truth" until it proclaimed him a Liar—
The Truth never flaunted a Sign—

Simplicity fled from his counterfeit presence   *5*
As Gold the Pyrites would shun—
What confusion would cover the innocent Jesus
To meet so enabled a Man!

6, *Pyrites:* Iron pyrites, a mineral resembling gold; often called "fool's gold."

Ann Stanford [b. 1916]

THE LATE VISITOR

Listen, let me explain, it was not the fire
That burned in the hearth and kept me there.
It was no real fire, though I swear it did seem so
And to go out was to step into blackest snow,
And to stay was to lose, not find. Words only say   *5*
What is gone. Or are motions like flame and snow,

Slow circlings of something about to occur,
The birth of a salamander in the fire.

I am caught between never and now. You must tell me to go.

Kelly Cherry [b. 1940]

A SONG FOR SIGMUND FREUD

Did you think you could hide from me?
But I won't *let* you.
Too long I've loved your mad anger, soft,
Wry, unrelenting rationality.

Once in Vienna, when the rain fell,   *5*
I saw you sing
And munch on your syllables as if they were mushrooms.
You were always full of fear for something

In the dark that teased your throat
Like a dog.   *10*
I could have cooled and warmed you any autumn.
Oh but you made yourself remote

In a last resort. Be brave, mein liebchen, I won't bite.
Look at my sunny face. I'm bright! I'm fun.
So kiss me, Siggy! . . . Hold me tight.   *15*
And I'll waltz with you when the Nazis come.

Sigmund Freud (1856–1939), major contributor to the literature and practice of psychoanalysis. 13, *mein liebchen:* German; my sweetheart.

Sir Walter Ralegh [1552?–1618]

THE LIE

Go, Soul, the body's guest,
Upon a thankless arrant:
Fear not to touch the best;
The truth shall be thy warrant:
Go, since I needs must die,   *5*
And give the world the lie.

Say to the court, it glows
And shines like rotten wood;

Say to the church it shows
What's good, and doth no good:
If church and court reply,
Then give them both the lie.

Tell potentates, they live
Acting by others' action;
Not loved unless they give,
Not strong but by affection:
If potentates reply,
Give potentates the lie.

Tell men of high condition
That manage the estate,
Their purpose is ambition,
Their practice only hate:
And if they once reply,
Then give them all the lie.

Tell them that brave it most
They beg for more by spending,
Who, in their greatest cost,
Seek nothing but commending:
And if they make reply,
Then give them all the lie.

Tell zeal it wants devotion,
Tell love it is but lust;
Tell time it metes but motion,
Tell flesh it is but dust:
And wish them not reply,
For thou must give the lie.

Tell age it daily wasteth;
Tell honor how it alters;
Tell beauty how she blasteth;
Tell favor how it falters:
And as they shall reply,
Give every one the lie.

Tell wit how much it wrangles
In tickle points of niceness;
Tell wisdom she entangles
Herself in over-wiseness:
And when they do reply,
Straight give them both the lie.

Tell physic of her boldness;
Tell skill it is pretension;
Tell charity of coldness;
Tell law it is contention:
And as they do reply,
So give them still the lie.

Tell fortune of her blindness;
Tell nature of decay;
Tell friendship of unkindness;
Tell justice of delay:
And if they will reply,
Then give them all the lie.

Tell arts they have no soundness,
But vary by esteeming;
Tell schools they want profoundness,
And stand too much on seeming:
If arts and schools reply,
Give arts and schools the lie.

Tell faith it's fled the city;
Tell how the country erreth;
Tell manhood shakes off pity
And virtue least preferreth:
And if they do reply,
Spare not to give the lie.

So when thou hast, as I
Commanded thee, done blabbing
— Although to give the lie
Deserves no less than stabbing —
Stab at thee he that will,
No stab thy soul can kill.

50

55

60

65

70

75

2, *arrant:* errand. 33, *metes:* measures. 39, *blasteth:* blights, goes to waste.

William Shakespeare [1564–1616]

SONNET 138

When my love swears that she is made of truth,
I do believe her, though I know she lies,
That she might think me some untutor'd youth,
Unlearned in the world's false subtleties.

Thus vainly thinking that she thinks me young, Although she knows my days are past the best, Simply I credit her false-speaking tongue: On both sides thus is simple truth supprest. But wherefore says she not she is unjust? And wherefore say not I that I am old? O, love's best habit is in seeming trust, And age in love loves not to have years told: Therefore I lie with her, and she with me, And in our faults by lies we flatter'd be.

9, *unjust:* untruthful.

James Tate [b. 1943]

THE BOOK OF LIES

I'd like to have a word
with you. Could we be alone
for a minute? I have been lying
until now. Do you believe

I believe myself? Do you believe
yourself when you believe me? Lying
is natural. Forgive me. Could we be alone
forever? Forgive us all. The word

is my enemy. I have never been alone;
bribes, betrayals. I am lying
even now. Can you believe
that? I give you my word.

e. e. cummings [1894–1962]

"NEXT TO OF COURSE GOD AMERICA I

"next to of course god america i
love you land of the pilgrims' and so forth oh
say can you see by the dawn's early my
country 'tis of centuries come and go
and are no more what of it we should worry
in every language even deafanddumb
thy sons acclaim your glorious name by gorry
by jingo by gee by gosh by gum

why talk of beauty what could be more beaut-
iful than these heroic happy dead   *10*
who rushed like lions to the roaring slaughter
they did not stop to think they died instead
then shall the voice of liberty be mute?"

He spoke. And drank rapidly a glass of water

Al Young [b. 1939]

A DANCE FOR MILITANT DILETTANTES

No one's going to read
or take you seriously,
a hip friend advises,
until you start coming down on them
like the black poet you truly are   *5*
& ink in lots of black in your poems
soul is not enough
you need real color
shining out of real skin
nappy snaggly afro hair   *10*
baby grow up & dig on *that!*

You got to learn to put in about
stone black fists
coming up against white jaws
& red blood splashing   *15*
down those fabled wine & urine-
stained hallways
black bombs blasting out real white estate
the sky itself black with what's to come:
final holocaust   *20*
the settling up

Don't nobody want no nice nigger no more
these honkies man that put out
these books & things
they want an angry splib   *25*
a furious nigrah
they don't want no bourgeois woogie
they want them a militant nigger
in a fiji haircut
fresh out of some secret boot camp   *30*
with a bad book in one hand

& a molotov cocktail in the other
subject to turn up at one of their conferences
or soirees
& shake the shit out of them   *35*

25, *splib:* a faintly derogatory term for a black person.

Ann M. Craig [b. 1952]

HYPOCRITE

You know me
    I'm the one who prays
  As if to say
Just in case you are there
      But I'm no fool   *5*
        if you aren't

Right after
    singing protest songs
      lying down

Chanting "Whitey ain't right"   *10*
    in my angry voice
  while living peacefully
    at his door

Needing a change today
    to let it wait   *15*
  an anxious tomorrow
    that might come
if someone does
    what I only talk about

Hey you know me   *20*
    I'm the one whose militancy
    never progresses
    beyond the stage of thinking

Anthony Hecht [b. 1923]

EPITAPH

Here lies fierce Strephon, whose poetic rage
Lashed out on Viet Nam from page and stage;
Whereby from basements of Bohemia he

Rose to the lofts of sweet celebrity;
Being, by Fortune, (our Eternal Whore)   5
One of the few to profit by that war;
A fate he shared—it bears much thinking on—
With certain persons at the Pentagon.

1, *Strephon:* conventional classical name for an imaginary character.

W. H. Auden [1907–1973]

THE UNKNOWN CITIZEN

(TO JS/07/M/378
THIS MARBLE MONUMENT
IS ERECTED BY THE STATE

He was found by the Bureau of Statistics to be
One against whom there was no official complaint,
And all the reports on his conduct agree
That, in the modern sense of an old-fashioned word, he was a saint,
For in everything he did he served the Greater Community.   5
Except for the War till the day he retired
He worked in a factory and never got fired,
But satisfied his employers, Fudge Motors Inc.
Yet he wasn't a scab or odd in his views,
For his Union reports that he paid his dues,   10
(Our report on his Union shows it was sound)
And our Social Psychology workers found
That he was popular with his mates and liked a drink.
The Press are convinced that he bought a paper every day
And that his reactions to advertisements were normal in every way.   15
Policies taken out in his name prove that he was fully insured,
And his Health-card shows he was once in hospital but left it cured.
Both Producers Research and High-Grade Living declare
He was fully sensible to the advantages of the Installment Plan
And had everything necessary to the Modern Man,   20
A phonograph, a radio, a car and a frigidaire.
Our researchers into Public Opinion are content
That he held the proper opinions for the time of year;
When there was peace, he was for peace; when there was war, he
    went.
He was married and added five children to the population,   25
Which our Eugenist says was the right number for a parent of his
    generation,
And our teachers report that he never interfered with their
    education.
Was he free? Was he happy? The question is absurd:
Had anything been wrong, we should certainly have heard.

Walter de la Mare [1873–1956]

THE LISTENERS

'Is there anybody there?' said the Traveller,
   Knocking on the moonlit door;
And his horse in the silence champ'd the grasses
   Of the forest's ferny floor:
And a bird flew up out of the turret,   5
   Above the Traveller's head:
And he smote upon the door again a second time;
   'Is there anybody there?' he said.
But no one descended to the Traveller;
   No head from the leaf-fringed sill   10
Lean'd over and look'd into his grey eyes,
   Where he stood perplex'd and still.
But only a host of phantom listeners
   That dwelt in the lone house then
Stood listening in the quiet of the moonlight   15
   To that voice from the world of men:
Stood thronging the faint moonbeams on the dark stair,
   That goes down to the empty hall,
Hearkening in an air stirr'd and shaken
   By the lonely Traveller's call.   20
And he felt in his heart their strangeness,
   Their stillness answering his cry,
While his horse moved, cropping the dark turf,
   'Neath the starr'd and leafy sky;
For he suddenly smote on the door, even   25
   Louder, and lifted his head:—
'Tell them I came, and no one answer'd,
   That I kept my word,' he said.
Never the least stir made the listeners,
   Though every word he spake   30
Fell echoing through the shadowiness of the still house
   From the one man left awake:
Ay, they heard his foot upon the stirrup,
   And the sound of iron on stone,
And how the silence surged softly backward,   35
   When the plunging hoofs were gone.

Donald Justice [b. 1925]

THE GRANDFATHERS

Why will they never speak,
The old ones, the grandfathers?

Always you find them sitting
On ruined porches, deep
In the back country, at dusk,   5
Hawking and spitting.
They might have sat there forever,
Tapping their sticks,
Peevish, discredited gods.
Ask of the traveler how   10
At road-end they will fix
You maybe with the cold
Eye of a snake or a bird
And answer not a word,
Only these dark, oracular   15
Head-shakes or head-nods.

Walt Whitman [1819–1892]

WHEN I HEARD THE LEARN'D ASTRONOMER

When I heard the learn'd astronomer,
When the proofs, the figures, were ranged in columns before me,
When I was shown the charts and diagrams, to add, divide, and
    measure them,
When I sitting heard the astronomer where he lectured with much
    applause in the lecture room,
How soon unaccountable I became tired and sick,   5
Till rising and gliding out I wander'd off by myself,
In the mystical moist night-air, and from time to time,
Look'd up in perfect silence at the stars.

Percy Bysshe Shelley [1792–1822]

OZYMANDIAS

I met a traveler from an antique land
Who said: Two vast and trunkless legs of stone
Stand in the desert . . . Near them, on the sand,
Half sunk, a shattered visage lies, whose frown,
And wrinkled lip, and sneer of cold command,   5
Tell that its sculptor well those passions read
Which yet survive, stamped on these lifeless things,
The hand that mocked them, and the heart that fed:
And on the pedestal these words appear:
"My name is Ozymandias, king of kings: 10

Look on my works, ye Mighty, and despair!"
Nothing beside remains. Round the decay
Of that colossal wreck, boundless and bare
The lone and level sands stretch far away.

Ozymandias was Ramses II, an Egyptian pharaoh of the thirteenth century B.C.

May Sarton [b. 1912]

BAROQUE IMAGE

(for Any Artist)

He angled the bright shield
To catch the setting sun,
And dazzled the whole field,
Enemy, friend, as one.

Who had the nerve to borrow   5
That sheen in a dark hour,
The arrows of Apollo
And the god's blinding power?

They did not sense the wound
Behind that tilted shield—   10
For he could hardly stand
Who dazzled the whole field!

7–8, *Apollo*: in Greek mythology, the god of the sun, and of music and poetry.

6
The National Habit

Politics

John Byrom [1692–1763]

**EXTEMPORE VERSES INTENDED TO ALLAY
THE VIOLENCE OF PARTY-SPIRIT**

God bless the King, I mean the Faith's Defender;
God bless—no Harm in blessing—the Pretender;
But who Pretender is, or who is King,
God bless us all—that's quite another Thing.

The king here is George II, of the house of Hanover. The Hanoverian monarchs of England succeeded the Stuart monarchs at the death of Queen Anne in 1714. Thereafter, James Stuart (1688–1766), son of James II, and Charles Stuart (1720–1788) were known as Pretenders to the throne. The "party-spirit" referred to in the title arose between the Whigs, who were loyal to the Hanoverians, and the Tories, who professed allegiance to the Stuarts.

William Cowper [1731–1800]

THE STATESMAN IN RETIREMENT

from RETIREMENT

Ye groves (the statesman at his desk exclaims,
Sick of a thousand disappointed aims)
My patrimonial treasure and my pride,
Beneath your shades your gray possessor hide,
Receive me languishing for that repose   5
The servant of the public never knows.
Ye saw me once (ah those regretted days
When boyish innocence was all my praise)

Hour after hour delightfully allot
To studies then familiar, since forgot,   10
And cultivate a taste for ancient song,
Catching its ardour as I mus'd along;
Nor seldom, as propitious heav'n might send,
What once I valued and could boast, a friend
Were witnesses how cordially I press'd   15
His undissembling virtue to my breast;
Receive me now, not uncorrupt as then,
Nor guiltless of corrupting other men,
But vers'd in arts that, while they seem to stay
A falling empire, hasten its decay.   20
To the fair haven of my native home,
The wreck of what I was, fatigu'd I come;
For once I can approve the patriot's voice,
And make the course he recommends, my choice:
We meet at last in one sincere desire,   25
His wish and mine both prompt me to retire.
'Tis done—he steps into the welcome chaise,
Lolls at his ease behind four handsome bays,
That whirl away from business and debate
The disincumber'd Atlas of the state.   30
Ask not the boy, who when the breeze of morn
First shakes the glitt'ring drops from ev'ry thorn,
Unfolds his flock, then under bank or bush
Sits linking cherry stones or platting rush,
How fair is freedom?—he was always free: 35
To carve his rustic name upon a tree,
To snare the mole, or with ill-fashion'd hook
To draw th' incautious minnow from the brook,
Are life's prime pleasures in his simple view,
His flock the chief concern he ever knew: 40
She shines but little in his heedless eyes,
The good we never miss, we rarely prize:
But ask the noble drudge in state affairs,
Escap'd from office and its constant cares,
What charms he sees in freedom's smile express'd,   45
In freedom lost so long, now repossess'd,
The tongue whose strains were cogent as commands,
Rever'd at home, and felt in foreign lands,
Shall own itself a stamm'rer in that cause,
Or plead its silence as its best applause.   50
He knows indeed that, whether dress'd or rude,
Wild without art, or artfully subdu'd,
Nature in ev'ry form inspires delight,

But never mark'd her with so just a sight.
Her hedge-row shrubs, a variegated store,   55
With woodbine and wild roses mantled o'er,
Green baulks and furrow'd lands, the stream that spreads
Its cooling vapour o'er the dewy meads,
Downs that almost escape th' enquiring eye,
That melt and fade into the distant sky,   60
Beauties he lately slighted as he pass'd,
Seem all created since he travell'd last.
Master of all th' enjoyments he design'd,
No rough annoyance rankling in his mind,
What early philosophic hours he keeps,   65
How regular his meals, how sound he sleeps!
Not sounder he that on the mainmast head,
While morning kindles with a windy red,
Begins a long look-out for distant land,
Nor quits, till ev'ning watch, his giddy stand,   70
Then swift descending with a seaman's haste,
Slips to his hammock, and forgets the blast.
He chooses company, but not the squire's,
Whose wit is rudeness, whose good breeding tires;
Nor yet the parson's, who would gladly come,   75
Obsequious when abroad, though proud at home;
Nor can he much affect the neighb'ring peer,
Whose toe of emulation treads too near;
But wisely seeks a more convenient friend,
With whom, dismissing forms, he may unbend!   80
A man whom marks of condescending grace
Teach, while they flatter him, his proper place:
Who comes when call'd, and at a word withdraws,
Speaks with reserve, and listens with applause;
Some plain mechanic, who, without pretence   85
To birth or wit, nor gives nor takes offence;
On whom he rests well-pleas'd his weary pow'rs,
And talks and laughs away his vacant hours.
The tide of life, swift always in its course,
May run in cities with a brisker force,   90
But no where with a current so serene,
Or half so clear, as in the rural scene.
Yet how fallacious is all earthly bliss,
What obvious truths the wisest heads may miss;
Some pleasures live a month, and some a year,   95
But short the date of all we gather here;
No happiness is felt, except the true,
That does not charm the more for being new.

This observation, as it chanc'd, not made,
Or if the thought occurr'd, not duly weigh'd,   *100*
He sighs—for after all, by slow degrees,
The spot he lov'd has lost the pow'r to please;
To cross his ambling pony day by day,
Seems at the best but dreaming life away;
The prospect, such as might enchant despair,   *105*
He views it not, or sees no beauty there;
With aching heart, and discontented looks,
Returns at noon, to billiards or to books,
But feels, while grasping at his faded joys,
A secret thirst of his renounc'd employs.   *110*
He chides the tardiness of ev'ry post,
Pants to be told of battles won or lost,
Blames his own indolence, observes, though late.
'Tis criminal to leave a sinking state,
Flies to the levee, and, receiv'd with grace,   *115*
Kneels, kisses hands, and shines again in place.

Richard Wilbur [b. 1921]

SHAME

It is a cramped little state with no foreign policy,
Save to be thought inoffensive. The grammar of the language
Has never been fathomed, owing to the national habit
Of allowing each sentence to trail off in confusion.
Those who have visited Scusi, the capital city,   *5*
Report that the railway-route from Schuldig passes
Through country best described as unrelieved.
Sheep are the national product. The faint inscription
Over the city gates may perhaps be rendered,
"I'm afraid you won't find much of interest here."   *10*
Census-reports which give the population
As zero are, of course, not to be trusted,
Save as reflecting the natives' flustered insistence
That they do not count, as well as their modest horror
Of letting one's sex be known in so many words.   *15*
The uniform grey of the nondescript buildings, the absence
Of churches or comfort-stations, have given observers
An odd impression of ostentatious meanness,
And it must be said of the citizens (muttering by
In their ratty sheepskins, shying at cracks in the sidewalk)   *20*
That they lack the peace of mind of the truly humble.
The tenor of life is careful, even in the stiff

Unsmiling carelessness of the border-guards
And *douaniers,* who admit, whenever they can,
Not merely the usual carloads of deodorant   25
But gypsies, g-strings, hasheesh, and contraband pigments.
Their complete negligence is reserved, however,
For the hoped-for invasion, at which time the happy people
(Sniggering, ruddily naked, and shamelessly drunk)
Will stun the foe by their overwhelming submission,   30
Corrupt the generals, infiltrate the staff,
Usurp the throne, proclaim themselves to be sun-gods,
And bring about the collapse of the whole empire.

5, *Scusi:* an imaginary name. In Italian, the word means "I beg your pardon." 6,
Schuldig: also imaginary. In German, it means guilty or blameworthy. 24, *douaniers:*
French; customs officers.

James Den Boer [b. 1937]

CASTING A VOTE

November 1968

In the eyes of the brown bear
back of Wellman Burn there is
a cloud, and I will clear
them, open deep in their retinas
my own vision;   5
he will see me walking the canyon,
holding myself tight
under the contracting gray sky —

poems in the eyes of old bears!
I think I will vote   10
for him for President or Senator,
to hear him growl in Congress,
cracking plaster in White House
walls, white dust drifting
slowly down on the President's desk!   15

I work up the canyon
looking for sign; two doe
rise from a thicket,
sailing without sound down
the dry meadows. A cloud   20

clears from my eye, sun burning
away dead scar tissue;
heat in the look opens mind.

Bear talk! pure harsh sound
walks water up creek, rock   25
by rock, to where I chew hard sausage,
a handful of nuts — he is voting
with his left front paw in water,
snapping the air, upwind.

Louis Simpson [b. 1923]

ON THE LAWN AT THE VILLA

On the lawn at the villa —
That's the way to start, eh, reader?
We know where we stand — somewhere expensive —
You and I *imperturbes*, as Walt would say,
Before the diversions of wealth, you and I *engagés*.   5

On the lawn at the villa
Sat a manufacturer of explosives,
His wife from Paris,
And a young man named Bruno,

And myself, being American,   10
Willing to talk to these malefactors,
The manufacturer of explosives, and so on,
But somehow superior. By that I mean democratic.
It's complicated, being an American,
Having the money and the bad conscience, both at the same time.   15
Perhaps, after all, this is not the right subject for a poem.

We were all sitting there paralyzed
In the hot Tuscan afternoon,
And the bodies of the machine-gun crew were draped over the
    balcony.
So we sat there all afternoon.   20

4, *imperturbes*: unperturbed; *Walt*: Walt Whitman. 5, *engagés*: French; involved,
committed.

Paul Lawson [b. 1916]

THE AMBASSADORS

When we heard it announced
that our country had been abolished
we looked around from the top of the embassy
loving the station
no way to tell the sky from the water   5
and
sickened
went inside and started packing

back of the funny tick-tick
we sensed lions dreaming our bones   10

in the infirmary was a man who'd
had his bowels removed
thankful that his stomach was left in

when the embarkation tickets were distributed
without names (to underline our identity)   15
and we realized we wouldn't have a home again
we knew we had to be something other than a nation
and went back to packing
and unpacking
discarding, reclaiming   20
questioning
hurting one another
waiting for a destination
listening to everyone cry
and occasionally thinking of the stomach man   25

someone mentioned Pocahontas
who left England for Virginia
in sixteen seventeen
and died off Gravesend

Pocahontas (ca. 1595–1617), daughter of Powhatan, chief of the Powhatan Indians. She married John Rolfe of Captain John Smith's party, went to England, where she became ill. When she realized that she might die, she began a return voyage to Virginia, but died shortly after the boat had departed. Gravesend is on the Thames below London.

John Milton [1608–1674]

ON THE NEW FORCERS OF CONSCIENCE
UNDER THE LONG PARLIAMENT

Because you have thrown off your prelate lord,
    And with stiff vows renounced his liturgy,
    To seize the widowed whore Plurality
    From them whose sin ye envied, not abhorred,
Dare ye for this adjure the civil sword   5
    To force our consciences that Christ set free,
    And ride us with a classic hierarchy
    Taught ye by mere A. S. and Rutherford?
Men whose life, learning, faith, and pure intent
    Would have been held in high esteem with Paul   10
    Must now be named and printed heretics
By shallow Edwards and Scotch what d'ye call:
    But we do hope to find out all your tricks,
    Your plots and packing worse than those of Trent,
        That so the Parliament   15
May with their wholesome and preventive shears
Clip your phylacteries, though balk your ears,
And succour our just fears
When they shall read this clearly in your charge:
New presbyter is but *old priest* writ large.   20

The Long Parliament was called by Charles I in 1640 and dissolved by Cromwell in 1653. The "new forcers of conscience" are the Presbyterians, whose power under the Long Parliament exceeded that of the Episcopalians.

1, *prelate lord:* bishop. 3, *Plurality:* the practice of one priest's holding more than one living at the same time. 8, *A.S.* and *Rutherford:* Adam Stuart and Samuel Rutherford, Presbyterian pamphleteers. 12: Thomas Edwards, author of *Gangraena*, a description of heresies which included an attack on Milton's statements in favor of divorce; *Scotch what d'ye call:* a dismissal of all the Scottish Presbyterian writers. 14, *Trent:* The Council of Trent (1545–1563) sat at intervals to formalize the doctrines of the Catholic Church, as opposed to those of the Reformation. 15–20: these are the "tails" of an Italian form called the "Tailed Sonnet"; there are two here, each two and one-half lines long. 17, *phylacteries:* here a symbol of superstition, these were small vials containing scrolls of the Law, worn by Orthodox Jews.

William Wordsworth [1770–1850]

ON THE EXTINCTION OF
THE VENETIAN REPUBLIC, 1802

Once did she hold the gorgeous East in fee;
    And was the safeguard of the West: the worth

Of Venice did not fall below her birth,
Venice, the eldest Child of Liberty.
She was a maiden City, bright and free;   5
    No guile seduced, no force could violate;
    And, when she took unto herself a mate,
She must espouse the everlasting Sea.
And what if she had seen those glories fade,
    Those titles vanish, and that strength decay;   10
Yet shall some tribute of regret be paid
    When her long life hath reach'd its final day:
Men are we, and must grieve when even the Shade
    Of that which once was great is pass'd away.

In 1792, Napoleon divided what was left of the Venetian Empire between Austria
and France.

1, *in fee:* as a landlord; see "On First Looking Into Chapman's Homer" (page 329),
line 4 and note. 13, *Shade:* ghost.

Percy Bysshe Shelley [1792–1822]

ENGLAND IN 1819

An old, mad, blind, despised, and dying king, —
Princes, the dregs of their dull race, who flow
Through public scorn — mud from a muddy spring;
Rulers, who neither see, nor feel, nor know,
But leech-like to their fainting country cling,   5
Till they drop, blind in blood, without a blow;
A people starved and stabbed in the untilled field, —
An army, which liberticide and prey
Makes as a two-edged sword to all who wield;
Golden and sanguine laws which tempt and slay;   10
Religion Christless, Godless — a book sealed;
A Senate, — Time's worst statute unrepealed, —
Are graves, from which a glorious Phantom may
Burst, to illumine our tempestuous day.

1–5: The king was George III, who was insane; his son, who became King George
IV, had been ruling as Prince Regent since 1811. The regent's brothers were an un-
savory lot; one reportedly murdered his wife and valet, and the other made an illegal
marriage with a commoner, fathering many children, and then deserted his wife and
left Parliament to pay the bills. 7: a reference to a severe economic depression suffered
in England after the Napoleonic wars. 10: i.e., laws passed by means of bribery, and
enforced by violence. 12, *Time's worst statute:* the Test Act, which limited the politi-
cal freedoms of Catholics. 13, *Phantom:* liberty.

Robinson Jeffers [1887–1962]

SHINE, PERISHING REPUBLIC

While this America settles in the mold of its vulgarity, heavily thick-
 ening to empire,
And protest, only a bubble in the molten mass, pops and sighs out,
 and the mass hardens,

I sadly smiling remember that the flower fades to make fruit, the fruit
 rots to make earth.
Out of the mother; and through the spring exultances, ripeness and
 decadence; and home to the mother.

You making haste haste on decay: not blameworthy; life is good, be it
 stubbornly long or suddenly   5
A mortal splendor; meteors are not needed less than mountains:
 shine, perishing republic.

But for my children, I would have them keep their distance from the
 thickening center; corruption
Never has been compulsory, when the cities lie at the monster's feet
 there are left the mountains.

And boys, be in nothing so moderate as in love of man, a clever ser-
 vant, insufferable master.
There is the trap that catches noblest spirits, that caught — they say —
 God, when he walked on earth.   10

Robert Watson [b. 1925]

LINES FOR A PRESIDENT

The Inauguration and Shortly After
You could not stop the snow the sky dumped down,
The cold, the lectern smoking when the priest
Invoked the Lord. Did the Lord in answer jab
Your poet blind? Was that your high silk hat
They held against the sun for Robert Frost?   5
And still he could not see his words for you.
Coatless, then, as if winter were not here
You blow cold words, your hand chops air.

Your wife's French chef breaks skulls
Of eggs. Upstairs her dresser   10

Gardens in her hair.
A maid brings scented pearls,
The world of Louis and Molière,
Her conquest of Versailles
And Athens, Downstairs   15
You praise the Spartans.

At the Funeral
Let all those who would stop a war
Sit in a chair and rock
And stare at a woman with flowered hair;
Have her chef prepare   20
A banquet for all the heads of state:
Let them advance between the Spartan guards,
And past the priest and past the poet.
Let the music play, have them dance,
And rocking in your rocking chair,   25
Point to a state of possibility:
The fragile arts of peace
Shatter the weather of war.

Now six grey horses draw you to where you are,
Not to Versailles, Sparta, or Athens.   30
The seventh horse is wild and black
And riderless and paws the streets of Washington
Where you are rocking and will always rock.

John Fitzgerald Kennedy,
You could not stop the shells,   35
The drowning of your boat in war;
You could not stop the snow the sky dumped down,
The cold, the lectern smoking when your priest invoked
The Lord, your poet struck blind, the bullets in your head,
The six grey horses drawing you to where you are   40
Rocking and will always rock.

The seventh horse is riderless, wild and black.

13, *Louis* and *Molière*: Louis XIV of France and Jean-Baptiste Poquelin de Molière (1622–1673), French playwright; they represent an age of extreme refinement; Versailles was Louis's creation.

John Berryman [1914–1972]

DREAM SONG #105

As a kid I believed in democracy: I
'saw no alternative'—teaching at The Big Place I ah
put it in practice:
we'd time for one long novel: to a vote—
Gone with the Wind they voted: I crunched 'No'   *5*
and we sat down with *War & Peace.*

As a man I believed in democracy (nobody
ever learns *any*thing): only one lazy day
my assistant, called James Dow,
& I were chatting, in a failure of meeting of minds,   *10*
and I said curious 'What are your real politics?'
'Oh, I'm a monarchist.'

Finishing his dissertation, in Political Science.
I resign. The universal contempt for Mr Nixon,
whom never I liked but who   *15*
alert & gutsy served us years under a dope.
since dynasty K swarmed in. Let's have a King
maybe, before a few mindless votes.

2, *The Big Place:* Berryman's speaker, Henry (see page 39), has many experiences similar to Berryman's own; the university in question was perhaps a large midwestern institution like the University of Minnesota, where Berryman taught. 17, *dynasty K:* a reference to the Kennedy family—John, Robert, Edward, and others.

Kenneth Patchen [1911–1972]

IN ORDER TO

Apply for the position (I've forgotten now for what) I had to marry the Second Mayor's daughter by twelve noon. The order arrived at three minutes of.

I already had a wife; the Second Mayor was childless: but I did it.

Next they told me to shave off my father's beard. All right. No matter that he'd been a eunuch, and had succumbed in early childhood: I did it, I shaved him.

Then they told me to burn a village; next, a fair-sized town; then, a city; a bigger city; a small down-at-heels country; then one of "the

great powers''; then another (another, another) — In fact, they went
right on until they'd told me to burn up every man-made thing on
the face of the earth! And I did it, I burned away every last trace, I
left nothing, nothing of any kind whatever.

Then they told me to blow it all to hell and gone! And I blew it all to
hell and gone (oh, didn't I) . . .   5

Now, they said, put it back together again; put it all back the way it
was when you started.

Well . . . it was my turn to tell *them* something! Shucks, I didn't want
any job that bad.

May Miller [b. 1900]

THE DIRECTION

Around, around,
All directions go around.
On our way to another place
We meet ourselves coming back.
Within the ends the means are self.   5
Even as the predatory beast adapts
To his golden flash
The camouflage of leaf and grass
We sift all points to our need,
The depth and ceiling one   10
Wherein naked and visible
We stand before bleak mirrors.
                    Behold the image.

There was a flood,
There was an ark.   15
Let none deny it.
In spite of bird and spring branch,
The lie is the new season,
For no one truly forgives.
                    Resist the memory.   20

They are believers in miracles
Who balance hours on pinpoints,
Who rivet shadows in song.
We slay our poets:
The old we reduce to absurdity,   25

The young we sell to skeptics.
The mighty keep their separate way
Tethering great eagles to bear arrows —
E pluribus unum.
A fish in every mound makes green;   30
Delirium cankers the air of cities;
Rot and red ruin corrode the dawn.
Money is made round to roll.
        Let it roll.

So are we heir to that, cursed and starred,   35
Which cries out for fulfillment:
Water, flame, ash in turn.
Yet fragments of asteroids exploded
Move in old restricted orbits
And do not clutter the universe.   40
        A shabby victory of sorts.

Howard Nemerov [b. 1920]

TO THE GOVERNOR & LEGISLATURE OF MASSACHUSETTS

When I took a job teaching in Massachusetts
I didn't know and no one told me that I'd have to sign
An oath of loyalty to the Commonwealth of Massachusetts.
Now that I'm hooked, though, with a house
And a mortgage on the house, the road ahead   5
Is clear: I sign. But I want you gentlemen to know
That till today it never occurred to me
To overthrow the Commonwealth of Massachusetts
By violence or subversion, or by preaching either.
But now I'm not so sure. It makes a fellow think,   10
Can such things be? Can such things be in the very crib
Of our liberties, and East of the Hudson, at that?

So if the day come that I should shove the Berkshire Hills
Over the border and annex them to Vermont,
Or snap Cape Cod off at the elbow and scatter   ·   15
Hyannis to Provincetown beyond the twelve-mile limit,
Proclaiming apocalypsopetls to my pupils
And with state troopers dripping from my fingertips
Squeaking, "You promised, you broke your promise!"
You gentlemen just sit there with my signature   20
And keep on lawyer-talking like nothing happened,
Lest I root out that wagon tongue on Bunker Hill

And fungo your Golden Dome right into Fenway Park
Like any red-celled American boy ought to done
Long ago in the first place, just to keep in practice.   25

12, *east of the Hudson*: i.e., in the civilized world. 17, *apocalypsopetls*: a coined
word combining *apocalypse*, the Book of Revelations — it means prophecy of doom —
and *petl*, a suffix used in the names of certain volcanic mountains, such as Popo-
catepetl in Mexico. The suggestion is of violent, destructive prophecies. 22, *wagon
tongue on Bunker Hill*: Bunker Hill Monument in Boston, the site of the first major
engagement of the Revolutionary War. 23, *fungo*: to hit with a baseball bat; *Golden
Dome*: dome of the state capitol of Massachusetts; *Fenway Park*: Boston's municipal
stadium.

Robert Browning [1812–1889]

THE LOST LEADER

I

Just for a handful of silver he left us,
   Just for a riband to stick in his coat —
Found the one gift of which fortune bereft us,
   Lost all the others she lets us devote;
They, with the gold to give, doled him out silver,   5
   So much was theirs who so little allowed:
How all our copper had gone for his service!
   Rags — were they purple, his heart had been proud!
We that had loved him so, followed him, honored him,
   Lived in his mild and magnificent eye,   10
Learned his great language, caught his clear accents,
   Made him our pattern to live and to die!
Shakespeare was of us, Milton was for us,
   Burns, Shelley, were with us, — they watch from their graves!
He alone breaks from the van and the freemen,   15
   — He alone sinks to the rear and the slaves!

II

We shall march prospering, — not thro' his presence;
   Songs may inspirit us, — not from his lyre;
Deeds will be done, — while he boasts his quiescence,
   Still bidding crouch whom the rest bade aspire: 20
Blot out his name, then, record one lost soul more,
   One task more declined, one more footpath untrod,
One more devils'-triumph and sorrow for angels,
   One wrong more to man, one more insult to God!
Life's night begins: let him never come back to us!   25
   There would be doubt, hesitation and pain,

Forced praise on our part—the glimmer of twilight,
 Never glad confident morning again!
Best fight on well, for we taught him—strike gallantly,
 Menace our heart ere we master his own;   *30*
Then let him receive the new knowledge and wait us,
 Pardoned in heaven, the first by the throne!

 William Wordsworth, liberal in his youth, grew conservative with age. When asked whether he meant to portray Wordsworth here, Browning replied, "I can only answer, with something of shame and contrition, that I undoubtedly had Wordsworth in my mind—but simply as a model . . . I thought of the great Poet's abandonment of liberalism at an unlucky juncture, and no repaying consequence that I could ever see. But once call my fancy-portrait *Wordsworth*—and how much more ought one to say!"

 15, *van:* vanguard.

W. S. Merwin [b. 1927]

CAESAR

My shoes are almost dead
And as I wait at the doors of ice
I hear the cry go up for him Caesar Caesar

But when I look out the window I see only the flatlands
And the slow vanishing of the windmills   *5*
The centuries draining the deep fields

Yet this is still my country
The thug on duty says What would you change
He looks at his watch he lifts
Emptiness out of the vases   *10*
And holds it up to examine

So it is evening
With the rain starting fo fall forever

One by one he calls night out of the teeth
And at last I take up   *15*
My duty

Wheeling the president past banks of flowers
Past the feet of empty stairs
Hoping he's dead

Robert Bly [b. 1926]

THOSE BEING EATEN BY AMERICA

The cry of those being eaten by America,
Others pale and soft being stored for later eating

And Jefferson
Who saw hope in new oats

The wild houses go on   5
With long hair growing from between their toes
The feet at night get up
And run down the long white roads by themselves

The dams reverse themselves and want to go stand alone in the
    desert

Ministers who dive headfirst into the earth   10
The pale flesh
Spreading guiltily into new literatures

That is why these poems are so sad
The long dead running over the fields

The mass sinking down   15
The light in children's faces fading at six or seven

The world will soon break up into small colonies of the saved

David Wagoner [b. 1926]

SONG TO ACCOMPANY THE BEARER OF BAD NEWS

Kings kill their messengers
Sometimes, slicing wildly
Through pages delivering their grief
And you may do the same
With this page under this poem   5
Tear it lengthwise first
With feeling, cutting off
Each phrase into meaningless halves
Then crossways, severing
The mild beginning from the bad ending   10

By now you know the worst
Having imagined the remainder
Down to the painful inch
Where something like your name
Closes this message   15
You needn't finish now
You may stop here
And puzzle it out later.

Kings kill
Sometimes, slicing   20
Through pages
And you may
With this page
Tear it
With feeling   25
Each phrase
Then crossways
The mild beginning
By now you know
Having imagined   30
Down to
Where something
Closes
You needn't finish
You may stop   35
And puzzle it out.

Their messengers
Wildly
Delivering their grief
Do the same   40
Under this poem
Lengthwise first
Cutting off
Into meaningless halves
Severing   45
The bad ending
The worst
The remainder
The painful inch
Like your name   50
This message
Now
Here
Later

You may   tear it   into meaningless halves   ⁵⁵
Lengthwise first   then crossways
Severing   something like   the painful inch
Later   under this poem   messengers
Delivering their grief   puzzle it out
Having imagined   the worst   ⁶⁰
Kings kill   wildly   through pages
Cutting off   the bad ending
Do the same   with this page
By now you know   the mild beginning
Down to where   your name   closes   ⁶⁵
With feeling   now   you may stop.

7
All
That
Mighty
Heart
Urban Complaints
and Celebrations

Thomas Nashe [1567–1601]

A LITANY IN TIME OF PLAGUE

Adieu, farewell, earth's bliss;
This world uncertain is;
Fond are life's lustful joys;
Death proves them all but toys;
None from his darts can fly;   5
I am sick, I must die.
   Lord, have mercy on us!

Rich men, trust not in wealth,
Gold cannot buy you health;
Physic himself must fade.   10
All things to end are made,
The plague full swift goes by;
I am sick, I must die.
   Lord, have mercy on us!

Beauty is but a flower   15
Which wrinkles will devour;
Brightness falls from the air;
Queens have died young and fair;
Dust hath closed Helen's eye.
I am sick, I must die.   20
   Lord, have mercy on us!

Strength stoops unto the grave,
Worms feed on Hector brave;
Swords may not fight with Fate,

Earth still holds ope her gate.

"Come, come!" the bells do cry.

I am sick, I must die.

   Lord, have mercy on us.

Wit with his wantonness

Tasteth death's bitterness;

Hell's executioner

Hath no ears for to hear

What vain art can reply.

I am sick, I must die.

   Lord, have mercy on us.

Haste, therefore, each degree,

To welcome destiny;

Heaven is our heritage,

Earth but a player's stage;

Mount we unto the sky.

I am sick, I must die.

   Lord, have mercy on us.

3, *Fond:* foolish. 19, *Helen:* Helen of Troy. 23, *Hector:* son of Priam; one of the bravest Trojans, he was killed by Achilles.

William Blake [1757–1827]

LONDON

I wander thro' each charter'd street,

Near where the charter'd Thames does flow,

And mark in every face I meet

Marks of weakness, marks of woe.

In every cry of every man,

In every Infant's cry of fear,

In every voice, in every ban,

The mind-forg'd manacles I hear.

How the Chimney-sweeper's cry

Every blackning church appalls;

And the hapless Soldier's sigh

Runs in blood down Palace walls.

London   [**217**]

But most thro' midnight streets I hear
How the youthful Harlot's curse
Blasts the new-born Infant's tear, 15
And blights with plagues the Marriage hearse.

---

1 & 2, *charter'd*: literally, established by charter or decree; the implication is that man has somehow managed to lay down not only the direction in which the streets must go, but also the course of the river Thames.

Jonathan Swift [1667–1745]

A DESCRIPTION OF A CITY SHOWER

Careful observers may foretell the hour
(By sure prognostics) when to dread a shower.
While rain depends, the pensive cat gives o'er
Her frolics, and pursues her tail no more.
Returning home at night, you'll find the sink 5
Strike your offended sense with double stink.
If you be wise, then go not far to dine;
You'll spend in coach-hire more than save in wine.
A coming shower your shooting corns presage,
Old aches throb, your hollow tooth will rage: 10
Sauntering in coffee-house is Dulman seen;
He damns the climate and complains of spleen.
   Meanwhile the South, rising with dabbled wings,
A sable cloud athwart the welkin flings,
That swilled more liquor than it could contain, 15
And, like a drunkard, gives it up again.
Brisk Susan whips her linen from the rope,
While the first drizzling shower is borne aslope:
Such is that sprinkling which some careless quean
Flirts on you from her mop, but not so clean: 20
You fly, invoke the gods; then turning, stop
To rail; she singing, still whirls on her mop,
Not yet the dust had shunned the unequal strife,
But, aided by the wind, fought still for life,
And wafted with its foe by violent gust, 25
'Twas doubtful which was rain and which was dust.
Ah! where must needy poet seek for aid,
When dust and rain at once his coat invade?
His only coat, where dust confused with rain

Erects the nap, and leaves a mingled stain.

30

Now in contiguous drops the flood comes down,
Threatening with deluge this devoted town.
To shops in crowds the daggled females fly,
Pretend to cheapen goods, but nothing buy.
The Templar spruce, while every spout's abroach,

35

Stays till 'tis fair, yet seems to call a coach.
The tucked-up sempstress walks with hasty strides,
While streams run down her oiled umbrella's sides.
Here various kinds, by various fortunes led,
Commence acquaintance underneath a shed.

40

Triumphant Tories and desponding Whigs
Forget their feuds, and join to save their wigs.
Boxed in a chair the beau impatient sits,
While spouts run clattering o'er the roof by fits,
And ever and anon with frightful din

45

The leather sounds; he trembles from within.
So when Troy chairmen bore the wooden steed,
Pregnant with Greeks impatient to be freed
(Those bully Greeks, who, as the moderns do,
Instead of paying chairmen, run them through),

50

Laocoön struck the outside with his spear,
And each imprisoned hero quaked for fear.
Now from all parts the swelling kennels flow,
And bear their trophies with them as they go:
Filth of all hues and odours seem to tell

55

What street they sailed from, by their sight and smell.
They, as each torrent drives with rapid force,
From Smithfield or St. Pulchre's shape their course,
And in huge confluent join at Snow Hill ridge,
Fall from the conduit prone to Holborn Bridge.

60

Sweeping from butchers' stalls, dung, guts, and blood,
Drowned puppies, stinking sprats, all drenched in mud,
Dead cats and turnip-tops come tumbling down the flood.

3, *depends:* is imminent. 5, *sink:* sewer. 11, *Dulman:* a type name from "dull man."
12, *spleen:* melancholy, 19, *quean:* wench. 30, *erects the nap:* stiffens the velvety
short fibers on the fabric. This is a good example of Swift's mock-heroic approach to
his subject. 33, *daggled:* spattered. 34, *cheapen:* to talk prices down. 35, *Templar:*
student of the law; *abroach:* flowing heavily. 41: when this poem was written, the
Tory party had just defeated the Whigs. Swift was involved with the Tories until
1714. 43, *chair:* sedan-chair. 46, *the leather:* the leather roof of the sedan-chair. 47–52:
reference to the story of the Trojan horse; Laocoön hurled a spear at the horse and was
subsequently drowned by sea-serpents. 53, *kennels:* gutters. 58–60: London localities;
St. Pulchre's is the Church of St. Sepulchre. 62, *sprats:* herrings.

Gwendolyn Brooks [b. 1915]

WE REAL COOL

The Pool Players.
Seven at the Golden Shovel.

We real cool. We
Left school. We

Lurk late. We   5
Strike straight. We

Sing sin. We
Thin gin. We

Jazz June. We
Die soon.   10

Oscar Wilde [1856–1900]

THE HARLOT'S HOUSE

We caught the tread of dancing feet,
We loitered down the moonlit street,
And stopped beneath the harlot's house.

Inside, above the din and fray,
We heard the loud musicians play   5
The "Treues Liebes Herz" of Strauss.

Like strange mechanical grotesques,
Making fantastic arabesques,
The shadows raced across the blind.

We watched the ghostly dancers spin   10
To sound of horn and violin,
Like black leaves wheeling in the wind.

Like wire pulled automatons,
Slim silhouetted skeletons
Went sidling through the slow quadrille.   15

They took each other by the hand,
And danced a stately saraband;
Their laughter echoed thin and shrill.

Sometimes a clockwork puppet pressed
A phantom lover to her breast,
Sometimes they seemed to try to sing.

Sometimes a horrible marionette
Came out, and smoked its cigarette
Upon the steps like a live thing.

Then, turning to my love, I said,
"The dead are dancing with the dead,
The dust is whirling with the dust."

But she—she heard the violin,
And left my side, and entered in:
Love passed into the house of lust.

Then suddenly the tune went false,
The dancers wearied of the waltz,
The shadows ceased to wheel and whirl.

And down the long and silent street,
The dawn, with silver-sandaled feet,
Crept like a frightened girl.

20

25

30

35

6: "Heart of True Love," a waltz by Johann Strauss (1825–1899). 15, *quadrille:* a kind of square dance. 17, *saraband:* a slow Spanish dance.

Thomas Hardy [1840–1928]

THE RUINED MAID

"O 'Melia, my dear, this does everything crown!
Who could have supposed I should meet you in Town?
And whence such fair garments, such prosperi-ty?"—
"O didn't you know I'd been ruined?" said she.

—"You left us in tatters, without shoes or socks,
Tired of digging potatoes, and spudding up docks;
And now you've gay bracelets and bright feathers three!"—
"Yes: that's how we dress when we're ruined," said she.

—"At home in the barton you said 'thee' and 'thou,'
And 'thik oon,' and 'theäs oon,' and 't'other'; but now

5

10

Your talking quite fits 'ee for high compa-ny!" —
"Some polish is gained with one's ruin," said she.

—"Your hands were like paws then, your face blue and bleak,
But now I'm bewitched by your delicate cheek,
And your little gloves fit as on any la-dy!" —   *15*
"We never do work when we're ruined," said she.

—"You used to call home-life a hag-ridden dream,
And you'd sigh, and you'd sock; but at present you seem
To know not of megrims or melancho-ly!" —
"True. One's pretty lively when ruined," said she.   *20*

—"I wish I had feathers, a fine sweeping gown,
And a delicate face, and could strut about Town!" —
"My dear — a raw country girl, such as you be,
Cannot quite expect that. You ain't ruined," said she.

6, *spudding up docks:* spading up weeds. 9, *barton:* farm. 10, *thik oon:* country
dialect for "this one"; *theäs oon:* "that one." 18, *sock:* groan. 19, *megrims:* bad moods.

T. S. Eliot [1888–1965]

PRELUDES

I

The winter evening settles down
With smell of steaks in passageways.
Six o'clock.
The burnt-out ends of smoky days.
And now a gusty shower wraps   *5*
The grimy scraps
Of withered leaves about your feet
And newspapers from vacant lots;
The showers beat
On broken blinds and chimney-pots,   *10*
And at the corner of the street
A lonely cab-horse steams and stamps.
And then the lighting of the lamps.

II

The morning comes to consciousness
Of faint stale smells of beer   *15*

From the sawdust-trampled street
With all its muddy feet that press
To early coffee-stands.
With the other masquerades
That time resumes,   20
One thinks of all the hands
That are raising dingy shades
In a thousand furnished rooms.

III
You tossed a blanket from the bed,
You lay upon your back, and waited;   25
You dozed, and watched the night revealing
The thousand sordid images
Of which your soul was constituted;
They flickered against the ceiling.
And when all the world came back   30
And the light crept up between the shutters
And you heard the sparrows in the gutters,
You had such a vision of the street
As the street hardly understands;
Sitting along the bed's edge, where   35
You curled the papers from your hair,
Or clasped the yellow soles of feet
In the palms of both soiled hands.

IV
His soul stretched tight across the skies
That fade behind a city block,   40
Or trampled by insistent feet
At four and five and six o'clock;
And short square fingers stuffing pipes,
And evening newspapers, and eyes
Assured of certain certainties,   45
The conscience of a blackened street
Impatient to assume the world.

    I am moved by fancies that are curled
Around these images, and cling:
The notion of some infinitely gentle   50
Infinitely suffering thing.

    Wipe your hand across your mouth, and laugh;
The worlds revolve like ancient women
Gathering fuel in vacant lots.

Barbara Howes [b. 1914]

CITY AFTERNOON

Far, far down
The earth rumbles in sleep;
Up through its iron grille,
The subway, black as a chimney-
Sweep, growls. An escalator rides   5
On dinosaur spines
Toward day. And on beyond,
Old bones, bottles,
A dismantled piano, sets
Of Mrs. Humphrey Ward all whirl   10
In the new disposal-unit; above
Its din, apartments are tenanted
Tight as hen-houses, people roosting
In every cupboard. Eighty storeys
Up, pigeons nest on the noise   15
Or strut above it; higher,
The outcast sun serves its lean meat
Of light.

The whinnying
Of Venetian blinds has ceased: we sit   20
Invisible in this room,
Behind glass. In a lull,
A chance abatement of sound, a scalping
Silence, far
Down we hear the Iron   25
Maiden whisper,
Closing upon her spikes.

10, *Mrs. Humphrey Ward:* Mary Augusta Ward (1851–1920), a prolific British novelist, 25–26, *Iron/Maiden:* a medieval instrument of torture, the iron maiden was an iron box of human shape and size, hinged at one side and lined with spikes which pierced anyone forced to get in the box and have it closed on him.

Stephen Spender [b. 1909]

AN ELEMENTARY SCHOOL CLASSROOM IN A SLUM

Far far from gusty waves, these children's faces.
Like rootless weeds the torn hair round their paleness.
The tall girl with her weighed-down head. The paper-

seeming boy with rat's eyes. The stunted unlucky heir
Of twisted bones, reciting a father's gnarled disease,   5
His lesson from his desk. At back of the dim class,
One unnoted, sweet and young: his eyes live in a dream
Of squirrels' game, in tree room, other than this.

On sour cream walls, donations. Shakespeare's head
Cloudless at dawn, civilized dome riding all cities.   10
Belled, flowery, Tyrolese valley. Open-handed map
Awarding the world its world. And yet, for these
Children, these windows, not this world, are world,
Where all their future's painted with a fog,
A narrow street sealed in with a lead sky,   15
Far far from rivers, capes, and stars of words.

Surely Shakespeare is wicked, the map a bad example
With ships and sun and love tempting them to steal —
For lives that slyly turn in their cramped holes
From fog to endless night? On their slag heap, these children   20
Wear skins peeped through by bones and spectacles of steel
With mended glass, like bottle bits on stones.
All of their time and space are foggy slum
So blot their maps with slums as big as doom.

Unless, governor, teacher, inspector, visitor,   25
This map becomes their window and these windows
That open on their lives like crouching tombs
Break, O break open, till they break the town
And show the children to the fields and all their world
Azure on their sands, to let their tongues   30
Run naked into books, the white and green leaves open
The history theirs whose language is the sun.

11, *Tyrolese:* the Tyrol is a region in the Alps of western Austria and northern Italy.
20, *slag heap:* a heap of the waste material left over from various kinds of mineral
refining.

John Vernon [b. 1943]

NOT HAVING A HISTORY

In the city, as soon as you fall someone is there to catch you,
in a moment an ambulance speeds you to the hospital,
expert fingers take off your shirt and pants.

Later you realize that none of this happened to you,
it happened to someone else.   5
Back at work, you realize you have no history.
Others who know where they've been
can say no or yes as they please
and the word funnels down from a decisive bulk of experience.
For them, history swarms up like a flock of birds in the skin,   10
there's no stopping it, they pound their fist
turning from the window, I have it!
take a letter!

But a man without a history is apt to look out the window for a long
    time,
to cancel all his appointments for the afternoon   15
thinking no, yes, what should I say,
and the light gleaming off the flint and glass
of the spacious and busy city outside
is apt to remind him of nothing.
He thinks of the primeval forest   20
where a man can die clutching ferns
and nobody finds him.

The city is better than the primeval forest.
If I had to choose anything to clutch
while the rest of me was letting go   25
it would be a pillow-case in a clean room
in a hospital overlooking the city.

William Jay Smith [b. 1918]

WHAT TRAIN WILL COME?

For Jack and Marty Hall
What train will come to bear me back across so wide a town?

—found scrawled in a subway station

Snow drifts melt in the streets, pock-marked at the curb
    as by newsprint, and the wind whips up the snow; the air tastes
    of black foam;

The world becomes a wet newspaper into whose blown pages now
    I step, snow mounting all around,

Smudged white walls where howling newsprint peels, tooth-white
  crevasses on which graffiti dance.

The wet dark rushes up as I descend where the black turnstile
  rests, an upended propeller,

And the steps at the edge of the platform echo as if from
  another deserted platform toward another on and on   5

Like the tapping of miners through the dark; and my heel clicks
  in the cold on a toothless silver comb . . .

                    What train will come?

Wet clings to my body; gray ash sifts down upon the track
  unwinding ahead, and I can hear far off — or is it far off in the
  mind? — the clang of car on car,

The human chain, the haunted sound; and before me a broken
  mirror swings in the void at the track's edge

And through it cracks spread from a dark center — veins
  like roots tunnelling through the ground —   10

And my step clicks on cement, and whichever way I move — from
  whichever way the train will come — the way is down . . .

While wheels — remembered wheels — turn dizzily before me
  with the broken glass

And in the glass a face that in the silence spreads and turns;
  and in my chest a heart-beat like a distant drum . . .

                    What train will come?

Glass glints; shoe creaks . . . A small child, I walked after
  a tornado in the city, holding my mother's hand,   15

The sky open again above us like a wound drained of blood, the
  pale edges folded in upon a pink center;

I strolled beside her, and she seemed to spin off from me in
  her dress of voile, her cartwheel hat;

And I gazed out on tilted and shattered telephone poles, their
   wires trailing over sidewalks like black spaghetti;

An acrid taste of burning bread hovered in the air; the most
   intimate parts of buildings had been ripped off, and here
   a bed dangled down

And there was the smell of buried flesh; and I was sick and
   wanted to hide my face and run to some green spot, gaze up
   at a proper sun-lit dome . . .   20

                        What train will come?

O violent earth: I think of the morning Darwin saw you,
   "the very emblem of all that is solid," a world

That had moved overnight beneath his feet "like a crust over
   a fluid," and when he sailed into Talcahuano Bay

All was strangely still: after the battering waves, water black and
   boiling where the seabed had seemed to crack open;

The shore was strewn with debris, ships keeling over on a
   plain of mud and soggy seaweed,   25

Burst cotton bales, dead animals, uprooted trees, housetops
   lay tossed about and huge rocks covered the beaches;

And there had been little warning: the first shocks, and then
   the curious twisting movement, making the ground open and
   then close again — as on a tomb . . .

                        What train will come?

But now we do not wait: we rip the earth apart ourselves,
   bulldoze the dead before us,

Make a desert of our blue earth, and explore the desert moon,
   bringing   30

Her rocks to add to those we pile upon our dead, while in an
   empty landscape of slag heaps

And smoking lagoons the black poor gather under a low sky, and
   trapped light hovers like false dawn;

The assassin's bullet is answered by a quiet voice: "Put
your banners down; go quietly home . . ."

And another bullet answers; and still the banners rage and
blaze and burn: Which way is back? Which way is home?

What train will come?

35

Violence breeds violence until the chain binds and slashes
over burned-over ground

And the distant war is brought closer, diminished on the TV
screen: men kill men, and all three inches tall . . .

In a small skirmish — "little activity, two or three dead,
nothing extraordinary,"

In a country that is soft and wet and hot; now under whirling
chopper blades the grass huts blaze

And the little moon-faced people are lined up for a roll of
color film — men, women, children — and shot down   40

And with cadaver obedience heaped by rice paddy and rubble —
all to be neatly held one day upon a screen within a frame
of chrome . . .

What train will come?

Three inches tall (in memory) I wander up and down . . . Ah,
once I loved a stone, the shape of water winding through

Wild rose, sweet william, Indian paint brush, and in the woods
a woman (was it my mother?) walking in yellow lace

Through violet shadows, nodding and talking . . . And I left her
there by the stream . . . and then that night found her again   45

Locked in a little room at the top of the stairs, moaning and
calling as if from underground,

And the club that had beaten her rested like some heraldic
emblem beside the door where the drunken man had placed it;

And I knelt down, staring into my own vomit, helpless, dazed,
and dumb . . .

What Train Will Come? [**229**]

What train will come?

O dreadful night! . . . What train will come? . . . What tree is
   that? . . . a sycamore—the mottled bark stripped bare, *50*

Desolate in winter light against the track, and I continue
   on to the mudflats

By the roaring river where garbage, chicken coops, and houses
   rush by me on mud-crested waves,

And at my feet are dead fish—catfish, gars—and there in a
   little inlet

Come on a deserted camp, the tin can in which the hoboes brewed
   their coffee stained bitter black

As the cinders sweeping ahead under a milkweed-colored sky
   along a darkening track *55*

   And gaze into a slough's green stagnant foam,
     and know that the way out is never back,

       but down,

          down . . .

     What train will come

      to bear me back

     across so wide a town?

22–27: In *The Voyage of the Beagle*, Charles Darwin (1809–1882) describes the
eruption of a Chilean volcano and the results of an earthquake in the harbor of Con-
cepción, Chile.

Richard Wilbur [b. 1921]

JUNK

      Huru Welandes
           worc ne geswiceð
     monna ænigum

> Ꝇara ꝺe Mimming can
> heardne gehealdan.
>
> WALDERE

An axe angles
        from my neighbor's ashcan;
It is hell's handiwork,
        the wood not hickory,
The flow of the grain
        not faithfully followed.
The shivered shaft
        rises from a shellheap
Of plastic playthings,
        paper plates,   5
And the sheer shards
        of shattered tumblers
That were not annealed
        for the time needful.
At the same curbside,
        a cast-off cabinet
Of wavily-warped
        unseasoned wood
Waits to be trundled
        in the trash-man's truck.   10
Haul them off! Hide them!
        The heart winces
For junk and gimcrack,
        for jerrybuilt things
And the men who make them
        for a little money,
Bartering pride
        like the bought boxer
Who pulls his punches,
        or the paid-off jockey   15
Who in the home stretch
        holds in his horse.
Yet the things themselves
        in thoughtless honor
Have kept composure,
        like captives who would not
Talk under torture.
        Tossed from a tailgate
Where the dump displays
        its random dolmens,   20
Its black barrows
        and blazing valleys,

They shall waste in the weather
                    toward what they were.
The sun shall glory
             in the glitter of glass-chips,
Foreseeing the salvage
              of the prisoned sand,
And the blistering paint
                  peel off in patches,   25
That the good grain
              be discovered again.
Then burnt, bulldozed,
                they shall all be buried
To the depth of diamonds,
                 in the making dark
Where halt Hephaestus
              keeps his hammer
And Wayland's work
             is worn away.   30

"The epigraph, taken from a fragmentary Anglo-Saxon poem, concerns the legendary smith Wayland, and may roughly be translated: 'Truly, Wayland's handiwork — the sword Mimming which he made — will never fail any man who knows how to use it bravely.'" (Wilbur's note.)

20, *dolmens*: literally, a prehistoric monument made of stone. 29, *Hephaestus*: in Greek mythology, the god of fire and of the blacksmith's forge; he was lame ("halt").

Ezra Pound [1885–1972]

IN A STATION OF THE METRO

The apparition of these faces in the crowd;
Petals on a wet, black bough.

William Wordsworth [1770–1850]

COMPOSED UPON WESTMINSTER BRIDGE, SEPTEMBER 3, 1802

Earth has not anything to show more fair:
Dull would he be of soul who could pass by
A sight so touching in its majesty;
This City now doth, like a garment, wear
The beauty of the morning; silent, bare,   5
Ships, towers, domes, theatres, and temples lie
Open unto the fields, and to the sky;

All bright and glittering in the smokeless air.
Never did sun more beautifully steep
In his first splendor, valley, rock, or hill;   ¹⁰
Ne'er saw I, never felt, a calm so deep!
The river glideth at his own sweet will;
Dear God! the very houses seem asleep;
And all that mighty heart is lying still!

9, *steep:* immerse.

Allen Ginsberg [b. 1926]

A SUPERMARKET IN CALIFORNIA

What thoughts I have of you tonight, Walt Whitman, for I walked down the sidestreets under the trees with a headache self-conscious looking at the full moon.

In my hungry fatigue, and shopping for images, I went into the neon fruit supermarket, dreaming of your enumerations!

What peaches and what penumbras! Whole families shopping at night! Aisles full of husbands! Wives in the avocados, babies in the tomatoes! — and you, Garcia Lorca, what were you doing down by the watermelons?

I saw you, Walt Whitman, childless, lonely old grubber, poking among the meats in the refrigerator and eyeing the grocery boys.

I heard you asking questions of each: Who killed the pork chops? What price bananas? Are you my Angel?   5

I wandered in and out of the brilliant stacks of cans following you, and followed in my imagination by the store detective.

We strode down the open corridors together in our solitary fancy tasting artichokes, possessing every frozen delicacy, and never passing the cashier.

Where are we going, Walt Whitman? The doors close in an hour. Which way does your beard point tonight?

(I touch your book and dream of our odyssey in the supermarket and feel absurd.)

Will we walk all night through solitary streets? The trees add shade to shade, lights out in the houses, we'll both be lonely.   10

Will we stroll dreaming of the lost America of love past blue automobiles in driveways, home to our silent cottage?

Ah, dear father, graybeard, lonely old courage-teacher, what America

did you have when Charon quit poling his ferry and you got out on
a smoking bank and stood watching the boat disappear on the black
waters of Lethe?

1, *Walt Whitman*: the American poet; see pages 195, 242, 269, and 283. 3, *Garcia Lorca* (1899–1936): Spanish poet and dramatist. 12, *Charon*: in Greek mythology, the ferryman of the Underworld, who ferried dead souls across the rivers Styx and Acheron into the region of dead souls; *Lethe*: another river in Hades, which had the power of making souls forget their past lives before being reincarnated.

James Tate [b. 1943]

COMING DOWN CLEVELAND AVENUE

The fumes from all kinds
of machines have dirtied
the snow. You propose
to polish it, the miles
between home and wherever   5
you and your lily
of a woman might go. You
go, pail, brush, and
suds, scrubbing down
Cleveland Avenue   10
toward the Hartford Life
Insurance Company. No
one appreciates your
effort and one important
character calls you   15
a baboon. But pretty
soon your darling jumps
out of an elevator
and kisses you and you
sing and tell her to   20
walk the white plains
proudly. At one point
you even lay down
your coat, and she, in
turn, puts hers down for   25
you. And you put your
shirt down, and she, her
blouse, and your pants,
and her skirt, shoes—
removes her lavender   30
underwear and you slip
into her proud, white skin.

Josephine Miles [b. 1911]

REASON

Said, Pull her up a bit will you, Mac, I want to unload there.
Said, Pull her up my rear end, first come first serve.
Said, Give her the gun, Bud, he needs a taste of his own bumper.
Then the usher came out and got into the act:

Said, Pull her up, pull her up a bit, we need this space, sir.   5
Said, For God's sake, is this still a free country or what?
You go back and take care of Gary Cooper's horse
And leave me handle my own car.

Saw them unloading the lame old lady,
Ducked out under the wheel and gave her an elbow,   10
Said, All you needed to do was just explain;
Reason, Reason is my middle name.

David Ignatow [b. 1914]

THE BAGEL

I stopped to pick up the bagel
rolling away in the wind,
annoyed with myself
for having dropped it
as it were a portent.   5
Faster and faster it rolled,
with me running after it
bent low, gritting my teeth,
and I found myself doubled over
and rolling down the street   10
head over heels, one complete somersault
after another like a bagel
and strangely happy with myself.

R. H. W. Dillard [b. 1937]

DOWNTOWN ROANOKE

1.
The streetlights blink DONT WALK WALK
DONT WALK and the cars are filling
The air with burnt gas. And all will pass.
I often think and secretly suspect

Big Lick will come again and cows
Will graze in downtown Roanoke.

2.

A trip to the zoo: where we watch
The llamas chew and stare, stare
At the bears and pat the baby goats.
We walk by the crazy mirrors
Where we are stranger than the strangers
In the cages, furry and climbing
On the wire of their cages.
We ride the small train and wave
Out over the edge of the mountain,
Wave down at the valley, the puzzle
Of downtown Roanoke.

3.

The star on the mountain turns red
Whenever someone dies in the street,
But I have heard (although I have not seen)
That late at night in the earliest
Of morning, someone always turns
It red and then, I wonder, does
Someone gasp and stumble into a car
And die in downtown Roanoke?

4.

The mayor puffs on his cigar,
(The mayor is my dad), puffs
On his cigar, and the children
Dance around his legs, they sing
And toss petals in the smoky air,
And the mayor puffs on his cigar,
(The mayor is my dad), while people
Stare, he puffs, the little ones,
They dance and sing, the people
On the sidewalks think it strange, they
Do not understand in downtown Roanoke.

5.

From the airport the whisper jet
Rises on a wisp of black smoke
And a thunderous roar, draws me
To the door to observe. It is
A pale night and the lights
Of the plane are blinking green
And red. The star is white.

And the jet flies on while
The moon is full, as I think   45
Seriously of climbing in my car
And driving down 581 to see
The empty streets of downtown Roanoke.

6.

The Park and the Roanoke
And even the Rialto are parking   50
Lots. The Academy of Music
With its famed acoustics
Where Caruso and others sang
Is long down and gone.
There are many parking lots   55
And garages in downtown Roanoke.

7.

The Pakistani gentleman said,
In progress to a nearby college,
"I have lived in the vale of Kashmir
For much of my life, but I would   60
Gladly live and die in this valley."
The valley is green, the mountains blue,
All around downtown Roanoke.

8.

The furniture store across the street
From the main fire house has burned   65
Nearly to the ground three times.
The smoke hung low and red, the red
Stop lights blinked, but no sirens
Were required in downtown Roanoke.

9.

And when it rains, it pours water   70
In streams down the windows of the stores
And blurs the names, and down the windshields
Of heavy trucks and delivery vans. It wets
Down the dust and cleans the air and wets
The trainmen's high striped hats, makes   75
All the highways slick, and pours
Down all the undertakers' black umbrellas.
When it rains, the water runs down
The tombstones in each of the various cemeteries
And wears down the stone and wears down   80
The names into the ground where their dust
Lies. And when it rains, it wets the sides

Of buildings, and the building by the tracks
Built out of coal sheds long black streams
That crawl across the sidewalk, streak the gutters,   *85*
And run down the streets of downtown Roanoke.

10.

There was once a pool hall one flight
Down across the street from another
One just one flight up. The lower
One had a sign that read BILLIARDS.   *90*
The higher one is still there, one
Flight above downtown Roanoke.

11.

There are many birds in Roanoke.
I have seen: a great blue heron,
A green heron, the shy least bittern,   *95*
Orioles and robins, killdeers
Live near our house, and sandpipers,
Cow birds who pick the dung of cows,
Wrens and sparrows, the familiar
Cardinals and blue jays, martins   *100*
And swallows, warblers make the air
Yellow in the spring, grackles,
A hundred cedar waxwings my mother found
Eating berries in a dogwood tree,
And towhees, nighthawks, and high   *105*
Overhead, their wings ragged
And spread wide, vultures, black
And circling over downtown Roanoke.

12.

My wife is from Pittsburgh.
Our dog is from Georgia. My friends   *110*
Are from New York and South Carolina,
Florida, Texas and northern Virginia,
Norfolk and even Connecticut.
My grandparents and parents
Are all from south of here,   *115*
From Franklin and Henry counties.
My wife says I am the only native,
That all the other inhabitants
Are castaways in downtown Roanoke.

13.

At early dusk in Roanoke the lights go on,   *120*
Neon, they're red and green, are purple,
Never gold, blink, stammer and fizz,

And say the names of things to people
Driving through, walking the streets,
On Pullmans in the railway yards   125
Waiting for the porter to make their beds.
The sign for YELLOW CAB is red and shines
Through white smoke to make the center
Of the city blaze like the mouth of hell
At early dusk. And outside the light   130
With only one red neon light at night,
The topless go-go girls lift up their knees,
They shake their breasts and do the frug
And bugaloo, they never smile, dance
In the dark beyond the light in downtown Roanoke.   135

14.

There is a blind lady with tilting
Scales on the seal and flag of Roanoke,
With steaming railroad trains
Shuffling at her knees. She appears
To be a young lady, and there is a great   140
Cogwheel or gear beside her.
The flag is blue. When they took
The one in the Council chambers
Down to make a copy, it fell
Into many pieces. One small piece   145
With one full pan of the blind lady's
Scales flew out of the window,
Across the lawn and into the traffic
Grinding gears in downtown Roanoke.

15.

We are watching the night, and the wind   150
Is very high. It strums the TV antenna.
It blows the dog's ears and makes
The windows rattle. The large highway
Signs hum in the wind. It makes
The heavy neon and steel star shake.   155
Perhaps it will accidentally turn
Red. It blows around and all round
The valley, wrinkling the new pale
Leaves on the trees, blowing
An occasional bird's nest over   160
And scattering the eggs. The wind
Blows up the streets and slaps
A bus transfer against the window
Of an elementary school principal's
House. She stops grading papers   165

And thinks of calling the police.
It rattles a paper cup up Jefferson
Street from the viaduct, a right
Turn onto Campbell Avenue, wrong
Way onto a one way street, turns left   *170*
On First Street at Fine's Men's Shop
And passing Kirk winds up in a storm
Drain at the corner of First and Church.
The wind blows the flat metal signs
On the side streets, blows grit   *175*
Into a rookie policeman's eyes.
He almost draws his gun but instead
Steps into the pool hall door. It blows
All up and down the streets, moans
In the halls of the empty office   *180*
Buildings, rattles the mayor's door,
And the door of my dentist next door,
And the door of the Office of Smoke Control.
The wind blows the mercury vapor lamps
That keep it always light in downtown Roanoke.   *185*

5, *Big Lick:* this is the original name of the settlement on the Roanoke River in southwest Virginia which became the city of Roanoke (approximate population, 100,000). 27: "the mayor is my dad" is a phrase which might well be taken figuratively, but before going too far with such an interpretation, it is well to know that Benton O. Dillard, the poet's father, was in fact mayor of Roanoke for several years until 1968.

8
With
Multitudinous
Will

War

Henry Reed [b. 1914]

NAMING OF PARTS

from LESSONS OF THE WAR

Today we have naming of parts. Yesterday,
We had daily cleaning. And tomorrow morning,
We shall have what to do after firing. But today,
Today we have naming of parts. Japonica
Glistens like coral in all of the neighboring gardens,   5
    And today we have naming of parts.

This is the lower sling swivel. And this
Is the upper sling swivel, whose use you will see,
When you are given your slings. And this is the piling swivel,
Which in your case you have not got. The branches   10
Hold in the gardens their silent, eloquent gestures,
    Which in our case we have not got.

This is the safety-catch, which is always released
With an easy flick of the thumb. And please do not let me
See anyone using his finger. You can do it quite easy   15
If you have any strength in your thumb. The blossoms
Are fragile and motionless, never letting anyone see
    Any of them using their finger.

And this you can see is the bolt. The purpose of this
Is to open the breech, as you see. We can slide it   20
Rapidly backwards and forwards: we call this
Easing the spring. And rapidly backwards and forwards
The early bees are assaulting and fumbling the flowers:
    They call it easing the Spring.

They call it easing the Spring: it is perfectly easy 25
If you have any strength in your thumb: like the bolt,
And the breech, and the cocking-piece, and the point of balance,
Which in our case we have not got; and the almond-blossom
Silent in all of the gardens and the bees going backwards and
   forwards,
     For today we have naming of parts. 30

For a discussion of this poem, see pages 35–36.

Walt Whitman [1819–1892]

CAVALRY CROSSING A FORD

A line in long array where they wind betwixt green islands,
They take a serpentine course, their arms flash in the sun — hark
   to the musical clank,
Behold the silvery river, in it the splashing horses loitering stop to
   drink,
Behold the brown-faced men, each group, each person a picture,
   the negligent rest on the saddles,
Some emerge on the opposite bank, others are just entering the ford —
   while, 5
Scarlet and blue and snowy white,
The guidon flags flutter gayly in the wind.

7, *guidon flags:* small pennants carried by guides of mounted cavalry.

Robert Frost [1874–1963]

RANGE-FINDING

The battle rent a cobweb diamond-strung
And cut a flower beside a groundbird's nest
Before it stained a single human breast.
The stricken flower bent double and so hung.
And still the bird revisited her young. 5
A butterfly its fall had dispossessed,
A moment sought in air his flower of rest,
Then lightly stooped to it and fluttering clung.
On the bare upland pasture there had spread
O'ernight 'twixt mullein stalks a wheel of thread 10

And straining cables wet with silver dew.
A sudden passing bullet shook it dry.
The indwelling spider ran to greet the fly,
But finding nothing, sullenly withdrew.

10, *mullein*: a tall, coarse plant related to the snapdragon.

W. D. Snodgrass [b. 1926]

"AFTER EXPERIENCE TAUGHT ME . . ."

After experience taught me that all the ordinary
Surroundings of social life are futile and vain;

> I'm going to show you something very
> Ugly: someday, it might save your life.

Seeing that none of the things I feared contain   5
In themselves anything either good or bad

> What if you get caught without a knife;
> Nothing — even a loop of piano wire;

Excepting only in the effect they had
Upon my mind, I resolved to inquire   10

> Take the first two fingers of this hand;
> Fork them out — kind of a "V for Victory" —

Whether there might be something whose discovery
Would grant me supreme, unending happiness.

> And jam them into the eyes of your enemy.   15
> You have to do this hard. Very hard. Then press

No virtue can be thought to have priority
Over this endeavor to preserve one's being.

> Both fingers down around the cheekbone
> And setting your foot high into the chest   20

No man can desire to act rightly, to be blessed,
To live rightly, without simultaneously

You must call up every strength you own
And you can rip off the whole facial mask.

Wishing to be, to act, to live. He must ask   *25*
First, in other words, to actually exist.

    And you, whiner, who wastes your time
      Dawdling over the remorseless earth,
    What evil, what unspeakable crime
      Have you made your life worth?   *30*

    The pairs of lines nearest the left margin are an adaptation of the beginning of "On
the Improvement of the Understanding," by Baruch Spinoza (1632–1677), in the
translation by John Wild: "After experience has taught me that all the usual surround-
ings of social life are vain and futile; seeing that none of the objects of my fears con-
tained in themselves anything either good or bad, except in so far as the mind is af-
fected by them, I finally resolved to inquire whether there might be some real good
having power to communicate itself, which would affect the mind singly, to the ex-
clusion of all else; whether, in fact, there might be anything of which the discovery
and attainment would enable me to enjoy continuous, supreme, and unending hap-
piness."

Michael Drayton [1563–1631]

THE BALLAD OF AGINCOURT

Fair stood the wind for France,
When we our sails advance,
Nor now to prove our chance,
    Longer will tarry;
But putting to the main   *5*
At Kaux, the mouth of Seine,
With all his martial train,
    Landed King Harry.

And taking many a fort,
Furnished in warlike sort,   *10*
Marcheth towards Agincourt,
    In happy hour;
Skirmishing day by day
With those that stopped his way,
Where the French general lay   *15*
    With all his power.

Which in his height of pride,
King Henry to deride,

His ransom to provide
  To the King sending;
Which he neglects the while
As from a nation vile,
Yet with an angry smile,
  Their fall portending.

And turning to his men,
Quoth our brave Henry then:
"Though they to one be ten,
  Be not amazèd.
Yet have we well begun;
Battles so bravely won
Have ever to the sun
  By fame been raisèd.

"And for my self," quoth he,
"This my full rest shall be,
England ne'er mourn for me,
  Nor more esteem me;
Victor I will remain,
Or on this earth lie slain,
Never shall she sustain
  Loss to redeem me."

Poitiers and Crécy tell,
When most their pride did swell,
Under our swords they fell;
  No less our skill is
Than when our grandsire great,
Claiming the regal seat
By many a warlike feat,
  Lopped the French lilies.

The Duke of York so dread
The eager vaward led;
With the main Henry sped
  Amongst his henchmen.
Excester had the rear,
A braver man not there;
O Lord, how hot they were
  On the false Frenchmen!

They now to fight are gone,
Armor on armor shone,
Drum now to drum did groan;

To hear was wonder,
That with cries they make
The very earth did shake,
Trumpet to trumpet spake,
    Thunder to thunder.

Well it thine age became,
O noble Erpingham,
Which didst the signal aim
    To our hid forces;
When from a meadow by,
Like a storm suddenly,
The English archery
    Stuck the French horses.

With Spanish yew so strong,
Arrows a cloth-yard long,
That like to serpents stung,
    Piercing the weather;
None from his fellow starts,
But playing manly parts,
And like true English hearts,
    Stuck close together.

When down their bows they threw,
And forth their bilboes drew,
And on the French they flew,
    Not one was tardy;
Arms were from shoulders sent,
Scalps to the teeth were rent,
Down the French peasants went;
    Our men were hardy.

This while our noble King,
His broad sword brandishing,
Down the French host did ding,
    As to o'er-whelm it;
And many a deep wound lent,
His arms with blood besprent,
And many a cruel dent
    Bruisëd his helmet.

Gloster, that Duke so good,
Next of the royal blood,
For famous England stood

With his brave brother;
Clarence, in steel so bright,
Though but a maiden knight,
Yet in that furious fight,
    Scarce such another.

Warwick in blood did wade,
Oxford the foe invade,
And cruel slaughter made,
    Still as they ran up;
Suffolk his axe did ply,
Beaumont and Willoughby
Bare them right doughtily,
    Ferrers and Fanhope.

Upon Saint Crispin's day
Fought was this noble fray,
Which fame did not delay
    To England to carry;
O, when shall English men
With such acts fill a pen,
Or England breed again,
    Such a King Harry?

Agincourt: a small town in northern France where, on St. Crispin's Day (October 25) 1415, Henry V of England defeated the French. Another depiction of the battle occurs in Shakespeare's *Henry V*. 28, *amazëd*: perplexed. 41, *Poitiers and Crécy*: French cities, scenes of earlier English successes in the Hundred Years' War. 50, *vaward*: vanguard. 73–74: *Spanish yew* is a strong, resilient wood, useful in bows; a *cloth-yard* is a yard. 82, *bilboes*: swords. 91, *ding*: batter. 94, *besprent*: spattered. 102, *maiden knight*: a knight in his first battle.

Ralph Waldo Emerson [1803–1882]

CONCORD HYMN

Sung at the completion of the Battle Monument, July 4, 1837

By the rude bridge that arched the flood,
    Their flag to April's breeze unfurled,
Here once the embattled farmers stood
    And fired the shot heard round the world.

The foe long since in silence slept;
    Alike the conqueror silent sleeps;

And Time the ruined bridge has swept
   Down the dark stream which seaward creeps.

On this green bank, by this soft stream,
   We set to-day a votive stone;   *10*
That memory may their deed redeem,
   When, like our sires, our sons are gone.

Spirit, that made those heroes dare
   To die, and leave their children free,
Bid Time and Nature gently spare   *15*
    The shaft we raise to them and thee.

Alfred, Lord Tennyson [1809–1892]

THE CHARGE OF THE LIGHT BRIGADE

Half a league, half a league,
Half a league onward,
All in the valley of Death
   Rode the six hundred.
"Forward, the Light Brigade!   *5*
Charge for the guns!" he said.
Into the valley of Death
   Rode the six hundred.

"Forward, the Light Brigade!"
Was there a man dismayed?   *10*
Not though the soldier knew
   Some one had blundered:
Theirs not to make reply,
Theirs not to reason why,
Theirs but to do and die.   *15*
Into the valley of Death
   Rode the six hundred.

Cannon to right of them,
Cannon to left of them,
Cannon in front of them   *20*
   Volleyed and thundered;
Stormed at with shot and shell,
Boldly they rode and well,
Into the jaws of Death,
Into the mouth of Hell   *25*
   Rode the six hundred.

Flashed all their sabres bare,
Flashed as they turned in air
Sabring the gunners there,
Charging an army, while   30
   All the world wondered:
Plunged in the battery-smoke
Right through the line they broke;
Cossack and Russian
Reeled from the sabre-stroke   35
   Shattered and sundered.
Then they rode back, but not,
   Not the six hundred.

Cannon to right of them,
Cannon to left of them,   40
Cannon behind them
   Volleyed and thundered;
Stormed at with shot and shell,
While horse and hero fell,
They that had fought so well   45
Came through the jaws of Death,
Back from the mouth of Hell,
All that was left of them,
   Left of six hundred.

When can their glory fade?   50
O the wild charge they made!
   All the world wondered.
Honor the charge they made!
Honor the Light Brigade,
   Noble six hundred!   55

Emily Dickinson [1830–1886]

SUCCESS IS COUNTED SWEETEST

Success is counted sweetest
By those who ne'er succeed.
To comprehend a nectar
Requires sorest need.

Not one of all the purple Host   5
Who took the Flag today
Can tell the definition
So clear of Victory

As he defeated — dying —
On whose forbidden ear
The distant strains of triumph
Burst agonized and clear!

10

George Gordon, Lord Byron [1788–1824]

WATERLOO

from CHILDE HAROLD, Canto III, 21–25

There was a sound of revelry by night,
And Belgium's capital had gathered then
Her beauty and her chivalry, and bright
The lamps shone o'er fair women and brave men;
A thousand hearts beat happily; and when
Music arose with its voluptuous swell,
Soft eyes looked love to eyes which spake again,
And all went merry as a marriage-bell;
But hush! hark! a deep sound strikes like a rising knell!

5

Did ye not hear it? — No; 't was but the wind,
Or the car rattling o'er the stony street;
On with the dance! let joy be unconfined!
No sleep till morn when Youth and Pleasure meet
To chase the glowing Hours with flying feet, —
But, hark! — that heavy sound breaks in once more,
As if the clouds its echo would repeat;
And nearer, clearer, deadlier than before!
Arm! arm! it is — it is — the cannon's opening roar!

10

15

Within a windowed niche of that high hall
Sate Brunswick's fated chieftain; he did hear
That sound the first amidst the festival,
And caught its tone with Death's prophetic ear;
And when they smiled because he deemed it near,
His heart more truly knew that peal too well
Which stretched his father on a bloody bier,
And roused the vengeance blood alone could quell:
He rushed into the field, and, foremost fighting, fell.

20

25

Ah! then and there was hurrying to and fro,
And gathering tears, and tremblings of distress,
And cheeks all pale which but an hour ago
Blushed at the praise of their own loveliness;
And there were sudden partings, such as press
The life from out young hearts, and choking sighs

30

Which ne'er might be repeated: who would guess 35
If evermore should meet those mutual eyes,
Since upon night so sweet such awful morn could rise!

And there was mounting in hot haste: the steed,
The mustering squadron, and the clattering car,
Went pouring forward with impetuous speed,
And swiftly forming in the ranks of war; 40
And the deep thunder peal on peal afar;
And near, the beat of the alarming drum
Roused up the soldier ere the morning star;
While thronged the citizens with terror dumb,
Or whispering with white lips,—"The foe! they come! they come!" 45

Wilfred Owen [1893–1918]

ANTHEM FOR DOOMED YOUTH

What passing-bells for these who die as cattle?
   Only the monstrous anger of the guns.
Only the stuttering rifles' rapid rattle
   Can patter out their hasty orisons.
No mockeries now for them; no prayers nor bells, 5
   Nor any voice of mourning save the choirs,—
The shrill, demented choirs of wailing shells;
   And bugles calling for them from sad shires.

What candles may be held to speed them all?
   Not in the hands of boys, but in their eyes 10
Shall shine the holy glimmers of good-byes.
   The pallor of girls' brows shall be their pall;
Their flowers the tenderness of patient minds,
And each slow dusk a drawing-down of blinds.

4, *orisons:* prayers. 8, *shires:* districts in England generally analogous to counties.

A. E. Housman [1859–1936]

I DID NOT LOSE MY HEART

I did not lose my heart in summer's even
   When roses to the moonrise burst apart:
When plumes were under heel and lead was flying,
In blood and smoke and flame I lost my heart.

I lost it to a soldier and a foeman,
    A chap that did not kill me, but he tried;
That took the sabre straight and took it striking,
    And laughed and kissed his hand to me and died. ⁵

Robert Bly [b. 1926]

COUNTING SMALL-BONED BODIES

Let's count the bodies over again.

If we could only make the bodies smaller,
The size of skulls,
We could make a whole plain white with skulls in the moonlight!

If we could only make the bodies smaller, ⁵
Maybe we could get
A whole year's kill in front of us on a desk!

If we could only make the bodies smaller,
We could fit
A body into a finger-ring, for a keepsake forever. ¹⁰

Denise Levertov [b. 1923]

WHAT WERE THEY LIKE?

    (Questions and Answers)

1) Did the people of Viet Nam
   use lanterns of stone?
2) Did they hold ceremonies
   to reverence the opening of buds?
3) Were they inclined to rippling laughter? ⁵
4) Did they use bone and ivory,
   jade and silver, for ornament?
5) Had they an epic poem?
6) Did they distinguish between speech and singing?

1) Sir, their light hearts turned to stone. ¹⁰
   It is not remembered whether in gardens
   stone lanterns illumined pleasant ways.
2) Perhaps they gathered once to delight in blossom,
   but after the children were killed
   there were no more buds. ¹⁵

3) Sir, laughter is bitter to the burned mouth.
4) A dream ago, perhaps. Ornament is for joy.
   All the bones were charred.
5) It is not remembered. Remember,
   most were peasants; their life   20
   was in rice and bamboo.
   When peaceful clouds were reflected in the paddies
   and the water-buffalo stepped surely along terraces,
   maybe fathers told their sons old tales.
   When bombs smashed the mirrors   25
   there was time only to scream.
6) There is an echo yet, it is said,
   of their speech which was like a song.
   It is reported their singing resembled
   the flight of moths in moonlight.   30
   Who can say? It is silent now.

W. S. Merwin [b. 1927]

WHEN THE WAR IS OVER

When the war is over
We will be proud of course the air will be
Good for breathing at last
The water will have been improved the salmon
And the silence of heaven will migrate more perfectly   5
The dead will think the living are worth it we will know
Who we are
And we will all enlist again

Richard Eberhart [b. 1904]

THE FURY OF AERIAL BOMBARDMENT

You would think the fury of aerial bombardment
Would rouse God to relent; the infinite spaces
Are still silent. He looks on shock-pried faces.
History, even, does not know what is meant.

You would feel that after so many centuries   5
God would give man to repent; yet he can kill
As Cain could, but with multitudinous will,
No farther advanced than in his ancient furies.
Was man made stupid to see his own stupidity?
Is God by definition indifferent, beyond us all?   10

Is the eternal truth man's fighting soul
Wherein the Beast ravens in its own avidity?

Of Van Wettering I speak, and Averill,
Names on a list, whose faces I do not recall
But they are gone to early death, who late in school   15
Distinguished the belt feed lever from the belt holding pawl.

14–15, *list . . . school:* Eberhart was a Naval gunnery instructor during World War II.

Thomas Hardy [1840–1928]

IN TIME OF "THE BREAKING OF NATIONS"
1
Only a man harrowing clods
  In a slow silent walk
With an old horse that stumbles and nods
  Half asleep as they stalk.
2
Only thin smoke without flame   5
  From the heaps of couch-grass;
Yet this will go onward the same
  Though Dynasties pass.
3
Yonder a maid and her wight
  Come whispering by: 10
War's annals will cloud into night
  Ere their story die.

This poem was written during World War I; it takes issue with a prophecy of Jeremiah (Chapter 51, verses 21–23) to the effect that God will destroy Babylon. Jeremiah says that God will destroy "horse and rider," "old and young," "the young man and the maid," "the shepherd and his flock," "the husbandman and his yoke of oxen," and "captains and rulers."

6, *couch-grass:* a hardy but worthless grass which chokes out crops.

CHANNEL FIRING

That night your great guns, unawares,
Shook all our coffins as we lay,
And broke the chancel window-squares,
We thought it was the Judgment-day

And sat upright. While drearisome   5

Arose the howl of wakened hounds:
The mouse let fall the altar-crumb,
The worms drew back into the mounds,

The glebe cow drooled. Till God called, "No;   *10*
It's gunnery practice out at sea
Just as before you went below;
The world is as it used to be:

"All nations striving strong to make
Red war yet redder. Mad as hatters
They do no more for Christès sake   *15*
Than you who are helpless in such matters.

"That this is not the judgment-hour
For some of them's a blessed thing,
For if it were they'd have to scour
Hell's floor for so much threatening *20*

"Ha, ha. It will be warmer when
I blow the trumpet (if indeed
I ever do; for you are men,
And rest eternal sorely need)."

So down we lay again. "I wonder,   *25*
Will the world ever saner be,"
Said one, "than when he sent us under
In our indifferent century!"

And many a skeleton shook his head.
"Instead of preaching forty year,"   *30*
My neighbor Parson Thirdly said,
"I wish I had stuck to pipes and beer."

Again the guns disturbed the hour,
Roaring their readiness to avenge,
As far inland as Stourton Tower,   *35*
And Camelot, and starlit Stonehenge.

9, *glebe cow*: cow pastured on the glebe, a plot of land attached to the church grounds. 35, *Stourton Tower*: a small town in Staffordshire. 36, *Camelot*: the supposed seat of King Arthur's court; *Stonehenge*, an ancient stone structure on Salisbury Plain, presumably built by Druids as a place of worship.

John William Corrington [b. 1932]

MR CLEAN

All the houses on drastic street
crawl with uneasy dirt

   when sun quits there
 are no stars only lewd moths hungering
in the sputter of queasy lamps
 where rare metals suffer juice

And in the absolute
     inutterable dark of
  each development hutch the
  balkanized hearts clinch and
strain under their flannel pelts

 Where impatient lovers grope
  there is darkness
 where winos huddle
  there is darkness
 where wives moan untouched
 beside daddy taking the long count
 dreaming of gina and liz
  there is darkness

 On every roof tortured fingers
  probe the reddening sky
   and under them
whether beer and cheese or breakup
  or conception by accident
only the kiddles imagine tomorrow
  and fear no three o'clock dawn

 And the militant ones
  used to darkness
   barking countdown
   considering negation
squat in their hqs
  secret alcoves
  advance bases
  ready rooms with mechanical ears
tipped for things at twice sounds speed
  hurtling in from

                    Out
                        There

  Probably not tonight possibly not
        tomorrow   40
        maybe not this august
  please god not on christmas eve
but certainly
        all attachés agree
        out of fears overcast   45
sometime before we wake

     To end the darkness
  to cleanse the dirt
     to clobber the sensitive
  distribute the hurt   50

some afternoon or evening
        some certain hour and minute

Mr Clean will clean your whole house
        and everything thats in it

_____

6: i.e., where tungsten filaments suffer the flow of electricity. 10, *balkanized:* The
Balkan Peninsula is in southern Europe, and comprises Yugoslavia, Rumania, Bul-
garia, Albania, Greece, and European Turkey. The peninsula was broken up into
small states after World War II; since then, to *balkanize* has meant to break up into
small, mutually hostile political units.

Richard Wilbur [b. 1921]

ADVICE TO A PROPHET

When you come, as you soon must, to the streets of our city,
Mad-eyed from stating the obvious,
Not proclaiming our fall but begging us
In God's name to have self-pity,

Spare us all word of the weapons, their force and range,   5
The long numbers that rocket the mind;
Our slow, unreckoning hearts will be left behind,
Unable to fear what is too strange.

Nor shall you scare us with talk of the death of the race.
How should we dream of this place without us?— 10
The sun mere fire, the leaves untroubled about us,
A stone look on the stone's face?

Speak of the world's own change. Though we cannot conceive
Of an undreamt thing, we know to our cost
How the dreamt cloud crumbles, the vines are blackened by frost, 15
How the view alters. We could believe,

If you told us so, that the white-tailed deer will slip
Into perfect shade, grown perfectly shy,
The lark avoid the reaches of our eye,
The jack-pine lose its knuckled grip 20

On the cold ledge, and every torrent burn
As Xanthus once, its gliding trout
Stunned in a twinkling. What should we be without
The dolphin's arc, the dove's return,

These things in which we have seen ourselves and spoken? 25
Ask us, prophet, how we shall call
Our natures forth when that live tongue is all
Dispelled, that glass obscured or broken

In which we have said the rose of our love and the clean
Horse of our courage, in which beheld 30
The singing locust of the soul unshelled,
And all we mean or wish to mean.

Ask us, ask us whether with the worldless rose
Our hearts shall fail us; come demanding
Whether there shall be lofty or long standing 35
When the bronze annals of the oak tree close.

Hephaestus, invoked by Achilles, scalded the river Xanthus (Scamander) in
Iliad, xxi. (Wilbur's note.)

9
Seeking
What is
Yet Unfound

Frontiers and Illusions of Progress

Edward Kessler [b. 1927]

THE DODO

*The skeleton of a Dodo was discovered in a mudflat on Mauritius,
called La Mer des Rêves*

As if I needed some means to maintain
Myself from all that paradise around,
From Portugal trim Mascarenhas came
Singling out, like Adam, the sights he saw.

He saw me lumbering through torrid green,   5
Yelled *Dóudo, Dóudo* to his shipmates on the beach —
Meaning, I learned, a clumsy oaf, a fool —
And caught me for a feast he couldn't eat.

Soon bored with my abundant uselessness
He sailed for Lisbon on the favorable tide,   10
Leaving upon the beach some goats and hogs,
A legacy of garbage, and my name.

A century I languished in my trees,
Perfectly anonymous as the island air,
Until the sea cast up another man: 15
Jacob Cornelius Van Neck, a Hollander.

He called me *Walghvogel*, and took me off
To sit for portraits in the English cold.
And when I died he willed my tired remains
To insatiable eyes in the Ashmolean Museum.   20

Much later, since I did not wear so well,
Calling attention from the artifacts

By the persistent odor of myself,
Vice-Chancellor Huddesford ordered me burned.

By the seventeenth century I was extinct,   25
Mythical as the phoenix or the roc,
My body's fact obscure as any
Hippogriff. One more heraldic beast.

But scientists are always ill at ease
With names or myths or anything not here.   30
An expedition proved my isle again
And in *la mer des rêves* they found these bones.

So here they stand, assembled and serene
As any work of art that tames your eye.
Too odd to last, I someday may return   35
A visitor to your most awkward dream.

The dodo was a large bird formerly found on the island of Mauritius; it is now ex-
tinct. Kessler's historical facts are self-explanatory, and accurate.

La Mer des Rêves: French; the Sea of Dreams. 20, *Ashmolean Museum:* at Oxford
University, named for Elias Ashmole (1617–1692), who donated to Oxford his col-
lection of curiosities and his library. 24, *Huddesford:* Vice-Chancellor of Oxford
University. 26, *phoenix:* mythical bird that rose anew from the ashes of its own
funeral pyre; *roc:* a mythical bird of gigantic size; see *Arabian Nights.* 28, *Hippo-
griff:* mythical animal, half griffin and half horse.

Gilbert Keith Chesterton [1874–1936]

THE ROLLING ENGLISH ROAD

Before the Roman came to Rye or out to Severn strode,
The rolling English drunkard made the rolling English road.
A reeling road, a rolling road, that rambles round the shire,
And after him the parson ran, the sexton and the squire;
A merry road, a mazy road, and such as we did tread   5
The night we went to Birmingham by way of Beachy Head.

I knew no harm of Bonaparte and plenty of the Squire,
And for to fight the Frenchman I did not much desire;
But I did bash their baggonets because they came array'd
To straighten out the crooked road an English drunkard made,   10
Where you and I went down the lane with ale-mugs in our hands,
The night we went to Glastonbury by way of Goodwin Sands.

His sins they were forgiven him; or why do flowers run
Behind him; and the hedges all strengthening in the sun?
The wild thing went from left to right and knew not which was
    which,   15
But the wild rose was above him when they found him in the ditch.
God pardon us, nor harden us; we did not see so clear
The night we went to Bannockburn by way of Brighton Pier.

My friends, we will not go again or ape an ancient rage,
Or stretch the folly of our youth to be the shame of age,   20
But walk with clearer eyes and ears this path that wandereth,
And see undrugg'd in evening light the decent inn of death;
For there is good news yet to hear and fine things to be seen,
Before we go to Paradise by way of Kensal Green.

1, *Rye* and *Severn*: areas in southern England among those settled by the Romans.
6, 12, 18, and 24: the place names here identify pairs of towns a great distance apart.
Brighton, for example, is on the Channel south of London, and Bannockburn is in
Scotland, north of Glasgow. 9, *baggonets*: dialect pronunciation of bayonet.

William McGonagall [1825–1902]

THE RAILWAY BRIDGE OF THE SILVERY TAY

Beautiful Railway Bridge of the Silvery Tay!
With your numerous arches and pillars in so grand array,
And your central girders, which seem to the eye
To be almost towering to the sky.
The greatest wonder of the day,   5
And a great beautification to the River Tay,
Most beautiful to be seen,
Near by Dundee and the Magdalen Green.

Beautiful Railway Bridge of the Silvery Tay!
That has caused the Emperor of Brazil to leave   10
His home far away, *incognito* in his dress,
And view thee ere he passed along *en route* to Inverness.

Beautiful Railway Bridge of the Silvery Tay!
The longest of the present day
That has ever crossed o'er a tidal river stream,   15
Most gigantic to be seen,
Near by Dundee and the Magdalen Green.

Beautiful Railway Bridge of the Silvery Tay!
Which will cause great rejoicing on the opening day,
And hundreds of people will come from far away,   20
Also the Queen, most gorgeous to be seen,
Near by Dundee and the Magdalen Green.

Beautiful Railway Bridge of the Silvery Tay!
And prosperity to Provost Cox, who has given
Thirty thousand pounds and upwards away   25
In helping to erect the Bridge of the Tay,
Most handsome to be seen,
Near by Dundee and the Magdalen Green.

Beautiful Railway Bridge of the Silvery Tay!
I hope that God will protect all passengers   30
By night and by day,
And that no accident will befall them while crossing
The Bridge of the Silvery Tay,
For that would be most awful to be seen
Near by Dundee and the Magdalen Green.   35

Beautiful Railway Bridge of the Silvery Tay!
And prosperity to Messrs. Bouche and Grothe,
The famous engineers of the present day,
Who have succeeded in erecting the Railway
Bridge of the Silvery Tay,   40
Which stands unequalled to be seen
Near by Dundee and the Magdalen Green.

from **THE TAY BRIDGE DISASTER**

Beautiful Railway Bridge of the Silv'ry Tay!
Alas! I am very sorry to say
That ninety lives have been taken away
On the last Sabbath day of 1879,
Which will be remember'd for a very long time.   5
. . . .
So the train mov'd slowly along the Bridge of Tay,
Until it was about midway,
Then the central girders with a crash gave way,
And down went the train and passengers into the Tay!
The Storm Fiend did loudly bray,   10
Because ninety lives had been taken away,
On the last Sabbath day of 1879,
Which will be remember'd for a very long time.

As soon as the catastrophe came to be known
The alarm from mouth to mouth was blown,   15
And the cry rang out all o'er the town,
Good Heavens! the Tay Bridge is blown down,
And a passenger train from Edinburgh,
Which fill'd all the people's hearts with sorrow,
And made them for to turn pale,   20
Because none of the passengers were sav'd to tell the tale,
How the disaster happen'd on the last Sabbath day of 1879,
Which will be remember'd for a very long time.

It must have been an awful sight,
To witness in the dusky moonlight,   25
While the Storm Fiend did laugh, and angry did bray,
Along the Railway Bridge of the Silv'ry Tay.
Oh! ill-fated Bridge of the Silv'ry Tay,
I must now conclude my lay
By telling the world fearlessly without the least dismay,   30
That your central girders would not have given way,
At least many sensible men do say,
Had they been supported on each side with buttresses,
At least many sensible men confesses,
For the stronger we our houses do build   35
The less chance we have of being kill'd.

from AN ADDRESS TO THE NEW TAY BRIDGE

Beautiful new railway bridge of the Silvery Tay,
With your strong brick piers and buttresses in so grand array,
And your thirteen central girders, which seem to my eye
Strong enough all windy storms to defy.
And as I gaze upon thee my heart feels gay,   5
Because thou art the greatest railway bridge of the present day . . .
Because thine equal nowhere can be seen,
Only near by Dundee and the bonnie Magdalen Green.

Beautiful new railway bridge of the Silvery Tay,
With thy beautiful side-screens along your railway,   10
Which will be a great protection on a windy day,
So as the railway carriages won't be blown away,
And ought to cheer the hearts of the passengers night and day
As they are conveyed along thy beautiful railway,
And towering above the Silvery Tay,   15
Spanning the beautiful river shore to shore
Upwards of two miles and more,

Which is most wonderful to be seen
Near by Dundee and the bonnie Magdalen Green.

Thy structure to my eye seems strong and grand,   20
And the workmanship most skillfully planned;
And I hope the designers, Messrs Barlow & Arrol, will prosper for
    many a day
For erecting thee across the beautiful Tay.
And I think nobody need have the least dismay
To cross o'er thee by night or by day,   25
Because thy strength is visible to be seen
Near by Dundee and the bonnie Magdalen Green.
. . . .

The New Yorkers boast about their Brooklyn Bridge,
But in comparison to thee it seems like a midge,
Because thou spannest the silvery Tay   30
A mile and more longer I venture to say;
Besides the railway carriages are pulled across by a rope,
Therefore Brooklyn Bridge cannot with thee cope;
And as you have been opened on the 20th day of June,
I hope Her Majesty Queen Victoria will visit thee very soon,   35
Because thou are worthy of a visit from Duke, Lord, or Queen,
And strong and securely built, which is most worthy to be seen
Near by Dundee and the bonnie Magdalen Green.

These three poems arise from (1) the construction, in 1877, of a railway bridge
over the Firth of Tay, on the eastern coast of Scotland north of Edinburgh; (2) its col-
lapse, some eighteen months later; (3) the construction of a new bridge, in 1887.
McGonagall always signed his name "William McGonagall, Poet and Tragedian."

George Berkeley [1685–1753]

VERSES ON THE PROSPECT OF PLANTING ARTS
AND LEARNING IN AMERICA

The Muse, disgusted at an age and clime
    Barren of every glorious theme,
In distant lands now waits a better time,
    Producing subjects worthy fame:

In happy climes where from the genial sun   5
    And virgin earth such scenes ensue,

The force of art by nature seems outdone,
    And fancied beauties by the true:

In happy climes, the seat of innocence,
    Where nature guides and virtue rules,   *10*
Where men shall not impose for truth and sense
    The pedantry of courts and schools:

There shall be sung another golden age,
    The rise of empire and of arts,
The good and great inspiring epic rage,   *15*
    The wisest heads and noblest hearts.

Not such as Europe breeds in her decay;
    Such as she bred when fresh and young,
When heavenly flame did animate her clay,
    By future poets shall be sung.   *20*

Westward the course of empire takes its way;
    The four first acts already past,
A fifth shall close the drama with the day;
    Time's noblest offspring is the last.

Emily Dickinson [1830–1886]

I LIKE TO SEE IT LAP THE MILES

I like to see it lap the Miles—
And lick the Valleys up—
And stop to feed itself at Tanks
And then—prodigious step

Around a Pile of Mountains—   *5*
And supercilious peer
In Shanties—by the sides of Roads—
And then a Quarry pare

To fit its Ribs
And crawl between   *10*
Complaining all the while
In horrid—hooting stanza—
Then chase itself down Hill—

And neigh like Boanerges—
Then—punctual as a Star   *15*

Stop—docile and omnipotent
At its own stable door—

14, *Boanerges:* literally, "sons of Thunder"; the name was given by Christ to James
and John (Mark iii:17).

Robert Creeley [b. 1926]

I KNOW A MAN

As I sd to my
friend, because I am
always talking,—John, I

sd, which was not his
name, the darkness sur-
rounds us, what

can we do against
it, or else, shall we &
why not, buy a goddamn big car,

drive, he sd, for
christ's sake, look
out where yr going.

Melvin DeBruhl [b. 1950]

AT LAST

At last
man has reached
the first point
in a line leading
to mysterious universe
and spreads peace
to another world
claiming it in the
name of humanity

a little blue boy
waits for
the flying machine
that never can get
off the ground

hoping it will drop   *15*
a growing seed
in a swollen stomach
but hopes go
with a blast
or with a slow   *20*
death in a road

Edgar Allan Poe [1809–1849]

SONNET – TO SCIENCE

Science! true daughter of Old Time thou art!
  Who alterest all things with thy peering eyes.
Why preyest thou thus upon the poet's heart,
  Vulture, whose wings are dull realities?
How should he love thee? or how deem thee wise?   *5*
  Who wouldst not leave him in his wandering
To seek for treasure in the jeweled skies,
  Albeit he soared with an undaunted wing?
Hast thou not dragged Diana from her car?
  And driven the Hamadryad from the wood   *10*
To seek a shelter in some happier star?
  Hast thou not torn the Naiad from her flood,
The Elfin from the green grass, and from me
The summer dream beneath the tamarind tree?

9: *Diana* was the Roman goddess of the hunt; her *car*, or chariot, was the moon.
10, *Hamadryad:* wood-nymph. 12, *Naiad:* river-nymph. 14, *tamarind:* an oriental
tree whose fruit is used as food and as medicine.

James Merrill [b. 1926]

LABORATORY POEM

Charles used to watch Naomi, taking heart
And a steel saw, open up turtles live.
While she swore they felt nothing, he would gag
At blood, at the blind twitching, even after
The murky dawn of entrails cleared, revealing   *5*
Contours he knew, egg-yellows like lamps paling.

Well then. She carried off the beating heart
To the kymograph and rigged it there, a rag
In fitful wind, now made to strain, now stopped

By her solutions tonic or malign   *10*
Alternately in which it would be steeped.
What the heart bore she noted on a chart,

For work did not stop only with the heart.
He thought of certain human hearts, their climb
Through violence into exquisite disciplines   *15*
Of which, as it now appeared, they all expired.
Soon she would fetch another and start over,
Easy in the presence of her lover.

Ben Belitt [b. 1911]

MOON WALK

It is time to re-invent life,
we say, smelling ammonia from Mars
in a photograph, seeing right angles
in galactic soda, a glass bead from a crater,
the color purple.   *5*

                    To that enormous death's head
we bring the constellation of Snoopy and Charlie Brown
in a comic-strip balloon of antiphonal beeps,
with a virus's chemical courage, trailing a ration
of air in plexiglass and nylon, printing   *10*
a square of carbon like a tennis court,
planting our human shadow and contamination.

A hammer taps: *It is later than you think.*
                                    We follow
the White Rabbit through the lunar asparagus,   *15*
gathering specimens for the radiologist, peer
into the pockets of Alice's pinafore, grown infinitesimal,
fall into the daydream of the hookah and the caterpillar
and the Sea of Tears.

7: *Snoopy and Charlie Brown* are the names of the lunar module and the command module of Apollo 10, the orbital flight which preceded Apollo 11, the first moon landing mission. 15, 17, and 18: The White Rabbit, Alice and the hookah-smoking caterpillar are all characters in *Alice's Adventures in Wonderland*. 19, *Sea of Tears:* an invention of the poet, echoing the names of certain areas of the moon.

William Meredith [b. 1919]

EARTH WALK

He drives onto the grassy shoulder and unfastens
his seat-belt. The aluminum buckle glistens.
He is watched from behind by two upholstered knobs.
He thinks: strapped to things we drive or fly,
helmeted for cycling and all the jobs   5
that peril our coconut heads, we rush
on our wheeled callings, hoping to avoid the crush,
the whooping car that blinks its bloody eye
—no Roman would be able to make sense
of our Latin name for it, an ambulance,   10
the rubber-walker with the spry attendants.

I was to go to the hospital tomorrow, but I thought
Why not today? Now I unstrap the rented Avis car
and, opening the hatch, step boldly out
onto the Planet Earth. My skull is bare,   15
thin animal hide is fitted to my feet.
The autumn air is fresh, a first pepperidge tree
has turned mahogany and red. This is a safe walk.
This turnpike is uninhabited. When I come back
I'll meet a trooper with a soft, wide hat   20
who will take away my Earth-rocks and debrief me.

10, *Latin name: ambulance* derives from the Latin verb *ambulare*, to walk or move.

Walt Whitman [1819–1892]

FACING WEST FROM CALIFORNIA'S SHORES

Facing west from California's shores,
Inquiring, tireless, seeking what is yet unfound,
I, a child, very old, over waves, towards the house of maternity, the
    land of migrations, look afar,
Look off the shores of my Western sea, the circle almost circled;
For starting westward from Hindustan, from the vales of Kashmere,   5
From Asia, from the north, from the God, the sage, and the hero,
From the south, from the flowery peninsulas and the spice islands,
Long having wander'd since, round the earth having wander'd,
Now I face home again, very pleas'd and joyous,
(But where is what I started for so long ago?   10
And why is it yet unfound?)

Robert Frost [1874–1963]

DESERT PLACES

Snow falling and night falling fast, oh, fast
In a field I looked into going past,
And the ground almost covered smooth in snow,
But a few weeds and stubble showing last.

The woods around it have it—it is theirs.   5
All animals are smothered in their lairs.
I am too absent-spirited to count;
The loneliness includes me unawares.

And lonely as it is, that loneliness
Will be more lonely ere it will be less—   10
A blanker whiteness of benighted snow
With no expression, nothing to express.

They cannot scare me with their empty spaces
Between stars—on stars where no human race is.
I have it in me so much nearer home   15
To scare myself with my own desert places.

William Meredith [b. 1919]

AN OLD FIELD MOWED FOR APPEARANCES' SAKE

My loud machine for making hay
Mutters about our work today;
Through bushes and small trees it flails—
Blueberry, sumac, cherry, bay.

I lay the little woods in swales   5
To burn them as the daylight fails
For no surviving horse or cow
Is fed such crazy salad bales.

They fall like jackstraws, anyhow,
Or like the forest, trunk and bough   10
That harder hands and will than these
Burned once, where it is meadow now.

I side with meadow against trees
Because of woodsmoke in the breeze,
The ghost of other foes—though both   15
Would find us puny enemies,
Second growth and second growth.

Thomas Reiter [b. 1940]

DINOLAND

1.

With grenades of sumac fruit
and with spears or wands
of the dried, forked stems of tiger lilies,
I hunted each horned and armored reptile
among the tourists in Dinoland.   5

But mostly I feared Tyrannosaurus Rex
would return by his prints in lava streambeds
to the souvenir shop of my parents, where
he would shatter the glazed ashtrays
of his tracks, crush in his jaws   10
plaster of Paris paths of crabs and mollusks
and the stomach stones preserved
in swallowed Mesozoic reptiles, perfect
for paperweights. The starfish and sea urchins
my father embedded in casting plastic   15
for pen & pencil sets, or mounted
in their shale graves on pedestals of stainless steel,
he would free to original seas.

2.

Soon an earlier darkness streamed each day
like springs from markings and tracks   20
and I was outdistanced.
Sending fewer and fewer tourists, the sun
behind our mountain quarry was where
the three-toed leaves of the maple led. Those hours
of *National Geographic*,   25
my father read aloud about the hunting people
who brought their wounded spearmen to touch
footprints that lay so profitably
on my father's workbench and shelves—the invoking
marks of the Spirit Beast   30
that stalked or healed the hunters, in its wisdom.

3.

Late one day as I waited for our gates
to be barred against the cold
from a hundred million years
as sharp as shale in my throat and eyes, everywhere   35
was the faintest snow like silt.
So I followed the newly-fallen strides
of Tyrannosaurus Rex.

But the next morning my father closed up Dinoland
till spring, and on top of a nearby hill   *40*
that arose in hunterless light to the level
of our quarry's earliest stratum, school began.

Clarice Short [b. 1910]

IMPERFECT SYMPATHIES

Kit Carson might be surprised
To see his grave stone with its edges chipped
Fluted, by relic seekers, to a blade.
He might be gratified that so many wished
Something to prove they had been near his bones   *5*
And found his country of long-leaved cottonwoods
Making a fragile shade against a sky
Immoderately blue, the adobe walls
Buttressed by purple shadow, the little voice
Of the irrigation ditch that spoke of mountains.   *10*

But he might feel a lack of fellowship
With these late comers. Only a century
Set him apart from them, but his had been
A less alleviated life which left
One little opportunity to ponder   *15*
What were man's greatest goods:
The cold, the thirst, the hunger making the answer,
The fire behind the windbreak, the scanty seep
In the bottom of the arroyo, the rabbit carcass.
It probably never occurred to him to question   *20*
The reason for suffering or man's existence.

Without antivenin or anesthetic
The hand bitten by the rattler, or the leg
Crushed by the falling horse engrossed the thought.
And why one lived was not a primary concern   *25*
With the trail steep, the darkness deepening, the snow falling.

1, *Kit Carson*: Christopher Carson (1809–1868), famous frontiersman who in 1826
made his home at Taos, New Mexico, where his grave is. 22, *antivenin*: antidote for
the venom of poisonous snakes.

Malcolm Cowley [b. 1898]

THE BLOWN DOOR

I watched for years a sidehill farm that died
   a little, day by day.
Branch after branch the dooryard maples died
and a buckwheat field was gullied into clay,

to the beat . . . beat of a loose board on the barn   5
   that flapped in the wind all night;
nobody came to drive a nail in it.
The farm died in a broken window light,

a broken pane upstairs in the east bedroom
   that let the northeast rain   10
beat down all night on the red Turkey carpet;
nobody puttied in another pane.

Nobody nailed a new slat on the corncrib;
   nobody mowed the hay
or swung a gate that sagged on rusty hinges.   15
The farm died when two boys went away,

or lived until the lame old man was buried.
   I came then, and once more
to see how sumac overspread the pasture,
to smell dead leaves and hear a gust of wind   20
somewhere inside the house blow shut a door.

11, *Turkey carpet:* Turkish carpet.

Edwin Arlington Robinson [1869–1935]

HOW ANNANDALE WENT OUT

"They called it Annandale—and I was there
To flourish, to find words, and to attend:
Liar, physician, hypocrite, and friend,
I watched him; and the sight was not so fair
As one or two that I have seen elsewhere: 5
An apparatus not for me to mend—
A wreck, with hell between him and the end,
Remained of Annandale; and I was there.
"I knew the ruin as I knew the man;

So put the two together, if you can,
Remembering the worst you know of me.
Now view yourself as I was, on the spot—
With a slight kind of engine. Do you see?
Like this . . . You wouldn't hang me? I thought not."

10
One Name
is Pain

Sports

Gary Gildner [b. 1938]

FIRST PRACTICE

After the doctor checked to see
we weren't ruptured,
the man with the short cigar took us
under the grade school,
where we went in case of attack   5
or storm, and said
he was Clifford Hill, he was
a man who believed dogs
ate dogs, he had once killed
for his country, and if   10
there were any girls present
for them to leave now.
                              No one
left. OK, he said, he said I take
that to mean you are hungry   15
men who hate to lose as much
as I do. OK. Then
he made two lines of us
facing each other,
and across the way, he said,   20
is the man you hate most
in the world,
and if we are to win
that title I want to see how.
But I don't want to see   25
any marks when you're dressed,
he said. He said, *Now*.

Thomas Whitbread [b. 1931]

N.B.A. PRELIM, BOSTON GARDEN

Two-pointer by New York! Boryla leaps!
    Neutral, the Boston crowd
  Makes medium, polite applause:
The Knicks now lead, 116–115.
      Five seconds left. Sure thing!   *5*
  But Philadelphia takes time out
      To stop the clock,
Jump the ball to midcourt (that's six Russell steps),
    And plan (ha, ha) a play.
The Knicks and most of the fans guess what it is: *10*
      They'll try
    To pass, quick as they can,
      To the angular man
      With tonight's on eye.
      That's what they do: *15*
        One
      To another
      And then
To Neil Johnston, waiting ten feet out on the right.
    He starts toward his soft right push   *20*
      But the ball stays where
      His torso was
      And his strained arm is:
      Instantaneous change!
      The fingers draw   *25*
      Him wholly back
And around, away, to complete control of the ball.
  His back to the hoop, no time to turn,
His right arm hooks the ball up over his head
In a high round arc which the buzzer cuts in half   *30*
And, everyone gasped, it goes without tickling a rim
      Through the swishing strings
     Just as Johnston turns around
And jumps! jumps up and down! jumps! jumps in one spot
And waves his arms, while the Celts' crowd roars, and jumps   *35*
Till his teammates hold him down with arms of joy.
    Only a game, a business, true,
        But as Pritchard said,
It was deeply moving, seeing Neil Johnston jump.

    Boryla and Johnston were both professional basketball players. *Pritchard*, line 38, is a friend of the poet's.

William Matthews [b. 1942]

OSCAR ROBERTSON: PERIPHERAL VISION

They clear the left side for him.
An eye-fake, dip and ripple
of a shoulder, he runs his man
into a pick. He's done this so many times
it hurts him the right way.   5
The ball blooms away from his wrist.
The body is most vulnerable
when it claims space,
shadows in the moist
and painfully kept open   10
corners of his eyes.

Robertson's peripheral vision is reputed to be extraordinary.

4, *pick:* one of Robertson's teammates, who is within a step and a half of the opponent defending against Robertson ("his man"), acts as interference so that Robertson can get past the defenseman.

Sir Philip Sidney [1554–1586]

from ASTROPHEL AND STELLA

41

Having this day my horse, my hand, my lance
Guided so well that I obtained the prize,
Both by the judgment of the English eyes
And of some sent from that sweet enemy, France,
Horsemen my skill in horsemanship advance,   5
Town-folks my strength; a daintier judge applies
His praise to sleight which from good use doth rise;
Some lucky wits impute it but to chance;
Others, because of both sides I do take
My blood from them who did excel in this,   10
Think nature me a man-at-arms did make.
How far they shoot awry! The true cause is,
Stella looked on, and from her heavenly face
Sent forth the beams which made so fair my race.

7, *sleight which from good use:* dexterity which from practice. 9–10, *both sides
... My blood:* the speaker claims ancestors on both sides who excelled at jousting.

James Dickey [b. 1923]

LISTENING TO FOXHOUNDS

When in that gold
Of fires, quietly sitting
With the men whose brothers are hounds,

You hear the first tone
Of a dog on scent, you look from face   5
To face, to see whose will light up.

When that light comes
Inside the dark light of the fire,
You know which chosen man has heard

A thing like his own dead   10
Speak out in a marvelous, helpless voice
That he has been straining to hear.

Miles away in the dark,
His enchanted dog can sense
How his features glow like a savior's,   15

And begins to hunt
In a frenzy of desperate pride.
Among us, no one's eyes give off a light

For the red fox
Playing in and out of his scent,   20
Leaping stones, doubling back over water.

Who runs with the fox
Must sit here like his own image,
Giving nothing of himself

To the sensitive flames,   25
With no human joy rising up,
Coming out of his face to be seen.

And it is hard,
When the fox leaps into his burrow,
To keep that singing down,   30

To sit with the fire
Drawn into one's secret features,
And all eyes turning around

From the dark wood
Until they come, amazed, upon
A face that does not shine

Back from itself,
That holds its own light and takes more,
Like the face of the dead, sitting still,

Giving no sign,
Making no outcry, no matter
Who may be straining to hear.

Brewster Ghiselin [b. 1903]

MARLIN

The wand of that fisherman witching the waves
Dips,
Feeling an abyss,
Lifts
Shuddering, buckling. It has hooked the tide.

Heartstring out of his reel
Screams, the sea
Fountains pieces of itself vomiting its vitals
Far from the boat
Something falling leaping

Skips like a keel—
Is up!
Brandishing, brandishing, a muscle, a rib: an arm,
Like God's
Torn off alive.

Tireless, until—as if the tide itself
Failed or the sea
Changed,
No more averse
Gave up its secret with strange irony

Under shrill-screaming unseemly seabirds' crisscross
Of augury—
Slow as a floating lily, mottled with sea-glyphs, fingered by the waters

Marlin [**279**]

Like an island,
Like its own sundown it glides in to die.   25

Marlin: a large but slim deep-sea fish related to the sailfish. 23, sea-glyphs: marks made by the sea; a glyph, strictly, is a carving.

Barbara Howes [b. 1914]

OUT FISHING

We went out, early one morning,
Over the loud marches of the sea,
In our walnut-shell boat,
Tip-tilting over that blue vacancy.

Combering, coming in,   5
The waves shellacked us, left us breathless, ill;
Hour on hour, out
Of this emptiness no fish rose, until

The great one struck that twine-
Wrapped flying-fish hard, turned and bolted   10
Off through the swelling sea
By a twist of his shoulder, with me tied fast; my rod

Held him, his hook held me,
In tug-of-war—sidesaddle on the ocean
I rode out the flaring waves,   15
Rode till the great fish sounded; by his submersion

He snapped the line, we lost
All contact; north, south, west, my adversary
Storms on through his world
Of water: I do not know him: he does not know me.   20

Alan Dugan [b. 1923]

ON HURRICANE JACKSON

Now his nose's bridge is broken, one eye
will not focus and the other is astray;
trainers whisper in his mouth while one ear
listens to itself, clenched like a fist;
generally shadow-boxing in a smoky room,   5

his mind hides like the aching boys
who lost a contest in the Pan-Hellenic games
and had to take the back roads home,
but someone else, his perfect youth,
laureled in newsprint and dollar bills,   *10*
triumphs forever on the great white way
to the statistical Sparta of the champs.

Hurricane Jackson: in the late fifties and early sixties, a contender for the Heavy-
weight Championship. 7, *Pan-Hellenic:* literally, "of all the Greek nations." The
reference here is to the early Olympic games.

R. Ernest Holmes [b. 1943]

BLACK LADY IN AN AFRO HAIRDO CHEERS FOR CASSIUS

Honey-hued beauty, you are;
in your gleaming white shorts,
gladiator shoes,
sparkling robe of satin cream,
bursting through the ropes,   *5*
piercing the arena smoke
with your confident eyes
of Kentucky brown.
Only *now* do I realize
what it must have been like   *10*
to have known Sweet Sugar
when he was King,
or to have prayed for Joe
when the ear of the ghetto
was pressed hard   *15*
to the sound machine.
But what you bring
to the ring, no
black champ has
ever brought before—   *20*
Sweet Cassius,
you are *my* pride
in these times of pain;
fast moving,
grooving in the ring   *25*
with that pepped-up cat
who acts so bold.
Child, your hands so fast

you make the young seem old!
So, mock him once or twice   30
for me, baby.
Sting him 'side the head,
spin, cool Daddy,
to the side.
Ease up a bit now   35
and let the man ride.
Now, in the eye —
jab, jab,
Ali Shuffle,
Ooh, heavens!!   40
The dude is down —
Did you see it?

Cassius: Muhammad Ali, formerly Cassius Clay. 11, *Sweet Sugar:* Sugar Ray
Robinson. 13, *Joe:* either Joe Louis or Jersey Joe Walcott.

John Betjeman [b. 1906]

A SUBALTERN'S LOVE SONG

Miss J. Hunter Dunn, Miss J. Hunter Dunn,
Furnish'd and burnish'd by Aldershot sun,
What strenuous singles we played after tea,
We in the tournament — you against me!

Love-thirty, love-forty, oh! weakness of joy,   5
The speed of a swallow, the grace of a boy,
With carefullest carelessness, gaily you won,
I am weak from your loveliness, Joan Hunter Dunn.

Miss Joan Hunter Dunn, Miss Joan Hunter Dunn,
How mad I am, sad I am, glad that you won.   10
The warm-handled racket is back in its press,
But my shock-headed victor, she loves me no less.

Her father's euonymus shines as we walk,
And swing past the summer-house, buried in talk,
And cool the verandah that welcomes us in   15
To the six-o'clock news and a lime-juice and gin.

The scent of the conifers, sound of the bath,
The view from my bedroom of moss-dappled path,

As I struggle with double-end evening tie,
For we dance at the Golf Club, my victor and I.   *20*

On the floor of her bedroom lie blazer and shorts
And the cream-colored walls are be-trophied with sports,
And westering, questioning settles the sun
On your low-leaded window, Miss Joan Hunter Dunn.

The Hillman is waiting, the light's in the hall,   *25*
The pictures of Egypt are bright on the wall,
My sweet, I am standing beside the oak stair
And there on the landing's the light on your hair.

By roads "not adopted", by woodlanded ways,
She drove to the club in the late summer haze,   *30*
Into nine-o'clock Camberly, heavy with bells
And mushroomy, pine-woody, evergreen smells.

Miss Joan Hunter Dunn, Miss Joan Hunter Dunn,
I can hear from the car-park the dance has begun.
Oh! full Surrey twilight! importunate band!   *35*
Oh! strongly adorable tennis-girl's hand!

Around us are Rovers and Austins afar,
Above us, the intimate roof of the car,
And here on my right is the girl of my choice,
With the tilt of her nose and the chime of her voice,   *40*

And the scent of her wrap, and the words never said,
And the ominous, ominous dancing ahead.
We sat in the car-park till twenty to one
And now I'm engaged to Miss Joan Hunter Dunn.

Aldershot, Surrey, and Camberly are British place-names; Hillmans, Rovers, and
Austins are British cars. 29, "not adopted": not officially maintained by the Ministry
of Works.

Walt Whitman [1819–1892]

THE RUNNER

On a flat road runs the well-train'd runner,
He is lean and sinewy with muscular legs,
He is thinly clothed, he leans forward as he runs,
With lightly closed fists and arms partially rais'd.

A. E. Housman [1859–1936]

TO AN ATHLETE DYING YOUNG

The time you won your town the race
We chaired you through the market-place;
Man and boy stood cheering by,
And home we brought you shoulder-high.

To-day, the road all runners come,   *5*
Shoulder-high we bring you home,
And set you at your threshold down,
Townsman of a stiller town.

Smart lad, to slip betimes away
From fields where glory does not stay   *10*
And early though the laurel grows
It withers quicker than the rose.

Eyes the shady night has shut
Cannot see the record cut,
And silence sounds no worse than cheers   *15*
After earth has stopped the ears:

Now you will not swell the rout
Of lads that wore their honors out,
Runners whom renown outran
And the name died before the man.   *20*

So set, before its echoes fade,
The fleet foot on the sill of shade,
And hold to the low lintel up
The still-defended challenge-cup.

And round that early-laureled head   *25*
Will flock to gaze the strengthless dead,
And find unwithered on its curls
The garland briefer than a girl's.

11, *laurel:* a wreath awarded in contests; see "The Garden" (page 95) and "Lycidas" (page 144). 12, *rose:* here symbolic of love; see last line of the poem.

Ernest Lawrence Thayer [1863–1940]

CASEY AT THE BAT

The outlook wasn't brilliant for the Mudville nine that day:
The score stood four to two with but one inning more to play.
And then when Cooney died at first, and Barrows did the same,
A sickly silence fell upon the patrons of the game.

A straggling few got up to go in deep despair. The rest 5
Clung to that hope which springs eternal in the human breast;
They thought if only Casey could but get a whack at that—
We'd put up even money now with Casey at the bat.

But Flynn preceded Casey, as did also Jimmy Blake,
And the former was a lulu and the latter was a cake; 10
So upon that stricken multitude grim melancholy sat,
For there seemed but little chance of Casey's getting to the bat.

But Flynn let drive a single, to the wonderment of all,
And Blake, the much despis-ed, tore the cover off the ball;
And when the dust had lifted, and the men saw what had occurred, 15
There was Jimmy safe at second and Flynn a-hugging third.

Then from 5,000 throats and more there rose a lusty yell;
It rumbled through the valley, it rattled in the dell;
It knocked upon the mountain and recoiled upon the flat,
For Casey, mighty Casey, was advancing to the bat. 20

There was ease in Casey's manner as he stepped into his place;
There was pride in Casey's bearing and a smile on Casey's face.
And when, responding to the cheers, he lightly doffed his hat,
No stranger in the crowd could doubt 'twas Casey at the bat.

Ten thousand eyes were on him as he rubbed his hands with dirt; 25
Five thousand tongues applauded when he wiped them on his shirt.
Then while the writhing pitcher ground the ball into his hip,
Defiance gleamed in Casey's eye, a sneer curled Casey's lip.

And now the leather-covered sphere came hurtling through the air,
And Casey stood a-watching it in haughty grandeur there. 30
Close by the sturdy batsman the ball unheeded sped—
"That ain't my style," said Casey. "Strike one," the umpire said.

From the benches black with people, there went up a muffled roar,
Like the beating of the storm-waves on a stern and distant shore.

"Kill him! Kill the umpire!" shouted some one on the stand;   35
And it's likely they'd have killed him had not Casey raised his hand.

With a smile of Christian charity great Casey's visage shone;
He stilled the rising tumult; he bade the game go on;
He signaled to the pitcher, and once more the spheroid flew;
But Casey still ignored it, and the umpire said, "Strike two."   40

"Fraud!" cried the maddened thousands, and echo answered fraud;
But one scornful look from Casey and the audience was awed.
They saw his face grow stern and cold, they saw his muscles strain,
And they knew that Casey wouldn't let that ball go by again.

The sneer is gone from Casey's lip, his teeth are clenched in hate;   45
He pounds with cruel violence his bat upon the plate.
And now the pitcher holds the ball, and now he lets it go,
And now the air is shattered by the force of Casey's blow.

Oh, somewhere in this favored land the sun is shining bright;
The band is playing somewhere, and somewhere hearts are light,   50
And somewhere men are laughing, and somewhere children shout;
But there is no joy in Mudville—mighty Casey has struck out.

Robert Francis [b. 1901]

THE BASE STEALER

Poised between going on and back, pulled
Both ways taut like a tightrope-walker,
Fingertips pointing the opposites,
Now bouncing tiptoe like a dropped ball
Or a kid skipping rope, come on, come on,
Running a scattering of steps sidewise,
How he teeters, skitters, tingles, teases,
Taunts them, hovers like an ecstatic bird,
He's only flirting, crowd him, crowd him,
Delicate, delicate, delicate, delicate—now!   10

Fred Chappell [b. 1936]

SPITBALLER

A poet because his hand goes first
to his head & then to his heart.

The catcher accepts the pitch
as a pool receives a dripping diver;
soaks up the curve like   5
cornflakes in milk.

The batter makes great
show of wringing out his bat.

On the mound he grins, tiger
in a tree, when the umpire   10
turns round & round the ball
magically dry as alum.

He draws a second salary as maintenance man.
Since while he pitches he waters the lawn.

John Malcolm Brinnin [b. 1916]

NUNS AT EVE

On St. Martin's evening green
Imaginary diamond, between
The vestry buttress and the convent wall,
Solemn as sea-birds in a sanctuary,
Under the statue of the Virgin they play baseball.   5
They are all named Mary,
Sister Mary, Mary Anthony or Mary Rose,
And when the softball flies
In the shadow of the cross
The little chaplet of the Virgin's hands   10
Contains their soft excitements like a house.

A flying habit traces
The unprecedented rounding of the bases
By Sister Mary Agatha, who thanks God
For the easy triple and turns her eyes toward home;   15
As *Mary, Mother, help me* echoes in her head,
Mild cries from the proud team
Encourage her, and the obliging sun,
Dazzling the pitcher's box
With a last celestial light upon   20
The gold-spiked halo of the Virgin in her niche,
Leads Sister Mary John to a wild pitch.

Prayer wins the game.
As Sister Mary Agatha comes sailing home
Through infield dusk, like birds fan-wise   25
In the vague cloisters of slow-rising mist,
Winners and losers gather in to praise
The fleetness of a bride of Christ.
Flushed and humble, Agatha collects the bats
And balls, while at her belt   30
Catcher's and pitcher's mitts
— Brute fingers, toes and gross lopsided heads —
Fumble the ropes of her long swinging beads.

Paul Ramsey [b. 1924]

WILLIE MAYS

You know the records. They are there to read.
The rest is private, and one name is pain.
How beautifully he runs to make a catch
Or circles second base and bluffs for third!
How graciously he laughs, and makes a joke,   5
And makes a catcher laugh. Yet what speaks there
Is not now a boy laughing, as it was,
But recognizes what there will not be,
A recognition hostile and alert
As on a desert under holy stars   10
The sand is entered into every breath,
A wound at last one writes upon the nerves.

William Jay Smith [b. 1918]

THE CLOSING OF THE RODEO

The lariat snaps; the cowboy rolls
    His pack, and mounts and rides away.
Back to the land the cowboy goes.

Plumes of smoke from the factory sway
    In the setting sun. The curtain falls,   5
A train in the darkness pulls away.

Good-by, says the rain on the iron roofs.
    Good-by, say the barber poles.
Dark drum the vanishing horses' hooves.

11
To Sight
the Stars

Movies

p. 289
to 309

John Updike [b. 1932]

MOVIE HOUSE

View it, by day, from the back,
from the parking lot in the rear,
for from this angle only
the beautiful brick blankness can be grasped.
Monumentality   5
wears one face in all ages.

No windows intrude real light
into this temple of shades,
and the size of it,
the size of the great rear wall measures   10
the breadth of the dreams we have had here.
It dwarfs the village bank,
outlooms the town hall,
and even in its decline
makes the bright-ceilinged supermarket seem mean.   15

Stark closet of stealthy rapture,
vast introspective camera
wherein our most daring self-projections
were given familiar names:
stand, stand by your macadam lake   20
and tell the aeons of our extinction
that we too could house our gods,
could secrete a pyramid
to sight the stars by.

Paul Ramsey [b. 1924]

MARILYN MONROE

She had a way with comedy and men.
She had a way with words. She loved to act.
Her shyness, beauty shall not come again,
And many of us are saddened by that fact.

John Hollander [b. 1929]

MOVIE-GOING

Drive-ins are out, to start with. One must always be
Able to see the over-painted Moorish ceiling
Whose pinchbeck jazz gleams even in the darkness, calling
The straying eye to feast on it, and glut, then fall
Back to the sterling screen again. One needs to feel   5
That the two empty, huddled, dark stage-boxes keep
Empty for kings. And having frequently to cope
With the abominable goodies, overflow
Bulk and (finally) exploring hands of flushed
Close neighbors gazing beadily out across glum   10
Distances is, after all, to keep the gleam
Alive of something rather serious, to keep
Faith, perhaps, with the City. When as children our cup
Of joys ran over the special section, and we clutched
Our ticket stubs and followed the bouncing ball, no clash   15
Of cymbals at the start of the stage-show could abash
Our third untiring time around. When we came back,
Older, to cop an endless series of feels, we sat
Unashamed beneath the bare art-nouveau bodies, set
High on the golden, after-glowing proscenium when   20
The break had come. And still, now as always, once
The show is over and we creep into the dull
Blaze of mid-afternoon sunshine, the hollow dole
Of the real descends on everything and we can know
That we have been in some place wholly elsewhere, a night   25
At noonday, not without dreams, whose portals shine
(Not ivory, not horn in ever-changing shapes)
But made of some weird, clear substance not often used for gates.
Stay for the second feature on a double bill
Always: it will teach you how to love, how not to live,   30
And how to leave the theater for that unlit, aloof
And empty world again. "B"-pictures showed us: shooting
More real than singing or making love; the shifting

Ashtray upon the mantel, moved by some idiot
Between takes, helping us learn beyond a trace of doubt   35
How fragile are imagined scenes; the dimming-out
Of all the brightness of the clear and highly lit
Interior of the hero's cockpit, when the stock shot
Of ancient dive-bombers peeling off cuts in, reshapes
Our sense of what is, finally, plausible; the grays   40
Of living rooms, the blacks of cars whose window glass
At night allows the strips of fake Times Square to pass
Jerkily by on the last ride; even the patch
Of sudden white, and inverted letters dashing
Up during the projectionist's daydream, dying   45
Quickly—these are the colors of our inner life.

Never ignore the stars, of course. But above all,
Follow the asteroids as well: though dark, they're more
Intense for never glittering; anyone can admire
Sparklings against a night sky, but against a bright   50
Background of prominence, to feel the Presences burnt
Into no fiery fame should be a more common virtue.
For, just as Vesta has no atmosphere, no verdure
Burgeons on barren Ceres, bit-players never surge
Into the rhythms of expansion and collapse, such   55
As all the flaming bodies live and move among.
But there, more steadfast than stars are, loved for their being,
Not for their burning, move the great Characters: see
Thin Donald Meek, that shuffling essence ever so
Affronting to Eros and to Pride; the pair of bloated   60
Capitalists, Walter Connolly and Eugene Pallette, seated
High in their offices above New York; the evil,
Blackening eyes of Sheldon Leonard, and the awful
Stare of Eduardo Cianelli. Remember those who have gone—
(Where's bat-squeaking Butterfly McQueen? Will we see again   65
That ever-anonymous drunk, waxed-moustached, rubber-legged
Caught in revolving doors?) and think of the light-years logged
Up in those humbly noble orbits, where no hot
Spotlight of solar grace consumes some blazing hearts,
Bestowing the flimsy immortality of stars   70
For some great distant instant. Out of the darkness stares
Venus, who seems to be what once we were, the fair
Form of emerging love, her nitrous atmosphere
Hiding her prizes. Into the black expanse peers
Mars, whom we in time will come to resemble: parched,   75
Xanthine desolations, dead Cimmerian seas, the far
Distant past preserved in the blood-colored crusts; fire

And water both remembered only. Having shined
Means having died. But having been real only, and shunned
Stardom, the planetoids are what we now are, humming
With us, above us, ever into the future, seeming
Ever to take the shapes of the world we wake to from dreams.

Always go in the morning if you can; it will
Be something more than habit if you do. Keep well
Away from most French farces. Try to see a set
Of old blue movies every so often, that the sight
Of animal doings out of the clothes of 'thirty-five
May remind you that even the natural act is phrased
In the terms and shapes of particular times and places.
Finally, remember always to honor the martyred dead.
The forces of darkness spread everywhere now, and the best
And brightest screens fade out, while many-antennaed beasts
Perch on the housetops, and along the grandest streets
Palaces crumble, one by one. The dimming starts
Slowly at first; the signs are few, as "Movies are
Better than Ever," "Get More out of Life. See a Movie" Or
Else there's no warning at all and, Whoosh! the theater falls,
Alas, transmogrified: no double-feature fills
A gleaming marquee with promises, now only lit
With "Pike and Whitefish Fresh Today" "Drano" and "Light
Or Dark Brown Sugar, Special." Try never to patronize
Such places (or pass them by one day a year). The noise
Of movie mansions changing form, caught in the toils
Of our lives' withering, rumbles, resounds and tolls
The knell of neighborhoods. Do not forget the old
Places, for everyone's home has been a battlefield.

I remember: the RKO COLONIAL; the cheap
ARDEN and ALDEN both; LOEW'S LINCOLN SQUARE's bright shape;
The NEWSREEL; the mandarin BEACON, resplendently arrayed;
The tiny SEVENTY-SEVENTH STREET, whose demise I rued
So long ago; the eighty-first street, sunrise-hued,
RKO; and then LOEW'S at eighty-third, which had
The colder pinks of sunset on it; and then, back
Across Broadway again, and up, you disembarked
At the YORKTOWN and then the STODDARD, with their dark
Marquees; the SYMPHONY had a decorative disk
With elongated 'twenties nudes whirling in it;
(Around the corner the THALIA, daughter of memory! owed
Her life to Foreign Hits, in days when you piled your coat
High on your lap and sat, sweating and cramped, to catch

"La Kermesse Heroique" every third week, and watched
Fritz Lang from among an audience of refugees, bewitched
By the sense of Crisis on and off that tiny bit
Of screen) Then north again: the RIVERSIDE, the bright
RIVIERA rubbing elbows with it; and right   125
Smack on a hundredth street, the MIDTOWN; and the rest
Of them: the CARLTON, EDISON, LOEW'S OLYMPIA, and best
Because, of course, the last of all, its final burst
Anonymous, the NEMO! These were once the pearls
Of two-and-a-half miles of Broadway! How many have paled   130
Into a supermarket's failure of the imagination?

Honor then all. Remember how once their splendor blazed
In sparkling necklaces across America's blasted
Distances and deserts: think how, at night, the fastest
Train might stop for water somewhere, waiting, faced   135
Westward, in deepening dusk, till ruby illuminations
Of something different from Everything Here, Now, shine
Out from the local Bijou, truest gem, the most bright
Because the most believed in, staving off the night
Perhaps for a while longer with its flickering light.   140

These fade. All fade. Let us honor them with our own fading sight.

19, *art-nouveau*: art and architecture popular at the end of the nineteenth century
that used free proportions and the forms of foliage in order to escape the rigidities of
classical conventions. 53, *Vesta*: a star named for the Roman goddess of fire. 54, *Ceres*:
a small planet or asteroid between Mars and Saturn; named for the Roman goddess of
agriculture. 60, *Eros*: in Greek mythology, god of love. 76, *Xanthine*: relating to Xan-
thus, an ancient ruined city in Asia Minor; *Cimmerian*: relating to the Cimmerii, a na-
tion of people supposed in ancient times to live in eternal darkness.

Paul Ramsey [b. 1924]

THE PHYSICAL IMPERFECTIONS OF OLD FILMS

We enter the darkened hall.
We look upon the dead
Who were sad even then.
The film is running. See,
He is kissing her. She   5
Lifts a hand to his face
As their faces touch. See,
Little lights from nowhere
Interpose their kiss. Let

The Physical Imperfections of Old Films   [293]

It be so, let light shine. 10
Let it be brown, odd light.
Let us not demand it.
For the faces which kiss
Are dead now, and lack means
Of bargaining. So we, 15
As we take our places,
Also lack means. Let us
Be ready for the light.
It is weakness which shines,
The celluloid's weakness, 20
But it is shining. It,
Unproposed, beautiful,
Is shining. It shines now.

C. Day-Lewis [1904–1972]

NEWSREEL

Enter the dream-house, brothers and sisters, leaving
Your debts asleep, your history at the door:
This is the home for heroes, and this loving
Darkness a fur you can afford.

Fish in their tank electrically heated 5
Nose without envy the glass wall: for them
Clerk, spy, nurse, killer, prince, the great and the defeated,
Move in a mute day-dream.

Bathed in this common source, you gape incurious
At what your active hours have willed— 10
Sleep-walking on that silver wall, the furious
Sick shapes and pregnant fancies of your world.

There is the mayor opening the oyster season:
A society wedding: the autumn hats look swell:
An old crock's race, and a politician 15
In fishing-waders to prove that all is well.

Oh, look at the warplanes! Screaming hysteric treble
In the long power-dive, like gannets they fall steep.
But what are they to trouble—
These silver shadows to trouble your watery, womb-deep sleep? 20

See the big guns, rising, groping, erected
To plant death in your world's soft womb.

Fire-bud, smoke-blossom, iron seed projected—
Are these exotics? They will grow nearer home:

Grow nearer home—and out of the dream-house stumbling
One night into a strangling air and the flung
Rags of children and thunder of stone niagaras tumbling,
You'll know you slept too long.

Norman Rosten [b. 1915]

NOBODY DIES LIKE HUMPHREY BOGART

Casual at the wheel, blinding rainstorm,
The usual blonde doll alongside—only
This time our man knows she's talked,
The double-c, and by his cold eyes
We can tell it's the end of the line for her.   5

It's all in the corner of his mouth:
Baby if we're gonna go we'll both go
My way, and his foot deep on the gas
With the needle (close-up) leaping to eighty.
She's shaky but ready to call his bluff.   10

Rain and the wipers clearing the glass
And dead ahead the good old roadblock.
Quick shot moll—the scream forming.
Quick shot Bogey—that endearing look
Which was his alone, face and soul.   15

Any way we go, baby, one or the other,
You'll look a lot prettier than me
When we're laid out in the last scene,
You in pink or blue with the angels,
Me with the same scar I was born in.   20

David Slavitt [b. 1935]

RIDE THE HIGH COUNTRY

I

The long red underwear of Randolph Scott,
the gold-rimmed spectacles of Joel McCrea,
underscore age, and through the reverend plot
the old gunfighters ride for one more day.

And Ladd was old in *Shane*, and in *High Noon*   5
old Coop had all his wrinkles emphasized
(with visible distaste he drew his gun).
The ritual of honor is disguised

and is an act of memory and will.
The pistol packing, popcorn eating child   10
feels the pretended stubble on his chin
and imagines his bones weary after the kill.
Even the movies' west is no longer wild,
its *virtu* now a trail bum, a has-been.

II

Odysseus, safe at home, can be our friend.   15
Orestes and the Furies come to terms
—our terms: we, craven, crave the tamest end,
the fireside remembrances of storms,

the hero's diminution. The old hand
is slower on the draw, the eyes are gone.   20
We may admire, but we understand
that nerve is all McCrea is working on,

that aged manliness becomes absurd.
He makes mistakes out on the trail, he has
fallen into their obvious trap, is hit,   25
and crumples with gun blazing. On the hard
ground he shakes our comfort as he dies,
affirming the agelessness of what is fit.

14, *virtu*: Italian; uprightness, valor, strength. 15, *Odysseus*: hero of the *Odyssey* of Homer. 16, *Orestes*: in Greek legend, the son of Agamemnon and Clytemnestra; he killed his mother, who had killed Agamemnon (see "Leda and the Swan," page 172, line 11 and note); *the Furies*: three spirits in Greek mythology who tortured those guilty of evil acts.

George Garrett [b. 1929]

GOODBYE, OLD PAINT, I'M LEAVING CHEYENNE

From the television set come shots and cries,
a hollow drum of hooves and then,
emerging from snowy chaos, the tall riders
plunging in a tumultuous surf of dust.
The Stage, it seems, is overdue.   5
My children, armed to the teeth, enchanted,

are, for the moment at least, quiet.
I see the Badmen riding for the Gulch,
all grins, not knowing as we do
("The rest of you guys follow me!")   10
the Hero's going to get there first.
And as the plot like a lariat spins out
a tricky noose, I shrink and become
a boy with a sweaty nickel in his palm
waiting to see two features and the serial   15
at the Rialto on a Saturday morning:
Buck Jones, the taciturn, Tom Mix
of silver spinning guns and a white horse,
and somebody left face to face with a buzz saw,
to writhe into next Saturday morning.   20

But how you have changed, my cavaliers,
how much we have had to grow up!
No Hero now is anything but cautious.
(We know the hole a .45 can make.)
No Badman's born that way.   25
("My mother loved me but she died.")
No buzz saw frightens like the whine
of a mind gone wild. No writhing's like
the spirit's on its bed of nails.
I clench my nickel tighter in my fist.   30
Children, this plot is new to me.
I watch the Hero take the wrong road
at the Fork and gallop away, grim-faced,
worn out from the exercise of choice.
I see the Badmen safely reach the Gulch,   35
then fight among themselves and die,
proving good luck is worse than any wound.
My spellbound children stare and couldn't care
less about my fit of raw nostalgia
or all the shabby ghosts I loved and lost.   40

Louis Coxe [b. 1918]

ON SEEING FILMS OF THE WAR

When will that war end? My whole house is still *apos.*
Except for the screen that lifts Pacific swells
Island by island in a rising host
And I live in an instant, out of real, false, *ant.*
And imagined passions, the old ache again   5
As though my heart yearned backward for old pain.

Empress Augusta Bay, Garapan town:
Glass raised to glass, the old names ring like coin
Pieces of the dead—my own dead self not least—
Whom I mourn yet give cold comfort in their rest   *10*
Under new lives, new wars, the unmemoried sift
Of distance that drifts with time on a feathered shaft.

Love's arrow poisoned and pointed by false hope *symb.*
Strikes home here—to me, now, before sleep—
Enslaving memory wounded with desire,   *15*
With youth and fervor: through a fog of war
Distance like a land-loom lifts the past
Brimmed with illusion like a rising glass.

7: both places mentioned are in the Pacific Islands south of Japan—Empress Augusta Bay in Bougainville Island in the Solomons, and Garapan on Saipan in the Marianas.

Edwin S. Godsey [1930–1966]

HOPPY

When Mary pulled the sorrel's reins from Stephen
The stunt man's hands, swung her buckskin squaw's skirt
Over, leaned up into his neck and, by God,
Was gone, Morris began screaming: "What are
You doing? Is she ruining me? Cut!   *5*
Hey, sweetheart! Somebody grab that woman. Cut!
She shouldn't be galloping in it here! Cut!"
I was the camera jockey on this series.
I got her last frames going over the rise.
Guitars were to volume up there for *The End*   *10*
With boys back here all lithe as cats, leaning
Against the fence and singing "Tumbleweed"
While Hoppy turned, waved, and rode away.

It was his riding off like that that took her,
I guess. It must have made the girl forget   *15*
Hoppy was phony. It's hard to understand, though.
She'd been around. She knew the camera angles.
You would say this one had quit pulling taffy.
One time I took her out myself. Just once.
She was O.K.—a little hard is all.   *20*
But that was back before they disappeared.

Way back before the war. You never know
About a person. Some people get mixed up.

I could have used a Hoppy, oh, my God,
At Anzio. Oh, you'd have been great, Hoppy,   25
The way you jingle-jumped from boulders, bullets
Whining in ricochet but plugged your ten
And came out clean ("Move in for the close-up, William."),
And gee-whiz coursed the outlaws through the hills,
Leaped on them horseback, rolled into the gulches   30
And whipped them silly in the sound effects.

Maybe she thought it was the real thing or
Something like that. It's hard to understand—
The Conestoga wagons, whiskey brawls,
Gold miners, Sioux with smuggled Winchesters—   35
They'd take your scalp—the gunfights at high noon.
But in that wild land she was safe with Hoppy.

It's interesting to think what they said when
She caught up with him. Hoppy would grin and nod:
"You keep a sharp eye out for Indians, Ma'am."   40
And she, "At last, I've found you, Hoppy. Hoppy,
I love you." "But Ma'am," he'd say, "no epic heroes
Have time for love—I mean, the family kind.
I can't be different. It's mostly killing here.
A hard country, here, to live in." "Better,"   45
She'd say. And he, "But this is no place for a
Woman or child." "Why it's a good place, Hoppy,
A good place. We'll have sons—trust me—more than
The sands of the desert. Every one a hero.
I've seen the signs." "We ought to make camp soon . . ."   50
(What could he say?) "You understand you'll have
To keep a sharp eye out." They'd build a campfire,
Drink coffee, eat sourdough hotcakes, and hear coyotes.
It wouldn't be as easy as a motel.

So all in buckskin love went riding on   55
Somewhere. At least they never reappeared.
Old actors say they ride the desert still
(At times they see a family resemblance
In one of the young crew but never so soft-
Spoken or beautiful as Hoppy was)—   60
She and the hero with the tall black Stetson
And easy grin of a boy, on the white steed.

They say they ride toward sunset by the mesquite,
Through the arroyos and beneath saguaros
That stand like giants in the land: Clip-clop,   65
Clippity, clippity, clippity, where the dust
Splashes like pools of water from those hoofs,
And twilight coming on in El Dorado.

It's nice to think like that, but what I think is
They ran into trouble at Los Alamos   70
Back in the forties, and needed to move fast
("Ma'am, what in hell is that?") and didn't make it—
And lost the way I lost at Anzio.

Hoppy: the character in this poem resembles in several respects the hero created
by William Boyd, known as Hopalong Cassidy. 24, *Anzio*: an Italian port, south of
Rome; it was the site of the Allied beachhead in the invasion of Italy in January, 1944.
68, *El Dorado*: Spanish for "the golden"; a name for a mythical place of incredible
wealth. 70, *Los Alamos*: a town in New Mexico not far from Santa Fe; it was estab-
lished as a center for the testing of atomic bombs.

Philip Legler [b. 1928]

LOVE AND AN OLD WESTERN
AT THE STARLITE DRIVE-IN THEATER

[*A Comic Opera*]

In from the roundup and dressed to kill
    (His tale begun), behind the neighs
By the Banker's ranch, the old corral
    And the Sheriff's Meg, Good Ranger Rod—
Whose eyes did woo, whose guns did blaze,   5
    Disguised, by the Law, as Outlaw Pete
Who strummed a tune that was prairie-sweet—
Stood ready to draw, one hulk of a lad
    While you put up with my ways.

Drawing four aces but playing no fiddle,   10
    Flashing a gun (You sighed) in the bar,
Killer, sighting the Law in his bottle,
    Bet the four aces, raised, then fanned
Sheriff whose blaze was less than his star;
    Shot Teller and Banker to rob from the safe   15
His golden deed—Sheriff's daughter as wife.
Killer he'd beg Mourning Meg for her hand
    As I mourned begging for more.

Five horses from town an abandoned mine
    (I touched you, knowing hidden gold   20
Was there), no longer claimed by a sign,
    Was willed to Meg. But the Hired Killer,
A scar for a cheek, and eyes gazing cold,
    He pumped poor Meg by the spring and bound
Her maiden arms. Would the gold be found?   25
For Killer was hard, hard on the daughter
    And I would be hard and bold.

When Killer he drew, Meg's body went dumb
    (We touched to kiss and, kissing, laid
A wager that Desperate Pete would come);   30
    But Pete, he was making a furious plan—
A way to get into that mine, not a raid
    On Hired Killer—when gallop, then horse
Came prancing to warn of Killer, of course.
And Meg, meanwhile, fought loose and she ran   35
    And you grew tense and afraid.

Killer and Pete, their parts were both short
    And alike (We knew the role): Gold buys
More than a share, and Pete would cavort
    Like Killer, going from glitter to worse.   40
But Rod, afraid of Pete's ways and Meg's sighs
    When fever swells in the head, his lust
Bit dust—he showed his hand—while his fast
Gun arm and the change of his Wanted Face
    Were my honor and only disguise.   45

Now Meg, Young Meg, she ran like a heifer;
    Killer ran, too (Your eyes gazed wide).
But Lucky Ranger, astride, galloped after
    To empty his chamber; then like a weed
Killer fell tumbling at Meg's best side,   50
    Never to take of her treasure, but cast
His shadow across her, the villain at last
As she and her Rod, in song, mounted steed
    And I was all ready to ride.

Then Meg grew saddened, pressing her luck   55
    (Sweeter than sugar), for Rod had no yen
To ride with a maiden or share in the rock.
    The sun was his gold; he'd ride and die
Out roaming the prairie—a legend to man,
    A lover to a woman who never would wed,   60

Love and an Old Western at the Starlite Drive-In Theater   **[301]**

A Ranger who rode with a price on his head.
But they rode, they rode away singing, and I
    Climbed back in the saddle again.

They jogged, two riders, over that prairie
    (We knew of thirst) till sunset cast   65
Its circle of shadow. Then down a valley—
    The mine, the mine; but Meg she sank pale,
For Ranger's westerly ways they did blast
    Not the rock but the partnership in the ore
That she and her song had long picked to share,   70
While Ranger rode off toward Sunset Trail
    And we knew these riches at last.

Now you may say, What's Ranger Rod's lot
    When he rids the town of a gunman's sins
And saves Brave Meg from God knows what.   75
    A Faithful Horse, of course, and I'm told
Because he's the hero his high-riding wins
    Smiles from the daughter, kisses his medal,
A twang from his singing guitar, and his saddle
To ride from his Meg, the mine and that gold,   80
    And that's where the tale begins.

Valery Nash [b. 1932]

WORKING FOR DR. NO

What sort of man could inspire fear
like that?

Perhaps it was the beautiful efficiency
Of the Doctor's organization,
or the attraction of strict discipline,
or the fact that everyone else was doing it—
the little luxuries that those on the payroll let show   5
like hints: a silk shirt, a bracelet, old wine
in unaccustomed, shaking hands . . .

Awake each morning at dawn, tossing
searching his rum-soaked brain
for details of the evening before: 10
the chance word slipped at the Club;
sweating under the sheets,

with always the image of two steel hands,
the round room, the echoing dark voice . . .

Does Professor Dent remember the days   15
before he worked for Doctor No?
Does he dream of leaving the island
retiring with his nest egg
to pursue geological research?

He would still waken sweating, trying   20
to remember where he slipped up . . .
And could he ever be sure?
He is safer staying where terror
becomes a way of life
as well-oiled as any other,   25
where there's no need to wonder what he fears.

Now his days are rigidly prescribed.
The order at Crab Key:
                    There.
                    On the table.   30
                    Pick it up.
Has the tarantula
reached through its cage to his skin?
Or is it his nerves dancing?

Dr. No: one of the films based on Ian Fleming's novels about James Bond.

William Meredith [b. 1919]

TWO FIGURES FROM THE MOVIES

I

The papers that clear him tucked in his inside pocket
And the grip of the plucky blond light on his bicep,
He holds the gang covered now, and backs for the door
That gives on the daylit street and the yare police.
But the regular customers know that before the end   5
With its kissing and money and adequate explanation,
He has still to back into the arms of the baldheaded man
With the huge signet ring and the favorable odds of surprise,
Somehow to outface the impossible arrogant stare,
And will his luck hold, they wonder, and has he the skill?   10

II

Pericles:

This is the rarest dream that e'er dull sleep
Did mock sad fools withal: this cannot be.
My daughter's buried . . .
                              O Helicanus!
Down on thy knees, thank the holy gods as loud
As thunder threatens us: this is Marina . . .
                              Mine own, Helicanus;
She is not dead at Tarsus, as she should have been . . .

They wouldn't dare to let it end like this:
Her lying still and silver on the screen.
Surely some recog recognition scene
Will cornily restore our stone-dead child,
Her who for reels beguiled us and who lies   *15*
Now mirror-undetected and called cold.

Part II: The epigraph comes from the fifth act of Shakespeare's *Pericles, Prince of
Tyre*, in which Pericles' daughter Marina is found years after she was assumed dead.
The last line of the poem refers to King Lear, Act V, Scene iii, in which Lear tries to
convince himself that his daughter Cordelia is alive by holding a feather and a look-
ing-glass to her nostrils.

R. H. W. Dillard [b. 1937]

THE DAY I STOPPED DREAMING ABOUT BARBARA STEELE

The drizzle shifted,
A bird drowsy with rain
Yawned into song,
The foghorn ran down.

Below the castle walls   *5*
Her head grisly with masks
The long slices of her sides
And the heavy dog's howl
(I hear the clamor of horses
     And the long rope to which I am attached   *10*
     Buckles beneath me)
The knotted arm
And the long sinew
That lays itself along
The long curve of her side.   *15*

Blond, her legs curved
To the horse's flank,
Making the sun dance
To the blue of her eyes

(Is the last dream before waking   20
More flesh than real,
More real than the dark before?)

The horse dances
And she is as purely naked
As the pine-needled dawn   25
And the dogs run lazy and smooth
In the tall grass.

The bronze door,
Stone,
A muffled cry,   30
The iron maiden,
And the sun
Crazy with its own size
In the moving lake
Where her horse lowers its head to drink   35
And she sleeps on his arching spine.

Barbara Steele: a British actress whose dark hair and mysterious features helped
her successful portrayals of evil women in various horror films.

Ben Belitt [**b. 1911**]

THE SPOOL

They splay at a bend of the road, rifles slung, the
shadows minimal, their hands tugging their slings by
the upper swivel to ease the routine of the march.
They have been moving since morning, and over each
has descended that singleness, mournful and   5
comatose, which is the mysterious gift of the march.
Their helmets shadow their eyes, their chinstraps
dangling. In the raddle of grasses their solitude
floats in a drift of identities, a common melancholy.
A captain enters the frame at the head of his   10

company. His face flashes. With his left hand he tilts
back his helmet, while with his right he draws the
length of an elbow across forehead and nose, his
stained armpits showing dark. A bracelet flashes
behind him. The column recedes, rifles close over the 15
canted belts, moving up, the packed backs vulnerable:
                    (Cut)
Late afternoon: in the halflight a handful of blazing
sticks, four infantrymen heating mess tins over an
eddy of smoke, a fifth on his hams, his eyes upcast
from the rim of his metal cup. Nearby a corporal 20
works a patch into the chamber of his rifle;
he repeats four syllables and smiles sleepily into
the camera. The camera moves to the bivouac area;
a group, their meatcans close to their mouths,
spooning the compost, chinese-fashion, and clowning 25
between mouthfuls. Very close; their jaws,
lightly bearded; the necks in their jacket collars
strained in an easy horseplay, the Adam's apples
rapidly raised and released in the human exertion
of eating. In deep shadow, the light failing, 30
very close: a private tugs at his boot by the toe
and the round of the heel. Deliberately, he draws
the boot clear of his foot, sets it aside with deep
satisfaction, massages his instep over a maternal
thickness of socks. He bends toward the other foot, 35
camera-shy, a half-smile breaking:
                    (Cut)
It is not yet possible to distinguish the forms
behind the camouflage netting. They move in the
central darkness of the gun, stacking shells and
bringing up powder charges. Only the bulk of the 40
howitzer is sure, the gun-barrel crossing the line
of the valley under the tented netting.
A village is burning in the valley. In the watery light,
smoke deepens over three hearthbeds of brightness.
A spire. A siding. 45
A ladder of rooftops.
The gun fires. The picture trembles.
                    (Cut)
An iron darkening.
The hip of a tank blackens a frame,
foreshortened, the treads close to the lens, 50
a rushing of hammers, rings. A second tank sprints
into focus at topspeed. The lens is cleared.
A cobbled street, a row of country-houses,

walled, a rosebush in the heavy light, blown
forward. Dust falls in the afterdraught,   55
a grain at a time. The camera is watchful.
A rifleman moves up the frame, his rifle at low port,
his shadow buffing the cobbles, crouched. He pauses
under the rosebush, his rifle hiked. A second figure
breaks through the frame, freezing between the   60
foreground and the far doorway. The man under
the rosetree sights carefully. The second man listens.
He raises his rifle, barrel backwards, and brings
the butt down heavily on the door panels.
The rifle rebounds.   65
He measures a second blow, his teeth bared
slightly in a reflex of anxiety. His eye is large.
The buttplate smashes over doorknob and lock,
the knocker flies upward once, the panel splinters
all at once. The man kicks the door open easily   70
with a booted foot. He listens, bent toward his
rifle-sights. He signals to the second man and enters
the doorway, stooped, like a man entering a cave:

                              (Cut)
Brightness through trees: a damascene.
At the edge of a clearing, a parked jeep.   75
Two medical corpsmen lash litters to the jeep
engine a few hundred yards behind front lines.
The litter-poles enter the lens over the arch
of the engine. On the litter, a swathed head, a shock
of broken hair, motionless, a fall of blankets.   80
The stretcher-bearers vault lightly to their seats
and move off at a crawl.
Roadmarker: *Battalion Aid Station*. A corner of
charred wall, rubble, glass, timber; legend: *Epicerie*.
The stretcher-bearers dismount.   85
The film is bad.
Presently a gloved hand in a surgeon's sheath,
holding a forceps. Briskly the hand moves over a
circlet of maimed flesh noosed in a bloody bandage.
A scalpel flashes between the living hand and the   90
human hurt, forcing the rind of the wound
filling the frame. The camera submits, framing
the wound like a surgeon's retractor, its gaze
nerveless and saline. The gauzes blacken swiftly,
too heavy for the jaws of the forceps.   95
The surgeon at full figure: a breeze finds the fold
of his tunic. In the distance, the litter-bearers are

leaning for the litter-poles. His eyes hold the optical
center of the lens, unanswered, his mouth rejects
contemplation, not yet relaxed, his hands are void   *100*
in their glimmering cicatrice of rubber.

84, *Epicerie:* French; grocery store. 101, *cicatrice:* scar.

Jerry Hammond [b. 1923]

FEATURE TIME

The doors have opened and
a ticket you can buy
any time you feel like it.
A pretty woman will
sell you some popcorn or   *5*
ice cream ahead of time
when the projector shines
lights through the old ratty
black velveteen curtain
that hangs between shows and   *10*
the credit lines flash on
and fade out why always
too fast to find out who
does what in the funny
flick today that stars you   *15*
which you will see only
after you are going
to lay down a very
dear price of admission
for the only seat in   *20*
the house that is behind
the balcony post.

Fred Chappell [b. 1936]

SKIN FLICK

The selfsame surface that billowed once with
The shapes of Trigger and Gene. New faces now
Are in the saddle. Tits and buttocks
Slide rattling down the beam as down
A coal chute; in the splotched light   *5*
The burning bush strikes dumb.

Different sort of cattle drive:
No water for miles and miles.

In the aisles, new bugs and rats
Though it's the same Old Paint.   10

Audience of lepers, hopeless and homeless,
Or like the buffalo, at home
In the wind only. No
Mushy love stuff for them.

They eye the violent innocence they always knew.   15
Is that the rancher's palomino daughter?
Is this her eastern finishing school?

Same old predicament:
No water for miles and miles,
The horizon breeds no cavalry.   20

Men, draw your wagons in a circle. Be ready.

12
Monuments
of Unageing
Intellect

Art and Artifice

William Blake [1757–1827]

THE TYGER

Tyger! Tyger! burning bright
In the forests of the night,
What immortal hand or eye
Could frame thy fearful symmetry?

In what distant deeps or skies   5
Burnt the fire of thine eyes?
On what wings dare he aspire?
What the hand, dare seize the fire?

And what shoulder, & what art,
Could twist the sinews of thy heart?   10
And when thy heart began to beat,
What dread hand? & what dread feet?

What the hammer? what the chain?
In what furnace was thy brain?
What the anvil? what dread grasp   15
Dare its deadly terrors clasp?

When the stars threw down their spears,
And water'd heaven with their tears,
Did he smile his work to see?
Did he who made the Lamb make thee?   20

Tyger! Tyger! burning bright
In the forests of the night,
What immortal hand or eye
Dare frame thy fearful symmetry?

Samuel Taylor Coleridge [1772–1834]

KUBLA KHAN

In Xanadu did Kubla Khan
A stately pleasure-dome decree:
Where Alph, the sacred river, ran
Through caverns measureless to man
  Down to a sunless sea.   *5*
So twice five miles of fertile ground
With walls and towers were girdled round:
And here were gardens bright with sinuous rills,
Where blossomed many an incense-bearing tree,
And here were forests ancient as the hills,   *10*
Enfolding sunny spots of greenery.

But oh! that deep romantic chasm which slanted
Down the green hill athwart a cedarn cover!
A savage place! as holy and enchanted
As e'er beneath a waning moon was haunted   *15*
By woman wailing for her demon-lover!
And from this chasm, with ceaseless turmoil seething,
As if this earth in fast thick pants were breathing,
A mighty fountain momently was forced,
Amid whose swift half-intermitted burst   *20*
Huge fragments vaulted like rebounding hail,
Or chaffy grain beneath the thresher's flail:
And 'mid these dancing rocks at once and ever
It flung up momently the sacred river.
Five miles meandering with a mazy motion   *25*
Through wood and dale the sacred river ran,
Then reached the caverns measureless to man,
And sank in tumult to a lifeless ocean:
And 'mid this tumult Kubla heard from far
Ancestral voices prophesying war!   *30*
    The shadow of the dome of pleasure
    Floated midway on the waves;
    Where was heard the mingled measure
    From the fountain and the caves.
It was a miracle of rare device,   *35*
A sunny pleasure-dome with caves of ice!
    A damsel with a dulcimer
    In a vision once I saw:
    It was an Abyssinian maid,
    And on her dulcimer she played.   *40*
    Singing of Mount Abora.

Could I revive within me
Her symphony and song,
To such a deep delight 'twould win me,
That music loud and long, 45
I would build that dome in air,
That sunny dome! those caves of ice!
And all who heard should see them there,
And all should cry, Beware! Beware!
His flashing eyes, his floating hair! 50
Weave a circle round him thrice,
And close your eyes with holy dread,
For he on honey-dew hath fed,
And drunk the milk of Paradise.

Kubla Khan: the first ruler of the Mongol dynasty in thirteenth-century China. The geographical and physical features described and named are imaginary. 37, *dulcimer:* a stringed instrument.

William Butler Yeats [1865–1939]

SAILING TO BYZANTIUM

I

That is no country for old men. The young
In one another's arms, birds in the trees
— Those dying generations — at their song,
The salmon-falls, the mackerel-crowded seas,
Fish, flesh, or fowl, commend all summer long 5
Whatever is begotten, born, and dies.
Caught in that sensual music all neglect
Monuments of unageing intellect.

II

An aged man is but a paltry thing,
A tattered coat upon a stick, unless 10
Soul clap its hands and sing, and louder sing
For every tatter in its mortal dress,
Nor is there singing school but studying
Monuments of its own magnificence;
And therefore I have sailed the seas and come 15
To the holy city of Byzantium.

III

O sages standing in God's holy fire
As in the gold mosaic of a wall,
Come from the holy fire, perne in a gyre,
And be the singing-masters of my soul. 20

Consume my heart away; sick with desire
And fastened to a dying animal
It knows not what it is; and gather me
Into the artifice of eternity.

IV

Once out of nature I shall never take   25
My bodily form from any natural thing,
But such a form as Grecian goldsmiths make
Of hammered gold and gold enamelling
To keep a drowsy Emperor awake;
Or set upon a golden bough to sing   30
To lords and ladies of Byzantium
Of what is past, or passing, or to come.

Byzantium became for Yeats a symbol of artistic perfection; he saw the impersonality of these artificers who made that city (now Istanbul) flourish in the fifth century A.D., and contrasted their impersonal devotion to art with the sensuality of natural life.

19, *perne in a gyre:* whirl in a spiralling fashion.

John Keats [1795–1821]

ODE ON A GRECIAN URN

Thou still unravished bride of quietness,
    Thou foster-child of silence and slow time,
Sylvan historian, who canst thus express
    A flowery tale more sweetly than our rhyme:
What leaf-fringed legend haunts about thy shape   5
    Of deities or mortals, or of both,
        In Tempe or the dales of Arcady?
What men or gods are these? What maidens loth?
    What mad pursuit? What struggle to escape?
        What pipes and timbrels? What wild ecstasy?   10

Heard melodies are sweet, but those unheard
    Are sweeter; therefore, ye soft pipes, play on;
Not to the sensual ear, but, more endeared,
    Pipe to the spirit ditties of no tone:
Fair youth, beneath the trees, thou canst not leave   15
    Thy song, nor ever can those trees be bare;
        Bold Lover, never, never canst thou kiss,
Though winning near the goal—yet, do not grieve;

She cannot fade, though thou hast not thy bliss,
    For ever wilt thou love, and she be fair!

Ah, happy, happy boughs! that cannot shed
  Your leaves, nor ever bid the spring adieu;
And, happy melodist, unwearièd,
  For ever piping songs for ever new;
More happy love! more happy, happy love!
    For ever warm and still to be enjoyed,
      For ever panting, and for ever young;
All breathing human passion far above,
    That leaves a heart high-sorrowful and cloyed,
      A burning forehead, and a parching tongue.

Who are these coming to the sacrifice?
  To what green altar, O mysterious priest,
Lead'st thou that heifer lowing at the skies,
    And all her silken flanks with garlands dressed?
What little town by river or sea shore,
  Or mountain-built with peaceful citadel,
    Is emptied of this folk, this pious morn?
And, little town, thy streets for evermore
  Will silent be; and not a soul to tell
    Why thou art desolate, can e'er return.

O Attic shape! Fair attitude! with brede
  Of marble men and maidens overwrought,
With forest branches and the trodden weed;
  Thou, silent form, dost tease us out of thought
As doth eternity: Cold Pastoral!
  When old age shall this generation waste,
    Thou shalt remain, in midst of other woe
Than ours, a friend to man, to whom thou say'st,
  "Beauty is truth, truth beauty,"—that is all
    Ye know on earth, and all ye need to know.

7, *Tempe* and *Arcady:* Greek localities famed in poetry for the beauty of their land-
scapes. 41, *Attic:* Greek; *brede:* woven design; compare *braid.*

W. H. Auden [1907–1973]

MUSÉE DES BEAUX ARTS

About suffering they were never wrong,
The Old Masters: how well they understood

Its human position; how it takes place
While someone else is eating or opening a window or just walking
    dully along;
How, when the aged are reverently, passionately waiting   *5*
For the miraculous birth, there always must be
Children who did not specially want it to happen, skating
On a pond at the edge of the wood:
They never forgot
That even the dreadful martyrdom must run its course   *10*
Anyhow in a corner, some untidy spot
Where the dogs go on with their doggy life and the torturer's horse
Scratches its innocent behind on a tree.

In Breughel's *Icarus*, for instance: how everything turns away
Quite leisurely from the disaster; the ploughman may   *15*
Have heard the splash, the forsaken cry,
But for him it was not an important failure; the sun shone
As it had to on the white legs disappearing into the green
Water; and the expensive delicate ship that must have seen
Something amazing, a boy falling out of the sky,   *20*
Had somewhere to get to and sailed calmly on.

Musée des Beaux Arts; Museum of Fine Arts. The museum in this poem is in
Brussels, where Breughel's *Icarus* hangs. 14, Breughel's *Icarus:* Icarus and his father,
Daedalus, flew with artificial wings made partly of wax; Icarus flew too near the sun,
which melted the wax, and so he plunged to his death. Pieter Breughel (ca. 1520–
1569) was a Flemish painter famous for his energetic depictions of peasant scenes;
his *Icarus* is as described in the poem: Icarus' legs are disappearing into the water in
a corner of the painting; the rest of the painting has nothing to do with the legend.

John Peale Bishop [1892–1944]

A RECOLLECTION

Famously she descended, her red hair
Unbound and bronzed by sea-reflections, caught
Crinkled with sea-pearls. The fine slender taut
Knees that let down her feet upon the air,

Young breasts, slim flanks and golden quarries were   *5*
Odder than when the young distraught
Unknown Venetian, painting her portrait, thought
He'd not imagined what he painted there.

And I too commerced with that golden cloud:
Lipped her delicious hands and had my ease   *10*
Faring fantastically, perversely proud.

All loveliness demands our courtesies.
Since she was dead I praised her as I could
Silently, among the Barberini bees.

14, *Barberini:* a prominent Venetian family, in whose coat of arms bees figure.

X. J. Kennedy [b. 1929]

NUDE DESCENDING A STAIRCASE

Toe upon toe, a snowing flesh,
A gold of lemon, root and rind,
She sifts in sunlight down the stairs
With nothing on. Nor on her mind.

We spy beneath the banister   *5*
A constant thresh of thigh on thigh—
Her lips imprint the swinging air
That parts to let her parts go by.

One-woman waterfall, she wears
Her slow descent like a long cape   *10*
And pausing, on the final stair
Collects her motions into shape.

Nude Descending a Staircase: a series of paintings by Marcel Duchamp (b. 1887), painted in the Cubist manner, with a series of five schematized human forms superimposed in procession down a winding staircase.

Ann Stanford [b. 1916]

EDWARD HICKS

"The Peaceable Kingdom"
Oil on wood, c. 1830

This was the peaceable kingdom: the river flows
like time beside it. This tiny slope,
grass covered, slants up to an impassable forest.

Half up the sky a natural bridge
curves like a rainbow. In such a place   5
Penn pledged his peace to all his Indian brothers.

He stands there, engraved, given to fat,
his friendly hands extended to the natives
who, lean as Caesar, accept his fatal gifts.

But that good Quaker in his peaceful country   10
is past and backdrop. On this crowded shore
herded together, the wolf and the lamb lie down

And the tiger looks at the kid as once
in the garden of Eden, innocent of blood.
The calf, the young lion, the fatling lie together.   15

And the cow and the bear share their ration of straw,
The lion and the ox beside one another, surprised.
The eagle and the dove eat from the hands of a child.

Another plays with the serpent. In all this mountain
there is no danger, for the earth is filled   20
with the word of the lord. There is no hunger.

How could this be? Even here, withdrawn on a mountain,
where the quail and dove walk at the grasses' edges,
I hear the world washing away my kingdom.
The deer go by, seeking the last wild ranges.   25

   Edward Hicks (1780–1849) was a Quaker minister and painter who became inter-
ested in the theme of the Peaceable Kingdom partly because of a schism in Quaker-
ism. He painted nearly fifty versions of the subject.

Bink Noll [b. 1927]

LANDSCAPE WITH PERVERT

(instructions to the painter on the
difficulties of pastoral conventions)

Once more, if you want, make many
into one geography that feeds
sheep and shepherds their hearty fare.

Start their tradition-hardened hands
playing flutes atop every hill.   5
With simplicity endow them,
and in one corner grow a wood
in whose thick, wrong shall be punished.

At once! villain and hauled child cross
through shadows you think you've rendered safe—   10
into some shrubs where he hugs her
till delight burns delight to ash.
While mirthful swains continue mirth
show him button up and sneak away.
You have to catch Outrage at work   15
for Nature and Imitation's sake,

fiend Outrage and his thousand kin
who pass privily over the map
and hide along its gentle paths.
No constabulary can catch   20
his multitude nor next thrash them
in that half-used, half-useful wood.
Instead you must smell out danger
and draw it stinking everywhere.

She is victimized whose surprise   25
cried out a field animal's cry:
she who supposed the world was kind
as parents: whose faces you soon
should change from innocence as hers changed
while he held her nose at his chest.   30
She smelled then how foully her hens
had scared in the fox's teeth.

Evening. They sit beneath the eaves,
a family who simply believe
their girl will grow up beautiful,   35
fill with a young wife's milkiness.
But across their ripening thoughts
news of murder flames and ignites
grief like a curse in heads less easy
than you first represented them.   40

Paint that. People the middle ground
with maidens composing posies,
mourners with elegiac scrolls,
musicians with flutes tuned sad behind

a rustic bier borne toward a green
where they've made a distant grave to lay
the child, wishing the doer were dead
with her, safe under varnished grass.

George Turberville   [1540?–1595?]

THAT NO MAN SHOULD WRITE BUT SUCH AS DO EXCEL

Should no man write, say you, but such as do excel?
This fond device of yours deserves a Bable and a Bell;

Then one alone should do, or very few indeed:
For that in every Art there can but one alone exceed.

Should others idle be, and waste their age in vain,   5
That might perhaps in after time the prick and price attain?

By practice skill is got, by practice wit is won.
At games you see how many do to win the wager run.

Yet one among the moe doth bear away the Bell:
Is that a cause to say the rest, in running, did not well?   10

If none in physic should but only Galen deal,
No doubt a thousand perish would whom Physic now doth heal.

Each one his talent hath, to use at his devise,
Which makes that many men as well as one are counted wise.

For if that wit alone in one should rest and reign,   15
Then God the skulls of other men did make but all in vain.

Let each one try his force, and do the best he can,
For thereunto appointed were the hand and head of man.

The poet Horace speaks against thy reason plain
Who says, 'tis somewhat to attempt, although thou not attain   20

The scope in every thing: to touch the highest degree
Is passing hard; to do the best, sufficing is for thee.

1, *Bable*: a scepter-like device carried by a Fool; *Bell*: prize; also, part of a Fool's costume. 6, *prick*: archer's term for the target; *price*: praise. 9, *moe*: others, many. 11, *Galen*: Greek physician of the second century A.D. 19, *Horace*: Quintus Horatius Flaccus, a Roman poet of the first century B.C.

Samuel Johnson [1709–1784]

LINES

Written in ridicule of certain
* poems published in 1777*

Wheresoe'er I turn my view,
All is strange, yet nothing new;
Endless labor all along,
Endless labor to be wrong;

Phrase that time has flung away,   *5*
Uncouth words in disarray,
Tricked in antique ruff and bonnet,
Ode, and elegy, and sonnet.

Alexander Pope [1688–1744]

from AN ESSAY ON CRITICISM

Part II

   Of all the causes which conspire to blind
Man's erring judgment, and misguide the mind,
What the weak head with strongest bias rules,
Is *Pride*, the never-failing vice of fools.
Whatever Nature has in worth denied,   *5*
She gives in large recruits of needful pride;
For as in bodies, thus in souls, we find
What wants in blood and spirits, swelled with wind:
Pride, where wit fails, steps in to our defence,
And fills up all the mighty void of sense.   *10*
If once right reason drives that cloud away,
Truth breaks upon us with resistless day.
Trust not yourself; but your defects to know,
Make use of ev'ry friend—and ev'ry foe.
   A little learning is a dang'rous thing;   *15*
Drink deep, or taste not the Pierian spring:
There shallow draughts intoxicate the brain,
And drinking largely sobers us again.
Fired at first sight with what the Muse imparts,
In fearless youth we tempt the heights of arts,   *20*
While from the bounded level of our mind,
Short views we take, nor see the lengths behind;
But more advanced, behold with strange surprise
New distant scenes of endless science rise!
So pleased at first the tow'ring Alps we try,   *25*
Mount o'er the vales, and seem to tread the sky,

Th' eternal snows appear already past,
And the first clouds and mountains seem the last:
But, those attained, we tremble to survey
The growing labours of the lengthened way, 30
Th' increasing prospect tires our wand'ring eyes,
Hills peep o'er hills, and Alps on Alps arise!
    A perfect judge will read each work of wit
With the same spirit that its author writ:
Survey the whole, nor seek slight faults to find 35
Where nature moves, and rapture warms the mind;
Nor lose, for that malignant dull delight,
The gen'rous pleasure to be charmed with wit.
But in such lays as neither ebb, nor flow,
Correctly cold, and regularly low, 40
That shunning faults, one quiet tenour keep;
We cannot blame indeed—but we may sleep.
In wit, as nature, what affects our hearts
Is not th' exactness of peculiar parts;
'Tis not a lip, or eye, we beauty call, 45
But the joint force and full result of all.
Thus when we view some well-proportioned dome,
(The world's just wonder, and ev'n thine, O Rome!)
No single parts unequally surprise,
All comes united to th' admiring eyes; 50
No monstrous height, or breadth, or length appear;
The whole at once is bold, and regular.
    Whoever thinks a faultless piece to see,
Thinks what ne'er was, nor is, nor e'er shall be.
In ev'ry work regard the writer's end, 55
Since none can compass more than they intend;
And if the means be just, the conduct true,
Applause, in spite of trivial faults, is due.
As men of breeding, sometimes men of wit,
T' avoid great errors, must the less commit: 60
Neglect the rules each verbal critic lays,
For not to know some trifles, is a praise.
Most critics, fond of some subservient art,
Still make the whole depend upon a part:
They talk of principles, but notions prize, 65
And all to one loved folly sacrifice.
    Once on a time, La Mancha's knight, they say,
A certain bard encount'ring on the way,
Discoursed in terms as just, with looks as sage,
As e'er could Dennis of the Grecian stage, 70
Concluding all were desp'rate sots and fools,

Who durst depart from Aristotle's rules.
Our author, happy in a judge so nice,
Produced his play, and begged the knight's advice;
Made him observe the subject, and the plot,   75
The manners, passions, unities; what not?
All which, exact to rule, were brought about,
Were but a combat in the lists left out.
"What! leave the combat out?" exclaims the knight;
"Yes, or we must renounce the Stagirite."   80
"Not so by Heav'n," he answers in a rage,
"Knights, squires, and steeds, must enter on the stage."
"So vast a throng the stage can ne'er contain."
"Then build a new, or act it in a plain."
    Thus critics, of less judgment than caprice,   85
Curious not knowing, not exact but nice,
Form short ideas; and offend in arts
(As in most manners) by a love to parts.
    Some to conceit alone their taste confine,
And glitt'ring thoughts struck out at ev'ry line;   90
Pleased with a work where nothing's just or fit;
One glaring chaos and wild heap of wit.
Poets, like painters, thus unskilled to trace
The naked nature and the living grace,
With gold and jewels cover ev'ry part,   95
And hide with ornaments their want of art.
True wit is nature to advantage dressed,
What oft was thought, but ne'er so well expressed;
Something, whose truth convinced at sight we find,
That gives us back the image of our mind.   100
As shades more sweetly recommend the light,
So modest plainness sets off sprightly wit.
For works may have more wit than does 'em good,
As bodies perish through excess of blood.
    Others for language all their care express,   105
And value books, as women men, for dress:
Their praise is still,—the style is excellent;
The sense, they humbly take upon content.
Words are like leaves; and where they most abound,
Much fruit of sense beneath is rarely found: 110
False eloquence, like the prismatic glass,
Its gaudy colours spreads on ev'ry place;
The face of nature we no more survey,
All glares alike, without distinction gay:
But true expression, like th' unchanging sun,   115
Clears and improves whate'er it shines upon,

It gilds all objects, but it alters none.
Expression is the dress of thought, and still
Appears more decent, as more suitable;
A vile conceit in pompous words expressed,   *120*
Is like a clown in regal purple dressed:
For diff'rent styles with diff'rent subjects sort,
As several garbs with country, town, and court.
Some by old words to fame have made pretence,
Ancients in phrase, mere moderns in their sense;   *125*
Such laboured nothings, in so strange a style,
Amaze th' unlearned, and make the learnèd smile.
Unlucky, as Fungoso in the play,
These sparks with awkward vanity display
What the fine gentleman wore yesterday;   *130*
And but so mimic ancient wits at best,
As apes our grandsires, in their doublets dressed.
In words, as fashions, the same rule will hold;
Alike fantastic, if too new, or old:
Be not the first by whom the new are tried,   *135*
Nor yet the last to lay the old aside.
    But most by numbers judge a poet's song;
And smooth or rough, with them is right or wrong:
In the bright Muse though thousand charms conspire,
Her voice is all these tuneful fools admire;   *140*
Who haunt Parnassus but to please their ear,
Not mend their minds; as some to church repair,
Not for the doctrine, but the music there.
These equal syllables alone require,
Though oft the ear the open vowels tire;   *145*
While expletives their feeble aid do join;
And ten low words oft creep in one dull line:
While they ring round the same unvaried chimes,
With sure returns of still expected rhymes.
Where'er you find "the cooling western breeze,"   *150*
In the next line, it "whispers through the trees;"
If crystal streams "with pleasing murmurs creep,"
The reader's threatened (not in vain) with "sleep."
Then, at the last and only couplet fraught
With some unmeaning thing they call a thought,   *155*
A needless Alexandrine ends the song,
That, like a wounded snake, drags its slow length along.
Leave such to tune their own dull rhymes, and know
What's roundly smooth, or languishingly slow;
And praise the easy vigour of a line,   *160*
Where Denham's strength, and Waller's sweetness join.

True ease in writing comes from art, not chance,
As those move easiest who have learned to dance.
'Tis not enough no harshness gives offence,
The sound must seem an echo to the sense: 165
Soft is the strain when Zephyr gently blows,
And the smooth stream in smoother numbers flows;
But when loud surges lash the sounding shore,
The hoarse, rough verse should like the torrent roar;
When Ajax strives some rock's vast weight to throw,   170
The line too labours, and the words move slow;
Not so, when swift Camilla scours the plain,
Flies o'er th' unbending corn, and skims along the main.
Hear how Timotheus' varied lays surprise,
And bid alternate passions fall and rise!   175
While, at each change, the son of Libyan Jove
Now burns with glory, and then melts with love;
Now his fierce eyes with sparkling fury glow,
Now sighs steal out, and tears begin to flow:
Persians and Greeks like turns of nature found,   180
And the world's victor stood subdued by sound!
The pow'r of music all our hearts allow,
And what Timotheus was, is Dryden now.
    Avoid extremes; and shun the fault of such,
Who still are pleased too little or too much.   185
At ev'ry trifle scorn to take offence,
That always shows great pride, or little sense;
Those heads, as stomachs, are not sure the best,
Which nauseate all, and nothing can digest.
Yet let not each gay turn thy rapture move;   190
For fools admire, but men of sense approve:
As things seem large which we through mists descry,
Dullness is ever apt to magnify.
    Some foreign writers, some our own despise;
The ancients only, or the moderns prize.   195
Thus wit, like faith, by each man is applied
To one small sect, and all are damned beside.
Meanly they seek the blessing to confine,
And force that sun but on a part to shine,
Which not alone the southern wit sublimes,   200
But ripens spirits in cold northern climes;
Which from the first has shone on ages past,
Enlights the present, and shall warm the last;
Though each may feel increases and decays,
And see now clearer and now darker days.   205
Regard not then if wit be old or new,

But blame the false, and value still the true.
   Some ne'er advance a judgment of their own,
But catch the spreading notion of the town;
They reason and conclude by precedent, 210
And own stale nonsense which they ne'er invent.
Some judge of author's names, not works, and then
Nor praise nor blame the writings, but the men.
Of all this servile herd, the worst is he
That in proud dullness joins with quality, 215
A constant critic at the great man's board,
To fetch and carry nonsense for my lord.
What woeful stuff this madrigal would be,
In some starved hackney sonneteer, or me?
But let a lord once own the happy lines, 220
How the wit brightens! how the style refines!
Before his sacred name flies ev'ry fault,
And each exalted stanza teems with thought!
   The vulgar thus through imitation err;
As oft the learn'd by being singular; 225
So much they scorn the crowd, that if the throng
By chance go right, they purposely go wrong:
So schismatics the plain believers quit,
And are but damned for having too much wit.
Some praise at morning what they blame at night; 230
But always think the last opinion right.
A Muse by these is like a mistress used,
This hour she's idolized, the next abused;
While their weak heads, like towns unfortified,
'Twixt sense and nonsense daily change their side. 235
Ask them the cause; they're wiser still, they say:
And still tomorrow's wiser than today.
We think our fathers fools, so wise we grow;
Our wiser sons, no doubt, will think us so.
Once school-divines this zealous isle o'erspread; 240
Who knew most sentences, was deepest read;
Faith, Gospel, all, seemed made to be disputed,
And none had sense enough to be confuted:
Scotists and Thomists, now, in peace remain,
Amidst their kindred cobwebs in Duck Lane. 245
If faith itself has diff'rent dresses worn,
What wonder modes in wit should take their turn?
Oft, leaving what is natural and fit,
The current folly proves the ready wit;
And authors think their reputation safe, 250
Which lives as long as fools are pleased to laugh.

Some, valuing those of their own side or mind,
Still make themselves the measure of mankind:
Fondly we think we honour merit then,
When we but praise ourselves in other men.   255
Parties in wit attend on those of state,
And public faction doubles private hate.
Pride, malice, folly, against Dryden rose,
In various shapes of parsons, critics, beaus;
But sense survived, when merry jests were past;   260
For rising merit will buoy up at last.
Might he return, and bless once more our eyes,
New Blackmores and new Milbourns must arise:
Nay, should great Homer lift his awful head,
Zoilus again would start up from the dead.   265
Envy will merit, as its shade, pursue;
But like a shadow, proves the substance true;
For envied wit, like Sol eclipsed, makes known
Th' opposing body's grossness, not its own.
When first that sun too pow'rful beams displays,   270
It draws up vapours which obscure its rays;
But ev'n those clouds at last adorn its way,
Reflect new glories, and augment the day.
    Be thou the first true merit to befriend;
His praise is lost, who stays till all commend.   275
Short is the date, alas, of modern rhymes,
And 'tis but just to let 'em live betimes.
No longer now that golden age appears,
When patriarch-wits survived a thousand years:
Now length of fame (our second life) is lost,   280
And bare threescore is all ev'n that can boast;
Our sons their fathers' failing language see,
And such as Chaucer is, shall Dryden be.
So when the faithful pencil has designed
Some bright idea of the master's mind,   285
Where a new world leaps out at his command,
And ready nature waits upon his hand;
When the ripe colours soften and unite,
And sweetly melt into just shade and light,
When mellowing years their full perfection give,   290
And each bold figure just begins to live,
The treach'rous colours the fair art betray,
And all the bright creation fades away!
    Unhappy wit, like most mistaken things,
Atones not for that envy which it brings.   295
In youth alone its empty praise we boast,

But soon the short-lived vanity is lost:
Like some fair flow'r the early spring supplies,
That gayly blooms, but ev'n in blooming dies.
What is this wit, which must our cares employ? 300
The owner's wife, that other men enjoy;
Then most our trouble still when most admired,
And still the more we give, the more required;
Whose fame with pains we guard, but lose with ease,
Sure some to vex, but never all to please; 305
'Tis what the vicious fear, the virtuous shun,
By fools 'tis hated, and by knaves undone!
   If Wit so much from ign'rance undergo,
Ah let not learning too commence its foe!
Of old, those met rewards who could excel, 310
And such were praised who but endeavoured well:
Though triumphs were to gen'rals only due,
Crowns were reserved to grace the soldiers too.
Now, they who reach Parnassus' lofty crown
Employ their pains to spurn some others down; 315
And while self-love each jealous writer rules,
Contending wits become the sport of fools:
But still the worst with most regret commend,
For each ill author is as bad a friend.
To what base ends, and by what abject ways, 320
Are mortals urged through sacred lust of praise!
Ah, ne'er so dire a thirst of glory boast,
Nor in the critic let the man be lost.
Good nature and good sense must ever join;
To err is human, to forgive, divine. 325
   But if in noble minds some dregs remain
Not yet purged off, of spleen and sour disdain;
Discharge that rage on more provoking crimes,
Nor fear a dearth in these flagitious times.
No pardon vile obscenity should find, 330
Though wit and art conspire to move your mind;
But dullness with obscenity must prove
As shameful sure as impotence in love.
In the fat age of pleasure, wealth, and ease,
Sprung the rank weed, and thrived with large increase: 335
When love was all an easy monarch's care;
Seldom at council, never in a war:
Jilts ruled the state, and statesmen farces writ;
Nay, wits had pensions, and young lords had wit:
The fair sat panting at a courtier's play, 340
And not a mask went unimprov'd away:

The modest fan was lifted up no more,
And virgins smiled at what they blushed before.
The following license of a foreign reign
Did all the dregs of bold Socinus drain;   *345*
Then unbelieving priests reformed the nation,
And taught more pleasant methods of salvation;
Where Heav'n's free subjects might their rights dispute,
Lest God himself should seem too absolute:
Pulpits their sacred satire learned to spare,   *350*
And vice admired to find a flatt'rer there!
Encouraged thus, wit's Titans braved the skies,
And the press groaned with licensed blasphemies.
These monsters, critics! with your darts engage,
Here point your thunder, and exhaust your rage!   *355*
Yet shun their fault, who, scandalously nice,
Will needs mistake an author into vice;
All seemed infected that th' infected spy,
As all looks yellow to the jaundiced eye.

16, *Pierian spring*: a spring sacred to the Muses of Greek mythology; hence, a source of poetic inspiration. 67, *La Mancha's knight*: Don Quixote. This episode does not appear in Cervantes. 70, *Dennis*: John Dennis (1657–1734), poet, playwright, and critic, and public foe of Pope. 72, *Aristotle's rules*: Aristotle (384–322 B.C.), the Greek philosopher, laid down rules for the construction of tragedy in his *Poetics*. 73, *nice*: precise. 80, *Stagirite*: a reference to Aristotle, who was born at Stageira, in Macedonia. 128, *Fungoso*: a bungling fop in *Every Man Out Of His Humour*, a play by Ben Jonson (1572–1637). 141, *Parnassus*: a Greek mountain sacred to Apollo and the nine Muses. 161, *Denham*: John Denham (1615–1659), neo-classical poet, author of "Cooper's Hill," in which these famous and exemplary lines on the Thames occur: "Oh, could I flow like thee, and make my stream/ My great example, as it is my theme;/ Though deep, yet clear; though gentle, yet not dull;/ Strong without rage, without o'erflowing, full." Edmund Waller (1606–1687) wrote some of the earliest examples of the heroic couplet in English. 166, *Zephyr*: Greek god of the west wind. 170, see page 36. 172, *Camilla*: in Roman mythology, a servant of Diana, goddess of the hunt. 174, *Timotheus*: (447–357 B.C.) court musician to Alexander the Great. 183, *Dryden*: John Dryden (1631–1700), neo-classical poet. 241, *sentences*: conclusions, aphorisms. 244, *Scotists and Thomists*: followers of the medieval theologians Duns Scotus (ca. 1265–ca. 1308) and St. Thomas Aquinas (1226–1274). 245, *Duck Lane*: London street, the location of second-hand book stores. 263, *Blackmore . . . Milbourn*: critics hostile to Dryden, in *Satire Against Wit* and *Notes on Dryden's Virgil*, respectively. 265, *Zoilus*: critic of Homer, of the period of Philip of Macedon. 283, *Chaucer*: see page 74; his poetry was all but incomprehensible to Pope and his contemporaries. 334, *fat age of pleasure*: reign of King Charles II, from 1660–1685. 334, *foreign reign*: reign of William and Mary, from 1689; Mary died in 1694, William in 1702. 345, *Socinus*: (1539–1604), Italian religious reformer.

John Keats [1795–1821]

ON FIRST LOOKING INTO CHAPMAN'S HOMER

Much have I traveled in the realms of gold,
   And many goodly states and kingdoms seen;
   Round many western islands have I been
Which bards in fealty to Apollo hold.
Oft of one wide expanse had I been told   5
   That deep-browed Homer ruled as his demesne;
   Yet did I never breathe its pure serene
Till I heard Chapman speak out loud and bold:
Then felt I like some watcher of the skies
   When a new planet swims into his ken;   10
Or like stout Cortez when with eagle eyes
   He stared at the Pacific—and all his men
Looked at each other with a wild surmise—
   Silent, upon a peak in Darien.

George Chapman (1559?–1634) translated the *Iliad* and the *Odyssey*.

4, *Apollo:* Greek god of poetry, here characterized as lord of the dominion of poetry; *fealty* is loyalty or allegiance. 11, *Cortez:* actually, Balboa was the discoverer of the Pacific; Cortez was the conqueror of Mexico. 14, *Darien:* a hill on the Isthmus of Panama.

Samuel Taylor Coleridge [1772–1834]

ON DONNE'S POETRY

With Donne, whose muse on dromedary trots,
Wreathe iron pokers into truelove knots;
Rhyme's sturdy cripple, fancy's maze and clue,
Wit's forge and fire-blast, meaning's press and screw.

See pages 24, 139, and 170.

Conrad Hilberry [b. 1928]

POET

"If the poet is tone-deaf as to sounds, it is best to rely upon the phonetic symbols above each group of rhyming words in the rhyming dictionary that terminates this book, or upon dictionary markings. Many people can not distinguish the obvious difference in sounds between this pair of words, which do not rhyme:

Take away the TH *sound, and many people still hear no difference between this pair of words, which do not rhyme:*

NOR, FORE.

Take away the R *sound, and some people still hear no difference between this pair of words, which do not rhyme:*

GNAW, FOE.

GNAW *plus* R *plus* TH *can not rhyme with* FOE *plus* R *plus* TH."

—CLEMENT WOOD, *The Complete Rhyming Dictionary and Poet's Craft Book*

O, lucky poet tone-deaf
As to something else than sounds!
(Tone-deaf to the turning leaf?
Tone-deaf to autumn wounds?)

He walks in step with what he hears,   5
Keeps both beat and pitch;
Without a circumflex he fares
Foe plus *r* plus *th.*

This striding, compass-perfect poet
Never strays to *know-earth.*   10
Impeccably he sounds the note
And sets his foot to *gnaw-earth.*

William Packard [b. 1933]

THE TEACHER OF POETRY

O what a lovely poem, Mrs. Jones.
One really has to read it once or twice.
And there are no disturbing overtones.

You say god's garden has all sorts of stones.
How pious, how incisive, how concise!   5
O what a lovely poem, Mrs. Jones.

You say god's flowers are our chaperones.
How civilized, and what a nice device!
And there are no disturbing overtones.

You say god's grace is like eau de cologne.   10
How apt, and how delightfully precise!
O what a lovely poem, Mrs. Jones.

You say we should be holy in our bones.
How gay, to have this taste of paradise!
And there are no disturbing overtones.   15

You do not deal with any vague unknowns.
You make your point, and give quite wise advice.
O what a lovely poem, Mrs. Jones.
And there are no disturbing overtones.

Tony Connor [b. 1930]

FASHIONABLE POET READING

He has forgone the razor for a year
to hide from himself his mooning eunuch smile.
His eye—a disease devouring detail—
finds poems in everything. Should he fail
to feed silence to death, he might think himself queer.   5

Page after page his active verbs perform
their masculine tricks, his syntax bares muscles
in a fighting stance through which the poor blood thrills
a wishful dream of health. He wills
significant scale on nothings, lest his infirm   10

grasp of the world appal him, and his claim
to deserved fame be openly suspect. Doubt
must still be howled down: sweating, he bellows out
his repertoire. Fat and guilt
begin to dissolve. He shouts. He is glad he came.   15

Samuel Hazo [b. 1928]

THE DAY THEY ATE THE BARITONE

They started with his best guitar,
crushed it like straw and tore it, string
by string, to splinters. Still, they cheered
him even as he tried to push
them back—typists in charcoal wigs,   5
shoppers with wedding rings, and girls
in halters and bikini briefs.

A widow ripped his shirt from sleeve
to gusset. Virgins trailed the slice
of fingernails across his cheeks.   10
One girl, hysterical and flushed,
would not release his ear. Under
the pain, he screamed, "For God's sake,
stop!" But she just pulled the harder,

laughing him deaf as if the ear   15
were hers by right. After they took
his shoes and slapped him down, they crawled
across his chest like foxes, each
deciding what was best to bite
and biting it before the teeth   20
of someone else could chew it loose.

Within an hour it was done.
The typists re-arranged their wigs.
One woman turned her wedding ring
around. A girl re-hooked her halter   25
while she searched for souvenirs
among torn socks, the scattered dice
of teeth, and here and there a bone.

See "Lycidas," page 144, lines 58–63 and note.

Gary Snyder [b. 1930]

RIPRAP

Lay down these words
Before your mind like rocks.
                        placed solid, by hands
In choice of place, set
Before the body of the mind   5
                        in space and time:
Solidity of bark, leaf, or wall
                        riprap of things:
Cobble of milky way,
                        straying planets,   10
These poems, people,
                        lost ponies with
Dragging saddles—
                        and rocky sure-foot trails.

The worlds like an endless
                    four-dimensional
Game of Go.   15
                    ants and pebbles
In the thin loam, each rock a word
                    a creek-washed stone   20
Granite: ingrained
                    with torment of fire and weight
Crystal and sediment linked hot
                    all change, in thoughts,
As well as things.   25

Riprap: a cobble of stone laid on slick mountain surfaces to make a trail for horses.

Wallace Stevens [1879–1955]

THE IDEA OF ORDER AT KEY WEST

She sang beyond the genius of the sea.
The water never formed to mind or voice,
Like a body wholly body, fluttering
Its empty sleeves; and yet its mimic motion
Made constant cry, caused constantly a cry,   5
That was not ours although we understood,
Inhuman, of the veritable ocean.

The sea was not a mask. No more was she.
The song and water were not medleyed sound
Even if what she sang was what she heard,   10
Since what she sang was uttered word by word.
It may be that in all her phrases stirred
The grinding water and the gasping wind;
But it was she and not the sea we heard.

For she was the maker of the song she sang.   15
The ever-hooded, tragic-gestured sea
Was merely a place by which she walked to sing.
Whose spirit is this? we said, because we knew
It was the spirit that we sought and knew
That we should ask this often as she sang.   20

If it was only the dark voice of the sea
That rose, or even colored by many waves;
If it was only the outer voice of sky

And cloud, of the sunken coral water-walled,
However clear, it would have been deep air,   *25*
The heaving speech of air, a summer sound
Repeated in a summer without end
And sound alone. But it was more than that,
More even than her voice, and ours, among
The meaningless plungings of water and the wind,   *30*
Theatrical distances, bronze shadows heaped
On high horizons, mountainous atmospheres
Of sky and sea.

             It was her voice that made
The sky acutest at its vanishing.
She measured to the hour its solitude.   *35*
She was the single artificer of the world
In which she sang. And when she sang, the sea,
Whatever self it had, became the self
That was her song, for she was the maker. Then we,
As we beheld her striding there alone,   *40*
Knew that there never was a world for her
Except the one she sang and, singing, made.

Ramon Fernandez, tell me, if you know,
Why, when the singing ended and we turned
Toward the town, tell why the glassy lights,   *45*
The lights in the fishing boats at anchor there,
As the night descended, tilting in the air,
Mastered the night and portioned out the sea,
Fixing emblazoned zones and fiery poles,
Arranging, deepening, enchanting night.   *50*

Oh! Blessed rage for order, pale Ramon,
The maker's rage to order words of the sea,
Words of the fragrant portals, dimly-starred,
And of ourselves and of our origins,
In ghostlier demarcations, keener sounds.   *55*

43, *Ramon Fernandez:* Though some readers of this poem have remarked that
Ramon Fernandez is the name of a twentieth-century aesthetician, there is no evi-
dence that Stevens did not select the name arbitrarily for the fictitious interlocutor
in this poem.

An
Epilogue

William Butler Yeats [1865–1939]

THE CIRCUS ANIMALS' DESERTION

I

I sought a theme and sought for it in vain,
I sought it daily for six weeks or so.
Maybe at last, being but a broken man,
I must be satisfied with my heart, although
Winter and summer till old age began   5
My circus animals were all on show,
Those stilted boys, that burnished chariot,
Lion and woman and the Lord knows what.

II

What can I but enumerate old themes?
First that sea-rider Oisin led by the nose   10
Through three enchanted islands, allegorical dreams,
Vain gaiety, vain battle, vain repose,
Themes of the embittered heart, or so it seems,
That might adorn old songs or courtly shows;
But what cared I that set him on to ride,   15
I, starved for the bosom of his faery bride?

And then a counter-truth filled out its play,
The Countess Cathleen was the name I gave it;
She, pity-crazed, had given her soul away,
But masterful Heaven had intervened to save it.   20
I thought my dear must her own soul destroy,
So did fanaticism and hate enslave it,
And this brought forth a dream and soon enough
This dream itself had all my thought and love.

And when the Fool and Blind Man stole the bread   *25*
Cuchulain fought the ungovernable sea;
Heart-mysteries there, and yet when all is said
It was the dream itself enchanted me:
Character isolated by a deed
To engross the present and dominate memory.   *30*
Players and painted stage took all my love,
And not those things that they were emblems of.

III

Those masterful images because complete
Grew in pure mind, but out of what began?
A mound of refuse or the sweepings of a street,   *35*
Old kettles, old bottles, and a broken can,
Old iron, old bones, old rags, that raving slut
Who keeps the till. Now that my ladder's gone,
I must lie down where all the ladders start,
In the foul rag-and-bone shop of the heart.   *40*

6–8: Yeats's "circus animals" are the images he used in his poetry. 10, *Oisin:* pronounced Ushéen: he was the hero of an ancient Irish legend and of Yeats's early poem, "The Wanderings of Oisin." 18–20: *The Countess Cathleen* is an early play by Yeats, in which the Countess sells her soul to the Devil in return for food for starving people; she goes to heaven anyway. 26, *Cuchulain:* pronounced Cuhúllen; another ancient Irish hero, and the hero of another of Yeats's plays.

Index of Titles
and Authors

Index of Terms